THE POWER TO SEE IN BOTH REALMS/WORLDS

FALLEN SCALES
Devotional Reading for a Spirit-Filled Life in Jesus Christ

By Joseph Harris

THE POWER TO SEE IN BOTH REALMS/WORLDS

FALLEN SCALES

Devotional Reading for a Spirit Filled Life in Jesus Christ

By Joseph Harris

Destiny House Publishing, LLC
Detroit, MI 48219

Fallen Scales
Published by Destiny House Publishing, LLC
Copyright © April 2012 Joseph Harris

ISBN: 13: 978-1936867516

Unless otherwise stated, all scripture quotations are from the Holy Bible, King James Version. Scripture references that do not have the Bible version noted are the author's paraphrase.

Cover design and Publication Layout: Destiny House Publishing, LLC

Editing: Destiny House Publishing, LLC

ALL RIGHTS RESERVED

All rights reserved under International Copyright law. No part of this book may be reproduced or transmitted in any form or by any means: electronic, mechanical, including photocopying and recording, or by any information storage and retrieval system, without permission in writing from the publisher.

Printed in the United States of America

For information:
Destiny House Publishing, LLC
www.destinyhousepublishing.com
email: inquiry@destinyhousepublishing.com
P.O. Box 19774
Detroit, MI 48219
888-890-9455

This book is designed to help you to seek God for Godly insight. This will help you overcome spiritual battles and principalities that are against your life as well as family and friends coming together. His word will help reveal your destiny for service in the ministry. These Biblical passages reveal Godly power that give sight to the blind, increase your faith and releases new revelation by the power of the Holy Spirit. This book will remind us daily of the power that is in our Lord, Jesus Christ who blesses us with every spiritual blessing throughout eternity. These daily devotions will help you to praise, worship, glorify Him, and get a closer relationship as you grow. His word will empower and transform you to stand in the power of His word. Today, ask the Lord to minister to you through His word. Read it today! Do not wait another day without Jesus Christ as the head of your life. Accept Him in your heart right now! This is the most important step in your life. Do not back down! God loves you more than you will ever comprehend or imagine. May the Love of Jesus Christ be revealed to you today and keep you and your family in his perfect will.

WORDS TO MEDITATE ON IN THE SPIRIT

THE LORD'S PRAYER

MATTHEW 6:9-13
    In this manner, therefore, pray:
    Our Father in heaven,
    Hallowed be your name.
    Your kingdom come.
    Your will be done
    On earth as it is in heaven.
    Give us this day our daily bread.
    And forgive us our debts,
    As we forgive our debtors.
    And do not lead us into temptation,
    But deliver us from the evil one.
    For Yours is the kingdom and the power and the glory
    forever. Amen.

THE LORD IS MY SHEPHERD

PSALM 23
    The LORD is my shepherd;
     I shall not want.
    He makes me to lie down in green pastures;
    He leads me beside the still waters.
    He restores my soul;
    He leads me in the paths of righteousness
    For His name's sake.
Yea, though I walk through the valley of the shadow of death,
    I will fear no evil;
    For You are with me;
    Your rod and Your staff, they comfort me.
You prepare a table before me in the presence of my enemies;

> You anoint my head with oil;
> My cup runs over.
> Surely goodness and mercy shall follow me
> All the days of my life;
> And I will dwell in the house of the LORD
> Forever.

PSALM 27:1-14

The LORD is my light and my salvation;
> Whom shall I fear?
> The LORD is the strength of my life;
> Of whom shall I be afraid?

When the wicked came against me
> To eat up my flesh,
> My enemies and foes,
> They stumbled and fell.

Though an army may encamp against me,
> My heart shall not fear;
> Though war may rise against me,
> In this I will be confident.

One thing I have desired of the LORD,
> That will I seek:
> That I may dwell in the house of the LORD
> All the days of my life,
> To behold the beauty of the LORD,
> And to inquire in His temple.

For in the time of trouble
> He shall hide me in His pavilion;
> In the secret place of His tabernacle
> He shall hide me;
> He shall set me high upon a rock.

And now my head shall be lifted up above my enemies all around me; Therefore I will
> offer sacrifices of joy in His tabernacle;
> I will sing, yes, I will sing praises to the LORD.

Hear, O LORD, when I cry with my voice!
> Have mercy also upon me, and answer me.

When You said, "Seek My face,"
    My heart said to You, "Your face, LORD, I will seek."
Do not hide Your face from me;
    Do not turn Your servant away in anger;
    You have been my help;
    Do not leave me nor forsake me,
    O God of my salvation.
When my father and my mother forsake me,
    Then the LORD will take care of me.
Teach me Your way, O LORD,
    And lead me in a smooth path, because of my enemies.
Do not deliver me to the will of my adversaries;
    For false witnesses have risen against me,
    And such as breathe out violence.
I would have lost heart, unless I had believed
    That I would see the goodness of the LORD
    In the land of the living.
Wait on the LORD;
    Be of good courage,
    And He shall strengthen your heart;
    Wait, I say, on the LORD!

PSALM 34

I will bless the LORD at all times;
    His praise shall continually be in my mouth.
My soul shall make its boast in the LORD;
    The humble shall hear of it and be glad.
Oh, magnify the LORD with me,
    And let us exalt His name together.

I sought the LORD, and He heard me,
    And delivered me from all my fears.
They looked to Him and were radiant,
    And their faces were not ashamed.
This poor man cried out, and the LORD heard him,
    And saved him out of all his troubles.
The angel of the LORD encamps all around those who fear Him,
    And delivers them.

Oh, taste and see that the LORD is good;

    Blessed is the man who trusts in Him!
Oh, fear the LORD, you His saints!
    There is no want to those who fear Him.
The young lions lack and suffer hunger;
    But those who seek the LORD shall not lack any good thing.
Come, you children, listen to me;
    I will teach you the fear of the LORD.
Who is the man who desires life,
    And loves many days, that he may see good?
Keep your tongue from evil,
    And your lips from speaking deceit.
Depart from evil and do good;
    Seek peace and pursue it.

The eyes of the LORD are on the righteous,
    And His ears are open to their cry.
The face of the LORD is against those who do evil,
    To cut off the remembrance of them from the earth.
The righteous cry out, and the LORD hears,
    And delivers them out of all their troubles.
The LORD is near to those who have a broken heart,
    And saves such as have a contrite spirit.

Many are the afflictions of the righteous,
    But the LORD delivers him out of them all.
He guards all his bones;
    Not one of them is broken.
Evil shall slay the wicked,
    And those who hate the righteous shall be condemned.
The LORD redeems the soul of His servants,
    And none of those who trust in Him shall be condemned.

PSALM 145

 I will extol You, my God, O King;
    And I will bless Your name forever and ever.
 Every day I will bless You,
    And I will praise Your name forever and ever.
 Great is the LORD, and greatly to be praised;
    And His greatness is unsearchable.

One generation shall praise Your works to another,
    And shall declare Your mighty acts.
I will meditate on the glorious splendor of Your majesty,
    And on Your wondrous works.[1]
Men shall speak of the might of Your awesome acts,
    And I will declare Your greatness.
They shall utter the memory of Your great goodness,
    And shall sing of Your righteousness.

The LORD is gracious and full of compassion,
    Slow to anger and great in mercy.
The LORD is good to all,
    And His tender mercies are over all His works.

All Your works shall praise You, O LORD,
    And Your saints shall bless You.
They shall speak of the glory of Your kingdom,
    And talk of Your power,
To make known to the sons of men His mighty acts,
    And the glorious majesty of His kingdom.
Your kingdom is an everlasting kingdom,
    And Your dominion endures throughout all generations.

The LORD upholds all who fall,
    And raises up all who are bowed down.
The eyes of all look expectantly to You,
    And You give them their food in due season.
You open Your hand
    And satisfy the desire of every living thing.

The LORD is righteous in all His ways,
    Gracious in all His works.
The LORD is near to all who call upon Him,
    To all who call upon Him in truth.
He will fulfill the desire of those who fear Him;
    He also will hear their cry and save them.
The LORD preserves all who love Him,
    But all the wicked He will destroy.
My mouth shall speak the praise of the LORD,
    And all flesh shall bless His holy name
    Forever and ever.

PSALM 135

Praise the LORD!
    Praise the name of the LORD;
    Praise Him, O you servants of the LORD!
You who stand in the house of the LORD,
    In the courts of the house of our God,
Praise the LORD, for the LORD is good;
    Sing praises to His name, for it is pleasant.
For the LORD has chosen Jacob for Himself,
    Israel for His special treasure.

For I know that the LORD is great,
    And our Lord is above all gods.
Whatever the LORD pleases He does,
    In heaven and in earth,
    In the seas and in all deep places.
He causes the vapors to ascend from the ends of the earth;
    He makes lightning for the rain;
    He brings the wind out of His treasuries.

He destroyed the firstborn of Egypt,
    Both of man and beast.
He sent signs and wonders into the midst of you, O Egypt,
    Upon Pharaoh and all his servants.
He defeated many nations
    And slew mighty kings—
Sihon king of the Amorites,
    Og king of Bashan,
    And all the kingdoms of Canaan—
And gave their land as a heritage,
    A heritage to Israel His people.

Your name, O LORD, endures forever,
    Your fame, O LORD, throughout all generations.
For the LORD will judge His people,
    And He will have compassion on His servants.

The idols of the nations are silver and gold,
    The work of men's hands.
They have mouths, but they do not speak;

  Eyes they have, but they do not see;
 They have ears, but they do not hear;
   Nor is there any breath in their mouths.
Those who make them are like them;
   So is everyone who trusts in them.

Bless the LORD, O house of Israel!
   Bless the LORD, O house of Aaron!
Bless the LORD, O house of Levi!
   You who fear the LORD, bless the LORD!
Blessed be the LORD out of Zion,
   Who dwells in Jerusalem!
   Praise the LORD!

PSALM 138
 I will praise You with my whole heart;
   Before the gods I will sing praises to You.
 I will worship toward Your holy temple,
   And praise Your name
   For Your lovingkindness and Your truth;
   For You have magnified Your word above all Your name.
 In the day when I cried out, You answered me,
   And made me bold with strength in my soul.

All the kings of the earth shall praise You, O LORD,
   When they hear the words of Your mouth.
Yes, they shall sing of the ways of the LORD,
   For great is the glory of the LORD.
Though the LORD is on high,
   Yet He regards the lowly;
   But the proud He knows from afar.

Though I walk in the midst of trouble, You will revive me;
   You will stretch out Your hand
   Against the wrath of my enemies,
   And Your right hand will save me.
 The LORD will perfect that which concerns me;
   Your mercy, O LORD, endures forever;
   Do not forsake the works of Your hands.

DEDICATION: This book is an inspired by my **Father in Heaven** and dedicated to my biological Father**, Joe Arthur Doyle and my Mother, Gussie Vance Doyle**, who introduced and taught me about my Lord, Jesus Christ. I pray that my parents rejoice in Heaven in the presence of our Lord Lord, Jesus Christ. My Father and my Mother was also responsible for my first baptism as the Holy Spirit led them. I thank God that both of them had vision to get their children in relationship with the Lord Jesus Christ. They knew the importance of relationship. My mother ensured each son and daughter went into the water, fully immersed, baptized in the name of the Father, the Son and the Holy Ghost (Matthew 28).

I will never forget the late Pastor, Reverend Bass who baptized me that day as a young boy around eight years old. Praise God! It was an experience for me that I never forgot. It was something about that moment that is spiritually embedded in my heart. One thing I learned from that is that my mother truly believed that God would bless us and keep us. She knew in her heart that God was and is the God of glory and eternal grace and mercy. She knew of His touch. And I believe she sought sound counsel from the Lord and my Father regarding her children's spiritual future. I believe both of them knew the power of God. I credit them for guiding me in the right direction of life. This helped me as I was growing up and even today to avoid and walk away from the dark side of life. I could have been dead and gone if it had not been for the Lord on my side. If it had not been for the Lord in my parents' life, I am not sure of where my life could have turned. We can't explain everything in life that happens but we do know that God has His way of directing our lives. So I am grateful that He gave me parents to care for me. It was their care that led to my blinders being removed at those set times in my life even to this day.

Later, I got baptized again because I understood much better who God was in my life at that time. I learned also of God's requirement of obedience regarding baptism. I am now aware of the symbolic meaning, sacredness and solemnity in baptism. My parents have since departed to be with the Lord, but I thank God and bow before Him in worship and the highest exaltation and praise. I thank God for all of my siblings who had a role in helping their little brother grow up in those early years of life. They played a crucial role in family love and trust. It is a blessing to have siblings that love and respect each other. Chris, Craig, Linda, Jacqueline, Joann, and Mary, you all are appreciated and loved. You all have always been in my heart. Thank each one of you for your love and prayers. I pray that the peace of over each person and hope that the Holy Spirit continue blessing and working on each person.

This book is also dedicated to the **Soldiers of the United States Army** who served throughout the world past, present and future. May God's blessings and arm of protection be with all soldiers and families during war and peace. I pray the power of Psalms 91 in their lives. If we trust God as the saints we are, we can go to Him and ask that His power continue to lift up our soldiers all over the world. We can pray for God's intervention with peace, love, healing and restoration. We pray that God always be the center of our lives and this country. I pray that the power of God's plan for our lives continue to manifest and that we be pleasing in His sight by walking in faith and the love of God. Father I thank you for family and friends. I thank you for all soldiers that dedicate themselves for the defense of this Nation. I thank you for the Priest that prays daily for peace throughout the world. In Jesus Name, Amen.

PURPOSE: This book highlights God's word in ways designed to help everyone see better in life's daily situations and get results. It is a book to encourage you to view the scripture in the spirit and life's events. The intent is to not only to witness to you as an ambassador of Jesus, however to help you be renewed in Christ. These scriptures in this book are to help you to walk in the Spirit. He alone can perform in our lives amazing and blessed things.

In this book, Jesus immediately transformed people continuously that came to Him looking for a life changing experience such as miracles and healing. He healed those who called upon His names. This book shares His power of love as a priority in our lives. This book will challenge you to see with new vision that God has given you. It is a book used for your future and generations to come. You will be encouraged in every scripture to live a better life by seeing with spiritual insight. Readers will be enabled to remove the blinder (scales) from their lives and specifically their eyes to see God more clearly in His glorious ways of blessing all of us, including families and friends. This is also designed to bless those of the Church of Jesus Christ, the one who died and rose from the dead.

This book is designed for you to see things in plain spiritual sight. You will be enabled by the power of the Holy Spirit to let go of the interruptions of life and seek God for new vision and purpose for your life. God is the one to lean on in life and He is the source of our being. You will be able to see it for yourself. All people need to understand that God is the God of love, church, worship, praise, fruit, seed, vision, prayer, deliverance and all things of Holiness. There is nothing too hard for Him and nothing that He is unable to change. There is nothing impossible for Him either. He can make anything happen according to His perfect will. There is nothing neither unseen nor unheard by Him. He sees, hears, and knows everything in our lives and everything that happens in creation. He is the creator and ruler of all that exist.

We have our inspirations, our challenges over the years of life. We have our disappointments and desires and ambitions. Many people have an abundance of blessings but there is still something missing. A void place exists that you may not be able to locate by yourself. Even when you aim at the best life can offer there is still something missing.

Sometimes life can even deal you a blow that shatters all that you have worked to gain and every dream you dreamed. Then reality sets in really fast once we are hurt and there is no one person who can comfort you and share the reality of your grief and heartache. Our minds tend to go out of control and build up unnecessary frustrations, negative thoughts and things against us that force us into seeking wrong sources of support and wrong dependencies. But you need to understand that there is someone to depend on in your life. God is our source of hope and the one to depend on. The hope of a life changing experience for the purpose of glorifying God is our desire. There is a hope that unites us with our Lord and makes us the kind of person who lives in expectation of God's outpouring power. We live to be pleasing in His eyes. Our purpose is to serve and glorify Him There is a hope that man can love like Jesus and live in the image that He purposely predestined for all mankind.

One of the most crucial obstacles that hinder people is the lack of ability to see through a glass lens, a microscropic lens, if you will. It is the lack of ability to pinpoint the obvious even when it's starring you in the face. But what is most important is that people begin to see with the spiritual eye. That is one of the major purposes of this book. You can blame many things on the culture, the fast pace of life, the past, the economic decline, recessions, interest rates, lack of employment, increase taxes, and broken healthcare and Medicare, government issues, and people in general, but reality is that you have to lift yourself up in the Lord and begin to see things in a different light. You need to begin to see things in a blessed attitude with vision for increase and multiple blessings and what you are planning to do to please God. Life goes on regardless of our surrounding and the world's point of view. It is high time to get your life together. No longer will you sit around and just applaud those that are successful in your eyes. You will be move for God and the angels in heaven will applaud you because you are being a blessing for God's glory.

You can even blame things on a diverse culture. You can blame it on the melting pot of Americans and other ethnicities. You can say that you are disadvantage people who have been torn and divided over differences of race, religion, culture, and poverty. But one thing for sure is that you have the ability to see in the spiritual realm if you are born again and if you want to remain or get out of those differences that you feel in bondage about. You have the ability to come out of this entire situation. God will show you how to see again if you have regressed or declined in your purpose for living. He will show you if it's your first time.

The good news is that when yours spiritual scales have fallen from your eyes like the Apostle Paul, your insight into who God is and what God wants your life to be for His Kingdom purpose will be even clearer for you. You will have the ability to correct circumstance that people tragically look over and ignore. You will become one of God's Kingdom warriors that witness and testify of His unfolding and everlasting love and salvation.

If you are not born again you have the ability to see in the natural realm. But you lack so much that God has in store for you. In fact, you miss out on so much that He has before your eyes that you miss over and over again. You want to catch those blessings today. Accept Jesus as Lord and Savior and know Him and the power of His resurrection. It is because you are not born again and you have no relationship with God.

Some people look at people who are not of Christ and they call it a cultural shock impacted by the increase population and the generational curse and generational change in that population. Many people, if a poll was taken today, would see so many things differently. The fact is that the view of people is from their own personal vision and personal eye sight depending on what they believe and comprehend. The question is have you embraced the necessity of life? Because if that person really embraces the necessity of life, that person would research and with their own eyes see that God is necessary to have in your life. He is more that any natural necessities. He is the God that destroys and denounces any false gods. He said there is no other God. He spoke to Moses and told Moses, tell Pharaoh, "I am, that I am" meaning, I am the only true and wise God. There is no other God. God wants you to put all your trust in him and believe that He is God. Tell all of your family and friends about his goodness. He is God and that is the end of it.

If you really believe about God's creations and man's different variations of scientific evidence and general hypothesis or ideas, then you need to take a look at your heart and mind to know for yourself. Read the word of God to learn of the God who made all things and who sits in heaven on the throne.

We are blessed because we see things in both the natural and the spiritual realm. We can see spiritual things when God allows us to see them. We just do not have a spiritual eye just because. God has to back us on everything. We see all around us in both conditions, natural and spiritual. In the natural we see our surroundings such as the birds, the trees, hard objects, concrete objects, and abstract objects. We only see things because God allows us to see it.

God formed everything that exists. He breathed the breath of life into man and man became a living creature. How about that? No one else has the authority or the ability to do so. What a mighty God we serve.

I love having the ability to see because it's fun and essential for life. Seeing causes the mind to register reactions to the object that you are viewing. Having the ability to see helps the communication flow in the highest level. When God allows a person to see in the natural and the spiritual realm, you have insight. You are also fortunate enough to witness to those that have similar cases. This kind of insight boggles the human mind and intellect. It would be good if everyone had such gift. An eye scale can be defined as a covering blanketed over the eyes of a sleeping person. It can also be defined as person who sight is spiritually flawed. This person has no idea of his or her spiritual surroundings. However, it is a scale that must come off to keep man from falling into the deep blindness and the grips of the enemy. You would never send a blind man out to survey an area that will someday be utilized for the uplifting of God's Kingdom. You would not send a blind man because they would not be expected to see what you expect someone with sight to see and someone to capture what God wants you to capture if they did not have the spiritual insight.

It is important to know that God is balancing our lives for His purpose. He takes every measure into His hand and makes the correct solution each time. He orders our lives, yet somehow allows us to make choices that either please Him or not. I am glad that He balances my life according to His perfect will. I am glad that He allows me to make choices because it is a reflection that I trust Him. I am thankful that God is the one who removes the scales from my eyes that I might know Him better and serve Him with all my heart. More importantly, I thank God for His everlasting love and salvation and the strength to glorify Him and His name only all of my days and in eternity.

TRANSFORMED TO PRIESTHOOD

ACTS 9:1-12 Then Saul, still breathing threats and murder against the disciples of the Lord, went to the high priest and asked letters from him to the synagogues of Damascus, so that if he found any who were of the Way, whether men or women, he might bring them bound to Jerusalem. As he journeyed he came near Damascus, and suddenly a light shone around him from heaven. Then he fell to the ground, and heard a voice saying to him, "Saul, Saul, why are you persecuting me?" And he said, "Who are You, Lord? "Then the Lord said, "I am Jesus, whom you are persecuting. It is hard for you to kick against the goads."So he, trembling and astonished, said, "Lord, what do You want me to do?" Then the Lord said to him, "Arise and go into the city, and you will be told what you must do." And the men who journeyed with him stood speechless, hearing a voice but seeing no one. Then Saul arose from the ground, and when his eyes were opened he saw no one. But they led him by the hand and brought him into Damascus. And he was three days without sight, and neither ate nor drank. Now there was a certain disciple at Damascus named Ananias; and to him the Lord said in a vision, "Ananias." And he said, "Here I am, Lord." So the Lord said to him, "Arise and go to the street called Straight, and inquire at the house of Judas for one called Saul of Tarsus, for behold, he is praying. And in a vision he has seen a man named Ananias coming in and putting his hand on him, so that he might receive his sight."

    A new beginning had begun in the life of Saul of Tarsus, who became the Apostle Paul, one of God's leading men that served as an instrumental witness on earth of God's everlasting salvation, grace and mercy. The Apostle experienced a touch of God that was as unique and needed as servants for the Most High God, Jesus Christ. He experienced a direct conversion by Jesus Christ Himself as he was on a journey to do evil to other Christians. Jesus Christ stopped him in his tracks and changed his life forever. All believers and ministers, those who operate in the five fold ministry, and those that are lost need to experience a touch of Jesus in specific areas of our lives. No one is exempt from His love and touch that fulfills his purpose that He has set for us.

    The Apostle Paul's life was converted by the touch of Jesus Himself who saw Saul on the road to destruction. Everyone in society needs a touch because of the sin that creeps in with its desire to reign over our lives. We need His touch everyday because we fall short of His glory. We need His touch because we all have been persecutors and violators of the faith in Christ in some form or fashion. Nevertheless, He is forever forgiving and always delivers us through our weakness and sin. We do not have to act all cute and prestigious and high society and set in our ways in this life. You see, everyone has something broken that will require God's attention. It is because everyone has something broken in their lives that requires only Jesus to restore or fix it. Jesus is the only one who can fix troubles and various situations in our lives. Whatever new thing God is about to do in your life, whether it is conversion or a blessing with wealth, healing, miracles or even if he wants you to step out in faith for what he is has been calling you to do, submit to his will. He is always ready to give you a new life with purpose. Ask God to do it and do it now that His name will be glorified. The enemy wants to stop you in your tracks, but God wants you to prosper in His Kingdom. You have a purpose in Christ. You purpose means more to the Lord than to the enemy because God sees you as one of His. The enemy is just a deterrent. He has a goal to make you turn your back on Jesus Christ. Do not give in to the enemy. And do not give up on God. Remember Jesus has all eternal power that is instantly manifested in your life for His Kingdom purpose.

    It is important to start lessons out giving the essential makeup of blessings and being able to explain the necessity of sight in the spiritual realm. It is much needed and has been avoided too long. Sometimes people cringe at the fact that there is a spiritual realm and two different spirits looking at you and both forces existing for different purposes.

    God desires to bless you and curse those who curse you. The enemy simply comes to still, kill and destroy. The question to you today is which one do you chose? I am sure you made the right choice today. If you have salvation in Jesus Christ, you will desire to see in the spiritual realm what God wants you to see and reveal to you.

    One of the most effective parts of Jesus ministry was the demonstration of restoring sight. Jesus is the only one who can restore and give sight. There is no other and certainly do not be fooled by the enemy. Jesus dealt with a blind man who needed sight because he was born with a birth defect from his mother's womb. He dealt with religious leaders who were confused about the new birth. They had no vision and no concept of the new birth, being born again. Their sights were limited by their spiritual conditions. Jesus made it very clear that you must be born again. They were too blind to understand and to see that the Son of God was in the midst of healing and revealing His gracious loving kindness. They were too caught up with the facts of the law, rather than the truth that was standing before their very eyes. They had different interpretations of the identity of Jesus.

The number one priority was to restore life in the people of God for the purpose of salvation, love, witness, grace and His never ending mercy. God is no respecter of persons. He rain on the just as well as the unjust. Jesus restored people for more than one reason. His primary reasons for restoring us are love, witness and testimony. He loves us more than a parent can. It was the demonstration of his love that rescued and blessed us. God sees all things and we see nothing without the blessing of spiritual sight that he gifts us with.

Christians alike have a unique lifestyle that must be projected and demonstrated at all times. People watch to see if you are walking and acting like a Godly person. What you do influences other people They want to know if you are a real Christian, who demonstrates the love of Jesus Christ. They want to know that you are filled with the Holy Ghost. So then show them that you are filled in the Spirit of Christ. Draw them to Christ under the anointing power of God. Use what you have to draw them. When the Apostle Paul was drawn in to Jesus Christ, he spent the remainder of his life drawing people to the Lord. In fact, that became his mission for Christ. He was a chosen vessel. When God removes your scales in the spirit, then you will see and become an effective witnesses for Jesus Christ.

When we expect to see things, we must be patient that God will reveal the blessing in time. Count on your Spiritual sight. The Apostle Paul said, **2 Corinthians 4:18 while we do not look at the things which are seen, but at the things which are not seen. For the things which are seen *are* temporary, but the things which are not seen *are* eternal.** I believe that once God changed the Apostle Paul's life, he could not help but to adopt this passage because of the anointing of God on his life. He desired to walk in obedience to his will and commands to receive the blessing of the Lord.

PRAYERS

Father, thank you for your transforming power to priesthood. Guide me by the power of your Holy Spirit as I seek, worship, serve and glorify you. ACTS 8,9

THE BLOOD OF JESUS APPLIED

JOHN 19:31-37 Therefore, because it was the Preparation Day, that the bodies should not remain on the cross on the Sabbath (for that Sabbath was a high day), the Jews asked Pilate that their legs might be broken, and that they might be taken away. Then the soldiers came and broke the legs of the first and of the other who was crucified with Him. But when they came to Jesus and saw that He was already dead, they did not break His legs. But one of the soldiers pierced His side with a spear, and immediately blood and water came out. And he who has seen has testified, and his testimony is true; and he knows that he is telling the truth, so that you may believe. For these things were done that the Scripture should be fulfilled, "Not one of His bones shall be broken." And again another Scripture says, "They shall look on Him whom they pierced.

One of the first times of hearing about blood issues was in the case surrounding Cain and Abel. The blood has impacted every life on earth in many ways especially with the Son of God, Jesus Christ. In the case of Cain, he slew his brother Abel. Cain killed his brother because he was jealous over the sacrifice that Abel had presented before God. He was jealous because God was pleased with that sacrifice. Cain did not please God with His offering of fruit. Do not misunderstand and think that fruit is not good because it is good. It was not the perfect offering that God was looking for, He was looking for obedience. The offering which was a sacrifice had to have blood involved in it. Abel pleased God with the offering of meat. He was the keeper of sheep. Meat is the reflection of the Lamb that would be slain someday for all of Israel and all of Gods people, including everyone lost in this world. The Lamb would be the perfect sacrifice because the lamb had to be slain so blood would have to be spilled. This would be a picture of Jesus Christ the lamb who was slain for the remission of sin. .

The fruit that Cain presented to God was good but it could not serve as a sacrifice. It did have its connection to the garden because the garden was filled with fruit and God had blessed everything. At the same time, God is looking for your best offering. What you give is noticed by the Lord. Do not allow sin to take your best offering away from God. The enemy specializes in provoking people into a sin filled lifestyle.

During that particular time, sin had taken its course and reflected on the first family. Whenever a family has been blessed you need to understand that the enemy will do everything in his power to destroy your family and anyone else involved. We are dealing with a force that has been defeated. However, this enemy still chose to raise his ugly head thinking that he has power to defeat you. Thank God that He is our refuge and strong tower. He covers us in His blood.

Scientist made a breakthrough discovery about DNA, the breakdown in identity of our individual blood. They use DNA for investigative crimes. Investigators know exactly who the person is that left the blood at the crime scene. They know who to track down at what height, weight, a full description. They trace different factors and characteristics about the blood DNA in specific people. They can do it for people and animals. They know your blood type.

When I was in the hospital years ago, I knew that my blood was my life line. I knew that if my blood was in trouble with a diseases or anything similar, I would be in trouble. God equips our mind to take care of our blood systems with vitamins and a proper diet. Because God supplies my needs, I came out of the hospital in the best of health.

God, on the other hand, has the power to know, to see things from any view. He sees all things in every possible way of life, spiritual and natural life. Abel's blood was on the ground and he was innocent. God could hear the blood crying from the ground. Cain was scared and did not want to tell the truth, but God already knew. He already knew the circumstance surrounding killing of his brother. He knew Cain had struck his brother over the jealousy of an offering.

In all history, one thing that every citizen, every person of God's Kingdom and those who have not committed to Him must know of without a doubt, is that the blood of Jesus Christ was applied to the hearts of those who believe. They must know that the blood is what saves us from being destroyed by God wrath.

We are reminded of the many wars that were fought that blood was shed for freedom. Some people are moved by the fact that wars were fought for freedom and peace. As a result of those wars, blood was shed on the battlefield, and the only help and relief you and I know is that God saw our relatives through those battles and wars. He is still protecting us now and bringing us through the wars that we constantly have with principalities demons and all of our enemies. God is all merciful and graceful in protecting us from harm and danger.

Today we live because the blood of Jesus was applied over our lives. He covers our heart, mind, soul, spirit and strengthens us which enables us to be victorious against Satan in every way. Satan was defeated by Jesus because of His love demonstrated on the cross and the power in His blood applied. When Jesus' blood was applied, He did not miss any of us. He covered us then and covers all of us now, the lost and those that feel abandoned. He covers us because He loves us more than we love ourselves. His love transcends imagination and any intellectual thoughts or ideas of man. He paid our debt to the Father. Because of His love for us, He washed us whiter than snow. He removed the sin stain from our lives so that we never would have to worry about it again Isaiah 64. He removed what the enemy wants you and I to keep in our lives which is sin. But thanks to the living God who has delivered us from darkness and the grips of sin.

Anybody can apply almost anything in life. But life has too many applications for one man to try to take hold of and cure them. Jesus is our cure anyway you want to see it. Any application outside the will of God will be useless because it is limited and it does not have the power of Christ in it. But the application of His word will bless us throughout eternity.

We apply money as purchasing power in our lives. But for so many they make it an essential substance of life. That is so far from the truth. We need to start understanding that there is nothing more powerful than the blood of the Lamb applied to our lives. There is nothing that can be compared to the precious blood of the Lamb. Money and power will not do the fix in your spiritual life. Winning the lottery will not fix your soul salvation. There is nothing wrong with having money. But we need to understand that Jesus died for us to give us life and give it more abundantly. He has made all things possible for us. So it really does not matter whatever else you apply in your life outside of the precious blood because the blood is the only thing that can save you. Today is your day to accept the Jesus Christ as the Lord of your life.

Rich people apply millions of dollars on Wall Street into the stock market and into banks. Nevertheless, there are millions of dollars to renew investments every day. Some would debate that these millions do not mean anything nor do they have the impact. I want to say to you that God has a blessing for you. Do not get discouraged. Just remember. Do not let Jesus pass you by with all of your investment every day. Instead grab hold of Him and get your blessings. Make Jesus the investment in your life from now on. He made you His! He washed you in His precious blood to atone you and I from the wrath and the grips of the enemy. Remember, you are covered in His blood and you are rich in His kingdom. You can't help but to be highly blessed.

Governments apply billions of dollars each month for war and foreign relations and foreign policy. They invest to maintain relationships and peace. They invest to use top dollar to bring war to a close and find peaceful solutions. Why not invest in Him who loves to bring peace to our hearts and minds. Invest in His Kingdom by first accepting Him in your life. It is then when you will know that the blood was applied.

Jesus defeated Satan on Calvary for the world to come back to Him as He took away the sin. His blood was our atonement. He identifies with us and His blood. Someone made a joke one day of who had made him clean through and through? He wanted to see the evidence of who cleaned him. He wanted to know how the blood was applied. God is able to do all of these things. Somehow in His own infinite wisdom, He broke us out of the prison of Satan and allowed us to sup with Him. You can be transformed by the renewing of you mind.

The blood applied is your way in to get to heaven and bow before His throne. He knows each of us by name. He knows the impact of His blood. We know that He is the God that blessed through the power of His blood.

We take communion now to recognize His blood and broken body. Corinthians 11:23-34. We identify with His death burial, resurrection. It appears that in order to get something to happen new and something to be victorious, it always had to be blood involved. I am so glad that Jesus was made the perfect sacrifice for my sin. He became sin on a cross for all my transgression, all of my mistakes, all of my failure in loving other people. He became the one and only perfect sacrifice. His bloodshed was and is the perfect purpose and means of new life. Jesus is the one who made life possible to live and worth living for in this world.

PRAYERS

Father, thank you for the blood of your son, Jesus Christ who sacrificed His life for the sin of this world. I bow before you Lord with Honor, glory, thanksgiving and praise. Hallelujah

JOHN 19

LOVE ON THE CROSS

JOHN 19:31-35 Therefore, because it was the Preparation Day, that the bodies should not remain on the cross on the Sabbath (for that Sabbath was a high day), the Jews asked Pilate that their legs might be broken, and that they might be taken away. Then the soldiers came and broke the legs of the first and of the other who was crucified with Him. But when they came to Jesus and saw that He was already dead, they did not break His legs. But one of the soldiers pierced His side with a spear, and immediately blood and water came out. And he who has seen has testified, and his testimony is true; and he knows that he is telling the truth, so that you may believe.

    That day was the day that every man, woman and child should always remember. No one has ever done anything like it before. Jesus demonstrated love beyond measure on the day He died on the cross. No other event in history or anything in our minds could compare to Jesus death for every human being. People cry when they think of the fact that one man fully divine, innocent of every charge that was place against Him, took a beating that no one else could have ever made it through. I was in the driver's seat one day when a man called me all kinds of names and was ready to run me over. What I learned about the driver's seat is that I am supposed to be in control for a certain amount of time especially behind the wheel. Jesus was in the driver's seat to make it to the cross and to be stretched high onto the cross. People cry when they think of the fact that He loves them so that He was willing to hang on a cross for someone that He in the flesh He wore never met us but still hang on the cross.
    To this day my heart still tries to imagine how He could love me so that He had to carry His own cross while being beaten then allow Himself to be nailed to a cross constructed by evil men. I still continue trying to imagine the fullness of His love for me to take on my sin, a person He created before time and never met. In Isaiah 53, it is written, "by His stripes we are healed." We were on our way to death by the wrath of God being poured out on us. He already recognized us as wretched people, yet precious enough in His eyes to save from death. Jesus stepped in with the power of love and save us from the Fathers wrath. The cross is precious to all people because Jesus carried it and died for our sin. In those times, they hang criminals on the cross

and wait for them to suffocate to death. This particular time they nailed Jesus to the cross and pierced Him in the side and blood came out with water.

When we see the cross, we see the most precious commitment and act of love that has ever existed in this world because of the blood of the lamb. He died for me and you. It is when people truly receive that truth in spirit and in the heart is when change in worship and heartfelt thanksgiving is activated on the inside. Some people may wear a cross as a symbol, but it is a reminder what Jesus did for a world entrenched in sin. It is a reminder that people have been redeemed. It is the evidence that sin was destroyed on the cross by the power of God invested in His precious Son Jesus. God destroyed sin in His son's body on the cross. There is simply no sacrifice that could take the place of Jesus. He was and is the only way out of sin. He is the only way to everlasting life. Jesus is the way the truth and the life and He is the only way to the Father.

PRAYERS

Father, thank you for sending your Son Jesus to die on the cross for my sin. Your love is unlimited. Your name is praised and glorified forever.

COLOSSIANS 2

WORSHIP GOD IN YOUR WHITE ROBE

REVELATION 7:13 Then one of the elders asked me, These in the white robes who are they, and where did they come? I answered, Sir, you know. And he said, These are they who have come out of the great tribulation; they have washed their robes and made them white in the blood of the Lamb.

John had a vision that allowed him to see in the heavenly realm. In fact he was taken to heaven in the Spirit to see what God wanted to reveal to Him. In that event, John was moved in the spirit, like in a time portal. He was allowed to see those dressed in white robes. He was allowed to see several things that would come to pass. Jesus even showed John Himself. He revealed the throne to John. He revealed the fountain of blood that never runs dry to John. He revealed what would take place in the future to John. In one scene, one of the elders in heaven saw John and responded to him. The Elder had identified the thousands and thousands of worshipers as those that came out of the great tribulation.

God blessed all worshipers in that He allowed their robes to be washed in the blood of the Lamb. These are those that believe and have accepted Christ Jesus as Lord and Savior. They made it through the roughest of tests of faith. There is no one else that can make robes white by the washing of the blood. Our Father in Heaven can do things beyond our comprehension and our wildest imagination. He washed us in the blood of the lamb.

God wants His people to see where they will spend eternity when they become one of His believers and followers. God wants His children to see the blessing of eternal life. It is the will of God that we spend eternity with Him. His will is for you to join Him in Heaven when the time comes. So believe in Him and worship Him and be watchful for when He breaks the sky wide open. Life will no longer be as you know it. He is Lord!

Our white robes are not ordinary robes. We wear robes for so many reasons. Some are for walking around in the comfort of your home. Some robes represent those that fight in the boxing arenas. There are robes that are specifically designed for Priest. We have been designated to wear the robe to represent priesthood. Jesus wore His robe and it was designed perfectly to fit our High Priest. You can worship in any clothing attire but the white robe that Jesus will place on us is to recognize and set apart those that made it through the tribulation. They are anchored in praise for the Most High God. Today is your day to know for sure that you will wear a white robe that was washed in the blood of the Lamb. Get God today and worship Him in the beauty of His holiness.

Please understand that the Lord washed those that followed Him and gave them a new identity in heaven. When the Lord gives you a new identity, it's time to act on it and use what you have from the Lord. Ask God to anoint you for His purpose.

Most people have identity crisis that plague their lives. Some have identity crisis that takes over their lives and their families as well. Today is a new day and the old day has passed away. It is high time for you to get your blessings. Look for your blessing that will get you to heaven.

When all the Christians get to heaven, they will have joyous time in worship and in praising His righteous name. There will be a continuous party in heaven. It will last forever because there is everlasting rejoicing in worshipping God. There is joy to be in His presence. So, can you imagine those that have and those that are destined to come out of the great tribulation? Those that are conquers in Jesus Christ will come out of the great tribulation. He said, in Romans that we are more than conquerors in Christ Jesus.

I believe it to be absolutely true because His word in Rev 7:17 says that "For the Lamb on the throne will be their shepherd. He will lead them to springs of life-giving water. And God will wipe every tear from their eye." These believers came out of the tribulation. You see when you worship and serve the Lord in faithfulness, He will bless you to the point of bringing you out of the tribulation to get your white robe and worship him. Then you will reign with Him forever. Praise to His Holy name **John 4.**

PRAYER

Father, thank you for your redeeming power. I am saved by your grace and look forward to the great day to be caught up in the air with you. Thank you for allowing me to reign with you. Praise to Jesus Christ our Lord.

ROMANS 8

WISE LEADERS

Proverbs 9:10 The fear of the Lord is the beginning of wisdom, And the knowledge of the Holy One is understanding. For by me your days will be multiplied, And years of life will be added to you.

Wise leaders must be in place everywhere you go especially for key decisions pertaining to life, death and everyday important business transactions. Wisdom is important for those jobs that require leadership and supervision. Wisdom comes from the fear of the Lord. In other words, you must reverence the Lord with all your might and with all of your heart, soul and mind. You have an understanding of who He really is in your life. Wisdom is a requirement to have an effective family life. You cannot lead your home if you do not have some wisdom. You might be making it by your coat tail but soon or later, you will see the need for wisdom.

Some of the most amazing questions asked are by children. They love to ask random questions such as where did God come from? Where is God right now? They like to ask question, Daddy why do you not attend church? Mother, who do I look like the most you or daddy? Mother, where does Jesus live? Why does He love me so much? Daddy what is the planet made out of? When will the earth come to an end? Mom, where is heaven? Yes they put all of them together at one time and ask a dozen of questions and expect an intelligent and accurate answer. Children do not only want an answer. They want reasoning behind the answer. They want to understand what is really going on.

A man without wisdom cannot truly answer those questions because He has no word in Him. He has no insight to who God really is. That why it so important that every man take that step of salvation and commit himself to the word of God. Get anchored in the wisdom of the Lord. You can learn more than you ever imagined in the word of God and be set free at that same time. There is nothing wrong with college degrees. You can have as many as you desire, but if you have no word, you just have degrees and you are flapping in the wind with zero wisdom. Wisdom will give you vision and boldness. You may gain worldly wisdom and get limited results, however Godly wisdom will give you maximum results and a better lifestyle. The other mistake is that he has not accepted Jesus Christ as his personal Savior and Lord.

This is a dangerous thing for his life and his family. You mean to tell me that there are men who are not training their children up in the way that they should go and not depart? It is a hurtful thing to know that I am not equipping them to have faith in the Most High God . They need that nourishment more than they need the food they eat each day.

I can never forget the day my daughter looked at me and asked her important questions about God. Daddy, how do I know I will go to heaven? I answered her with Romans 10:9. At that point, I became dedicated in serving the Lord and teaching scripture and asking them to memorize verses then recite them to me. I wanted ministering to happen all around my house. You see I had learned some of the key scriptures and knew that the Lord was working on something in my life and my family. It is good to have the word rooted inside your heart, at the same time knowing that nothing can separate me from the love of God. Jesus becomes your source of strength and you know it without a shadow of a doubt.

I learned early as a young boy growing up with my mother to fear God. When I began to understand that one day I would leave this earth and go to sleep and be put in the ground, I dreamed about living a long life. It became much clearer to me the value of living a good life and just having life inside me.

You see if a child is able to comprehend that God is needed in his life, surely adults can grasp the necessity of having God in their lives. The scripture says when I was a child, I thought as a child, but when I became a man, I put away foolish things. God is saying sometime in life, we have to grow up and be responsible for our lives and those we have a responsibility for as well. Wisdom tells me that God controls it all no matter what. Wisdom tells me that if you put all of your trust in God, you cannot fail with Him. He will take care of you in times of need. You need to know that you have a personal relationship with Jesus. That means that He knows you by name. Thank God that He links these words of wisdom together and sends them to us in spirit and truth. Thank God for revelation knowledge also which sends wisdom from above. He makes it clear that His wisdom is hidden however believers will find answers as long as God Himself reveals.
1 CORINTHIANS 2:7 But we speak the wisdom of God in a mystery, the hidden *wisdom* which God ordained before the ages for our glory

PRAYER

Father, thank you for perfect wisdom that comes from you alone. My heart desires your daily wisdom for my life.

JAMES 3

GET WISDOM IN YOUR HOUSE

Proverbs 9: 1 Wisdom has built her house, She has hewn out her seven pillars.

Wisdom can tell you that your house is the central focus of ministry. Of course Jesus must take first place and take root in your life. Everyone needs to start at their first level of ministry at home. Use your house to train the family in the word and power of God. He will provide answers. Jesus never leaves anything undone. Do you want your household to be complete in Jesus Christ? Do you also want to ask God to restore and bless your house so it is pleasing in His sight? The obvious answer is yes because all people want good things in life. Ask God to do a clean sweep through the house. Ask God to keep His anointing in houses, your body and your home. Ask God to take over your house. Do not leave it unattended to just run to church and leave it out of order. Church needs to start in the home. Take your concerns to the altar in your house. You can also take it to church to see your priest and bow at that altar. Nevertheless family matters start at home. Do not just leave your house just hanging. Why should I minister somewhere else before nurturing my family? Well, keep the focus on the family once you have taken it to the Lord.

Your very first step is to become a man or woman of God for His purpose. Once you have done that then focus on your family with even greater vigor. Seek God to help increase your faith. The old you has some focus but the new you, child of God will have better opportunity to minister at home. Start your practice at home and watch how the Lord moves in your life. This does not mean forget correcting your children. In fact teaching, correcting and nourishing them is a ministry itself. Start at home with love and kindness.

This scripture points to the fact that wisdom lacks nothing. It represents completeness in the will of God. The seven pillars appeal to so many because when you view the seven pillars. The number seven reminds us that God always completes what he has begun. It is God's business for Him to complete what He purposed for life. He does not leave anything undone. When He acts He blesses us in tremendous ways that we can never repay or even imagine. This wisdom in your house should reveal a house that is working on complete happiness and joy. Wisdom is also a way of saying; you are acting in perfection to satisfy your house. God's house is still His house. But you need to know that He is able to recover you and bless you in your house.

A well respected and friendly couple fought like cats and dogs at each other throat. They were all about impressing someone else and full of excuses why their marriage was not working. It got so bad to point of taking each other to court. But you need to understand that God shows in any court room and can change the heart of everyone involved including the Judge. God has wisdom that He gives the judge. The Lord can even give you wisdom before the court room. He can reconcile your marriage before you get to that point. You need to develop a sense of trusting the Most High God and developing a heart of wisdom.

A good woman who is in love with Jesus will demonstrate that wisdom works because she is responsible for her house and she posses the attitude of a helpmate to her husband. More importantly she has learned to submit and surrender to Jesus completely. When doing so her character changes for the good of the family and the ministering that God has laid aside for her.

Anytime a person has to deal with the sin God will immediately restore you from that entanglement. He wants you in His kingdom. You need wisdom so that you will not punish yourself with self guilt and self denial. God helps you to look up to the hills from whence cometh your help. God's wisdom will carry you over and help you to live in the blessings.

PRAYER

Father, thank you for your wisdom in my house. Lord that you give me and my household better understanding. Help us to know you better.

2 PETER 1:8

THE PRINCIPAL THING

PROVERBS 4:7 Wisdom is the principal thing; Therefore get wisdom. And in all your getting, get understanding .

Wisdom is extremely important to life's survival. Wisdom is vitally important to those in leadership roles appointed by God. King David wanted his son Solomon to know the importance of wisdom. He knew that His son would be the successor and he wanted him to be prepared because it was hard being a king to all of those people. You face so much adversity in this life. Then you will have many test that you need to past to be pleasing in God's sight. A person in a position of Pastor or Bishop must have wisdom to lead a congregation appointed by God.

Moses was definitely one who was appointed and ordained by God to bring God's children out of the bondage that Pharaoh had put them in. It took wisdom to go on such a journey to Egypt and be used by God. But the Key to it was that wisdom follows him. At one point Moses felt that he did not have the ability to speak. But because of God unfailing wisdom He assigned Aaron to go with him to speak on behalf of God to the king. Wisdom is what makes people listen. Although sometimes they still do not listen. If you want wisdom, you must pursue it. You must ask God for it. When ask God for wisdom, according to His purpose for you, you get wisdom.

Wisdom defined means the quality or state of being wise. It also means knowledge of what is true or right coupled with good judgment. Another meaning refers to scholarly knowledge or learning. You want the principle thing in all matters. When we talk about the principle it refers to the most important of a particular subject. You will not have wisdom if you do not understand or obtain knowledge in particular subjects or matters. Wisdom implies that you have to know something to have wisdom. Many families experience different things and the solutions sometime vary and are somewhat different in so many cases. Therefore you must have an anointing on your judgment toward situations.

The scriptures teach us about King Solomon who was said to be the wisest man who ever lived beside Jesus of course. God said there will be no one else like Him in wisdom. Most people remember the decision King Solomon made between two women who claimed the same baby. These two women both spoke up to the King stating that the baby belonged to each them.

The woman whom the baby was not related to was willing to allow the baby harm just to prove her point. The other woman had a different view. I believe we missed her judgment as well. She even displayed some wisdom. When King Solomon said to cut the baby in half, he knew exactly what was going to happen. Someone would step up because of their heart and bond to the baby. You see the original mother spoke up and told the King to spare the life of the baby. She told the King to give the baby to the other lady. The King knew that the biological mother's instinct would take over to ensure the utmost safety of the baby. God shows us multiple times that the truth will always come out and wisdom will prevail. 1 King 3:16-28

PRAYER

Lord, give me wisdom to walk this life of ministry led by the Holy Spirit. I open my heart for you to guide me. I know that if you guide me, I will be on the right path.

COL 1:9 -11

OVERCOME SIX PRIDE ISSUES

PROVERBS 6:16 These six things the Lord hates, Yes, seven are an abomination to Him: A proud look, A lying tongue, Hands that shed innocent blood, A heart that devises wicked plans, Feet that are swift in running to evil, A false witness who speaks lies, And one who sows discord among brethren. My son, keep your father's command, And do not forsake the law of your mother. Bind them continually upon your heart;

When people learn the power of love, it helps to overcome the power of hate. As longs as people keep their minds on the Lord instead of meditating and entertaining evil and hate, and then will you get your blessings. God is warning us to not walk in pride, hate or any manner of evil. Walk in love so that you will win souls. Walk under the influence of the Holy Spirit so that hate will not grip you.

God wants us to know the seven things that He hates. He wants us to keep our focus on His loving kindness and His character. Listen to what God is saying get wisdom to overcome. A proud look that makes you feel like you are above God. He is saying don't just concentrate on your image. Know who made you from speaking a word. He wants to remind us that our eyes have an impact in our lives because of how we see ourselves. In some case people see themselves higher than God.

I was in a group study who covered different variation of being a good employee in an environment that support wounded soldiers. In that class they emphasized goals. We normally make goals to remind us of the individual achievements we want to make. I believe that if you replace negatives with positives and evil and hate with a word of success and wisdom, then you will be able to make an impact.

Try something like this: Breaking a proud look: Keep your eyes on the Lord and not being prideful in self accomplishments. Do not lie on others because it is sinful and God sees it rolling off of the tongue of the person telling the lie and the hurt it causes the innocent. Don't murder or take the life of anyone because it is not the will of God that you live with such pain and regret. It is not the will of God that you shed innocent blood. God is able to deliver you out of that situation the enemy lowered you into. Keep your heart filled in the Spirit of Jesus Christ. If you have Jesus inside your heart then the wicked scheme cannot take root because you are now rooted in the will of God by His Son. Remember the story of Moses and Pharaoh, His heart had became harden for the purpose of giving God the glory without him even knowing it, yet with the intention of pouring out evil upon the children of Israel. God finally penetrated his heart and convince him at the Red Sea. But it took God to drown Pharaohs Army. God does not want us to run to evil and celebrate evil. That is what happens when the mind is on worldly things. Do not become a false witness that tell feel good stories that are really a lie on someone or thing. Whatever you do "follow peace with all men because without it, no man shall see God."

PRAYER

Father, I pray to walk under the authority of your Holy Spirit. Keep your servant humble under your power. Only allow me to stand in the wisdom you give. Keep me from pride.

1 PETER 5:6

ONE MAN'S OBEDIENCE

Romans 5:19 For as by one man's disobedience many were made sinners, so also by one Man's obedience many will be made righteous.

When the people of God began to understand His direction on obedience in their individual lives, then and only then will each believer begin to walk in power of His righteousness. Obedience is the key to direct access to righteousness. When you begin to walk in righteousness because you made a decision to subject yourself to the will of Gods' transforming power in obedience, the Holy Spirit will embrace it and bless you in tremendous ways. God wants us to be obedient and submit to His authority and purpose for our lives in every way. The Greek word for obedience is hupakoe. It means to hear under as a subordinate; to listen attentively and to heed or conform to a command and authority. It also means to hearken and submit. We do not submit partial man or woman to God. We submit ourselves totally unto the Lord. It is the power of the Holy Spirit that enables us in obedience and reveals to the Father our commitment to Him. Obedience enables us to be true worshipers and honor Him in the Spirit. Our Lord makes us righteous by our conversion. In the spirit of Christ in our hearts and minds, we are renewed being that walk in the spirit. The Lord takes hold of us and keeps us from being overcome of evil plots, manipulation and the grip of sin. Having been made righteous, we begin to reap the harvest because of our obedience and sowing. The righteous live for the uplifting of the Kingdom of God. Therefore our lives are ordered by the Lord.

God will show His people the blessings of the Lord in more abundance if we abide in Him with obedience. His blessings flow more and more each day in our lives because we believe in the power of His word and His will and promise through the scriptures. It is amazing how people still avoid the most fundamental requirement of God. God spells out in so many scriptures and in so many ways. The first thing in pleasing God is obedience. Why? It is because obedience demonstrates individual love for God and His love for us as well. Obedience is top priority in pleasing God. It is because the fruit of the Spirit, commitment, sacrifice, humility, holiness and relationship are all factors of obedience. The Holy Spirit helps us to be validated in God's eyes with these types of spiritual traits.

It is because He said to "love with all your heart and your entire mind and all your strength." Obedience is necessary to have order and everything that follows for the glorification of Him who called us out of darkness. Walking in the Spirit of the Lord will enable you to be obedient and worship Him with all your heart. Your walk will become faithful and life will be better because he will become real in your life, like never before. Anything on the outside is not of God and has no bearing in your praise life. You will become one who walks with praise on your lips and the depths of your heart will exalt His Holy name. You will be the one who worships in total admiration and glory to His righteous name. This will be because now you know Him.

There is an order that no man can stop from God. Man is incapable of stopping your servant heart. Man is incapable of stopping your heart of stewardship. Man is incapable of stopping the anointing on your life. Once God ordains it, man just need to say Lord what do you want me to do? How can I serve to glorify your Lord? Otherwise man will think that he is God.

There is an order in the home. The man must be the priest in your house or else you are open to the gateway of hell in your house. If a wife is not submissive to her husband then the house is out of order. You are blocking those multiple blessings that God set out for you to have and to overflow in your life.

Then there is the seed planter in the house. God gave man the ability to plant seed. He gave man the right to plant seed so that He would raise an heir in his house. You can look at Abraham's story and that the blessings on Abraham were significant that God had already planned on giving Abraham a son and heir. This simply means that God was waiting on Abraham to be obedient in faith and at the same time God wanted Abraham to trust in Him.

One of the things that I learned about God is that if you trust Him and wait on His promises, you are in for blessings of a lifetime. He will not let us down. You will overflow in the blessings of the Lord because He never goes against His promises and the blessings that are laid up for you and I are innumerable also. Not only will you be blessed, your entire household will be blessed. I am telling you right now that it is time to completely trust God for order, for promises and blessings in our lives. Walk in the power of faith that God will fulfill your heart's desires.

God still orders the house in other respects. You remember God giving Adam a woman. He gave him a woman in holy matrimony, a sealed marriage. Adam was so powerful that he announces that this woman is bone of my bone and flesh of my flesh. Adam was signifying that they are one under God in marriage. You see God did not stop there. He gave the woman the ability to birth. There is no other human being with that capability. Then Jesus said that every male that comes forth from a woman's womb is blessed. Jeremiah 1: 5. I just wanted to tell you that the birth process is never over and has the purpose to bruise the head of the serpent while the Lord is still blessing us. It was the Lord who gave the gift that He gave women.

PRAYER

Father, you made us righteous. I will trust you to walk in righteousness. Help me by the power of your Holy Spirit. Order my steps in obedience to receive righteousness.

DEUTERONOMY 11:26-28

HELP YOUR FAMILY SURVIVE

GENESIS 4:1-11 Now Adam knew Eve his wife, and she conceived and bore Cain, and said, "I have acquired a man from the LORD." Then she bore again, this time his brother Abel. Now Abel was a keeper of sheep, but Cain was a tiller of the ground. And in the process of time it came to pass that Cain brought an offering of the fruit of the ground to the LORD. Abel also brought of the firstborn of his flock and of their fat. And the LORD respected Abel and his offering, but He did not respect Cain and his offering. And Cain was very angry, and his countenance fell. So the LORD said to Cain, "Why are you angry? And why has your countenance fallen? If you do well, will you not be accepted? And if you do not do well, sin lies at the door. And its desire *is* for you, but you should rule over it." Now Cain talked with Abel his brother; and it came to pass, when they were in the field, that Cain rose up against Abel his brother and killed him. Then the LORD said to Cain, "Where *is* Abel your brother?" He said, "I do not know. *Am* I my brother's keeper?" And He said, "What have you done? The voice of your brother's blood cries out to Me from the ground.

Family is the core of our society with Jesus Christ as the head of the family. I cannot think of one family that is exempted from the necessity of surviving in this life. Family is so precious and vital to have in everyone's life. It is comforting to have that sense of belonging to people who love you. We mess up from time to time but the fact remains we need our families and we need God to lead each person in the family. We need the Lord and the family to help each of us straighten up our walk. You know how it is when you see a television show that projects the images of a loving family. It makes your heart warm and you want to act better. You want the real family love. One of the most important points of the family is the role they play in each sibling's life. Everyone is a keeper of the rest of the family. So stop feeling like you are the lost sheep of the family. Ask the Holy Spirit to lift your spirit. He will do it. So trust Him in all things. Trust Him to lead the family. God puts us in positions for some things we do not expect. You may have to take hold of the situation in your family and lead. God already knows best for you. He might just be calling you to lead them in some ways. But when we remember

Mother and her love in our hearts get back on track. We need to be reminded of how to survive as family and members.

The family must be a focused family under God's power and control. Family members must be introduced to Jesus as Lord and Savior. There will be more confusion if you do not have Christ as the center of your life. When you begin to focus on Jesus as the center of your life, prayer and worship time, then you will come to a point where you are pleasing God. He loves it when we give Him all the glory. Focusing on your family as it was originally designed for Adam and Eve was and still is one of God's priorities. Do not shift blame to one another when you fall short of the mark, just get up and get it right. God cast that kind of judgment out of the family. Make your family whole in Jesus Christ by allowing Him to come into the home.

Take life with your family serious to love them more by giving time in prayer, friendship, fellowship, family time, and devotion and just spending quality time. Remember to stay in the word together. It is the key to restoration and renewal in the family and the individual relationship with our Lord, Jesus Christ. Jesus Himself offers the greatest gift that you can receive, salvation through His word and His power. Family matters because of the blood of Jesus that washed us white as snow. I constantly run across families that have personal struggles. Through my observation, I have learned these families are not helping each other survive. They tend to cripple one another without even knowing it.

PRAYER

Father, help me in my Christian walk to make sacrifices pleasing in your sight. May my sacrifices be acceptable for service.

ROMANS 12

GOVERNING AUTHORITIES SUBJECT TO GOD'S AUTHORITY

ROMANS 13: 1-7 Let every soul be subject to the governing authorities. For there is no authority except from God, and the authorities that exist are appointed by God. Therefore whoever resists the authority resists the ordinance of God, and those who resist will bring judgment on themselves. For rulers are not a terror to good works, but to evil. Do you want to be unafraid of the authority? Do what is good, and you will have praise from the same. For he is God's minister to you for good. But if you do evil, be afraid; for he does not bear the sword in vain; for he is God's minister, an avenger to execute wrath on him who practices evil. Therefore you must be subject, not only because of wrath but also for conscience sake. For because of this you also pay taxes, for they are God's ministers attending continually to this very thing. Render therefore to all their due: taxes to whom taxes are due, customs to whom customs, fear to whom fear, honor to whom honor

    The Constitution of United States of America was written under the authority of men who had been persuaded to write about rules and order in a new land of freedom. Many believe that they had to set the foundation of the country under the influence of God in this document called the Constitution. This document meant several things but, one of its most influencing achievements was to incorporate Amendments 13 to abolish slavery and the 14 Amendment which gave the power to vote regardless of race, color or servitude . It finally recognized all men as created equal. It was also the law set forth that people should follow government orders, and make specific demands by law in order that these articles will be enforced to fall into place for the common good and order of the people and this Nation.

    They wrote the preamble, the Bill of Rights Amendments 1-10 and the entire 27 Amendments that serve as the law for this Nation. The constitution was designated to be the law of the land. But it still did not turn out to be a perfect system of government just because of the writings. It took men to go to war to set this nation free from its own inadequacies and sin nature to finally shape a nation for its own welfare and prosperity. We need sometimes to glance back at what happened to be reminded of freedom's cost and freedom gained. Thousands of men died for freedom during the Civil War and many other battles. We should always think of the goodness of our Lord who set things in order in man's heart and mind to begin the freedom process and healing process. Government should never think that it is free from God. Therefore faith and politics are integrated because God made everything and everybody. Most people have some of the same thoughts, dreams and hopes when it comes to peace and prosperity. They have a common bond when it comes to loving their neighbor.

Shaping views and character is extremely necessary in every country and in every household. The people make the government. The people are the centerpiece after God. But shaping faith and character is essential and you cannot go without it and be truthfully successful in the Lord . In fact, failure will approach every time in the absence of faith in God. Faith, integrity, character, truth, justice and the love for Christ and your neighbor is what God requires of all of people. They are at the highest of necessity. He will guide us by His Holy Spirit. Make up your mind today to follow His wisdom and blessings for your life, family and friends.

Faith and Politics sounds like something to so many that can never be work out or worked together. Well it is time to go against the grain, the old belief systems is just what it is, a belief system. It has no weight or bearing except being out of touch of reality. Politics may survive without sound faith in God. But Godly order and the appropriate politics must have God at the center to survive. I believe that this country is surviving and setting new standards that are making a difference. Politics may be the procedures, laws, and government controlled resources and spending. The deficient and the economy are elements that are a huge focus. We built it as God gave it. We should not worship it nor get off track with the Lord. We had faith in it all these years. Keep having faith so that things will get better. Make sure that your faith is in God first.

Faith is a Spiritual belief system that each person takes on an individual belief and personal relationship. For example, with me, I believe whole heartedly and with all my mind, soul, and spirit and strength that God is God and there is no one like Him. I believe that all of my blessings come from Him alone. I believe that He even allows others to bless you by blessing them. I believe that God sent His Son, Jesus and He lived on earth 33 years and died and rose from the grave on the third day. I believe that He died for my sin, my imperfections and disobedience. It is important to have faith because it puts you at a level of wise thinking and knowing that Jesus is your Savior and Redeemer who loves you unconditionally. Faith connects you with

God and therefore your political role becomes much more trusted and you become much more confident in what you are doing for the Church, community and the world. Blessings, Honor, and Glory to our Lord. Amen

PRAYER

Lord, I pray that your Holy Spirit guide the President of the United States, our government and the people. Lead this Nation, the Executive, Judicial, and legislative branches of Government under the God. Lead the President's cabinet and all supportive agencies within and external. I pray your angels stand with all the people of every nation for the sake of love, peace and joy throughout the world.

ROMANS 13

BREAKING THE PRISON MENTALITY

MATTHEW 25:36 I was naked and you clothed Me; I was sick and you visited Me; I was in prison, and ye came unto Me.

It is what you do in life that counts the most. If your actions please our Lord in Heaven, then you are on the path that God wants for you. You may be fulfilling the purpose and plan for your life. One thing is for sure, whatever has been holding you back from pleasing God, it is time to break that prison mentality.

It is what you do for the ministry of Christ Jesus that has everlasting blessings and rewards. You want to make life count regardless of what it looks like at this present moment in time. Make your life the best life that God has to offer. People will not think of you like you do yourself, so get ready to make changes to please God. The service in God's kingdom matters more than you and I could ever imagine in our minds. God is infinite in wisdom and mystery. God is infinite in His Glory and Holiness. His rewards are far greater than you and I could ever dream of. I am so glad that He is unlimited in the blessing of grace and love.

I just could not help thinking about the movie Private Ryan. It was a war story. It seems that war is one of the top issues that stimulate a certain amount of violence in our communities and worldwide. It was a story of young man who served in war. It happened that he had other brothers serving in the war as well and they all were killed. He was the last remaining son alive; the Army calls it "Sole Surviving." He was the only son left to carry on the family's name.

The Commanding General sent out a special Task Force to locate him and bring him home to his mother and family. War mentality is similar to prison mentality is so many ways. They both are the result of sin. Peace and order is violated because of war. Enemy tactic and strongholds are evident in both situations. If you are not careful your mind can remain locked up in both circumstances. I never forgot that one scene that still sticks with me today while viewing Private Ryan's rescue on the bridge in a heated battle. The actor Tom Hanks, starring as the CPT of the Special Tasks force in his dying words, he said to PVT Ryan "Make Life Count." No wonder millions watched the movie. Today come out of your prison and make life count! War can be a prison and a stronghold that keeps you mentally hurt and damaged. But you can overcome all things by the power of the Holy Spirit. Even if war causes hurt, death, pain, suffering, you have a healer and a comforter to help you through all of your times experiencing them. Remember Romans 10:9 no matter what happens in life. You have eternal life with Christ Jesus after this life is over. The effects of war and anything that bounds you and places you in depression and sets your life back from progression are prisons. But they do not have the power to hold you back forever. You have an advocate who is strong and mighty and His name is Jesus. You can break the prison mentality. You can break the war mentality that left you injured. You can overcome all wounds and hurts at their core. With all your might, call on the name of the Lord. He is our Strong Tower, He is our shelter in a storm, He is the one who rocks us in the midnight hour when no one else is there. He is the God who sends His angels to guard us in times of trouble. Trust Him right now.

You and I can always break the prison mentality by our submission and witness for Christ. You work for God to witness to the lost and to help restore those who need a helping hand. You have a mission in life today. You might as well get up and get to moving in your witness before the Lord. Jesus was talking about what people do counts as though they did it for Him. You see what we do for others gives God the glory and honor. God sees the good heart of your good deeds.

True, one of the most common mistakes in society is to have a prison mentality. There is a prison mentality that keeps so many men down in the pits of hell and locked up. The same mentality keeps men away from worship time to the Lord. There is a prison mentality that keeps the household down and under constant attack of the enemy. There is a prison mentality that is expected by the enemy and some people sad to say, keep falling into the same traps. This prison mentality is demonic because it persuades men and women with lies that there is no better life on the outside of prison bars. It constantly lies to everyone about the Lord. It will make you believe that God can not break your chain and shackles. Evil will make you believe that your life is over. But your life is never over because you have been redeemed, washed in the blood of the lamb. God wants you to get up and start making a difference in life today. Let God work a work in you that even those that look down on you will be baffled in amazement of what He has done and give praise to the Kingdom of God. Let them see what you contribute to society. Life is not over yet, stand up man! Stand up brother! Stand up you preacher! Stand up Christian soldier! Stand up women, Stand up child of God; you have work to do for the Kingdom sake.

How do you break the prison mentality? You break it by the power of prayer. In Luke 18:1-8, it states, "men ought to always pray." You break the prison mentality by meditating in the word of God. This should get at millions of people saved and delivered into God's Kingdom. You break the prison mentality by serving God in prison and wherever you are in life. You can be on the moon and still serve God. Your ministry in Christ Jesus is not limited by your condition. The only limits you have are the ones you accepted from the enemy and yourself. That is not God. So denounce it today in by the power of the Holy Spirit. God does not operate that way. You break the prison mentality by acknowledging Jesus as Lord and Savior. Once you get God on your side, there is nothing that He will not do for you. He can fix anything. You should ask to attend programs such as church service to keep you from fallen. He desires that we fellowship in the spirit and in the power of His love.

Bless His name because Jesus breaks every power that entangles the mind, soul, heart and strength. What I mean by that is He can get inside us and change us in every area of our lives. If the prison mindset is what you have, He can take it away. If you believe that Jesus is Lord of your life, He can strip you of any wrong mindsets and wrong heart conditions.

God has a ministry for everyone. Never think that you have been left out. Just because someone says it, does not mean it's true. In God's kingdom, work will never run out. Jesus said when I was in a condition, you took care of me. When I was in the hospital or at home on my sick bed, you visited me. When I was locked up for my mess ups, you visited me. You are not in the prison anymore. Break the prison mentality with the Spirit of Jesus Christ and His rest in your heart today. God is able to deliver you and me.

PRAYERS

Father, I pray to deny myself and pick up my cross that I may help someone in need that your name Lord, will be glorified.

MATTHEW 16:23-24

GOD KNOCKING AT YOUR HEART

MATTHEW 7:7 Ask, and it will be given to you; seek, and you will find; knock, and it will be opened to you. For everyone who asks receives, and he who seeks finds, and to him who knocks it will be opened.

Every time you get an opportunity to open your heart to God, do it and see what happens. Every time you hear God speaking to your heart, allow Him to do a work on the inside of you. It is important to understand that God is always working on the hearts of men and women. The Holy Spirit is always at work in the lives of both the believer and the unbeliever. He wants to convince the unbeliever who Jesus is and what the advantages there are to surrendering to Jesus Christ as Lord.

The question you have to ask yourself is what do you want in life? Jesus can help you with anything. Have you asked Him a question to your situation? He said ask, and it will be given to you. He did not limit anything because He already knows what you will ask for; maybe one good idea is to ask God to help you accomplish your dreams and destiny. If you ask and believe, then you need to trust Him. Faith in God is the solution to that thing you ask of God and receive. If you ask God for a new house because you need it, the God we are talking about supplies all of your needs. If you need your marriage to work because of distractions and enemy attacks on your marriage, God is the God that put marriages together in Corinthians 7. He will work on your marriage according to His purpose for your marriage.

Seek after God always because He is first in your life. If you had challenges or barriers in the past, make Him first and seek Him always. If you are searching for the Spirit of God in your life, make sure that you have accepted Him into your heart first. Some people believe that God is just with them. The bible declares that God saves us by His grace in Ephesians 2:8. When you know that you have been saved by grace. Seeking Him is always in the forefront of your mind because you know that God hears you and will answer you. Why are you seeking God? You seek God because you need Him to bless you. You seek God because you need someone to trust completely and with total authority and confidentiality. You need to see God because your life depends on it. You see the bible declares that the enemy comes to kill, steal, and destroy. The bible tells us that the enemy is like a roaring lion seeking and roaming this earth to see whom he may devour. The scripture says in Psalms 27, that the Lord is my strength and my salvation who shall I fear? The Lord is the strength of my life whom shall I be afraid? The power of His love is what saves you and me every time. Seek Him with all your heart. Isaiah says seek Him while He may be found. Today is your day to know Him better.

God is always knocking at the heart of man. He is knocking at the door of your heart to come in and stay with you. You just like everyone else has an entrance in your heart that God can come in and sup with you. He will come in and change your heart and transform you into the image of the person He wants you to be. Yes, God is just like that mail man knocking at your door to give you new mail that you receive so easily. You receive that 10,000 dollar check. If someone opens a door for you to become a millionaire, an actor, song artist, dancer, or any assistance of value to you including income, you will receive it because you believe that you deserve it. Well that is what Jesus is saying; you deserve the best at all time. You deserve to have Jesus in your heart. He is knocking to come into your heart. In **Romans 10:9, He says, "that if you confess with your mouth the Lord Jesus and believe in your heart that God has raised Him from the dead, you will be saved."** He is more important that all the other opportunities and blessings that you and I have gained in our lifetime. In fact, he is the reason for you gaining all your success and any accomplishment that awarded blessings.

PRAYERS

Father, you know how to be gentle when knocking at the heart. Lord come into my heart and minister to me daily. Use my heart for your glory by the power of your Holy Spirit.

1 SAMUEL 13

STEP OUT OF YOUR CONDITIONS

GENESIS 12:1-3 Now the LORD had said to Abram: "Get out of your country, From your family and from your father's house, To a land that I will show you. I will make you a great nation; I will bless you And make your name great; And you shall be a blessing. I will bless those who bless you, And I will curse him who curses you; And in you all the families of the earth shall be blessed."

    Some of the most commonly made mistakes in life is when a person does not listen to God and acts disobedience which also reveals the level of faith in God. What makes us a better person is when we turn it around and walk in obedience and faith. We can only doing by allowing the Holy Spirit to lead us. One of the primary solutions to turning things around is to step of your condition to listen to the voice of God when He speaks to you. He will give you specific steps and action in life that will please Him. We have to learn to conform to the Lord's word and what He asks of us. It is those same old conditions and specific circumstance that keep people in a place separated from God's purpose for your life. If God blessed you with ten million dollars, you would not remain in the same old house. Be for real! You know that you would immediately search for one of the biggest mansions you could find. Your entire mindset change because you desire to step out of the old beat up home to a better home. Today God wants you to depart from the old mindset and the old way of thinking. He wants us to depart from the old place that keeps us down. God might be telling you today to step out of those conditions that are holding you back from success. The question for you, do you hear His voice and will you obey God to get your blessing and glorify Him as well? The answer for you and I should be a resounding yes Lord, I will obey. I will conform to your will in my life. I will step out of all those stuck conditions, potholes, pits, and dark area and ask God to do a new thing in my life.

    Abram at a time in his life heard God's voice and moved by faith and obedience. It was his time to move. God set him up to move to be blessed. I know you can stand to be blessed! We may not move perfect in obedience, but if we move, God sees and rewards us because He knows why we are moving, why we are acting obedient. It is our destiny by faith to act in faith and accordingly when God speaks. He already knows! Nothing is a surprise to God, our Father. Stepping out of your condition to get your blessing is one of God's priorities for your life. Prostitutes and drug addicts must step out of their condition. Top priority is acting in faith and obedience to His commands. He speaks and sends us to safety. Today for every Christian the priority is to first get salvation. The simple step of opening your mouth in confession and opening your heart is a form of stepping out of your condition. Ask Jesus to come into your heart today. Then your faith walk will begin.

Abram was later rewarded for his faith and obedience in God. One of the things that impressed God so much was Abrams faith to say goodbye to any opposition in his life, to any thought of comfort or a comfort zone mentality, to any condition that had bondage. Yes, it meant existing false gods, any relative that did not see God the way he saw God. They have not had the same experience with God talking to them the exact same way and moment in time. You do not stop loving your relatives. You just do not have to live like anyone. You have been transformed to walk in the image of Christ. You have been born again.

Sometimes in life you have to strip yourself of things that are holding you back. Other people may not understand nor comprehend what is going on with you. But you need to know for yourself what God has for you. God has for you what God has for you. No one can take it away with their mentality or any kind of way. They may not understand what you are experiencing in Christ and that is fine. They might not understand the joy you feel in your heart because you know that you heard God speaking to you. They just don't know what you are experiencing! They may never know until you depart, taking the nearest exit route to get away from them that is holding you back. God wants His people to develop an attitude of stepping out in faith and on His word. His word is your path of life. His word will deliver you and enable you to prosper.

You may have heard plenty people talking about stepping out. The problem is they develop the when, where, why and how are you going to do it mentality. Those questions are fine but if you use them to make an excuse, then you will miss out on the blessing God has for you. Go wants us to get ourselves out of the picture. Ask the Lord to move in your life. Do not misunderstand, you may have to do some things to get things going. But you must operate under God's influence. If you are going to do anything that will succeed, you need to do it because of God and under the power of the Holy Spirit. Your moment and timing and intention must be because of God. Abram strictly moved because of God. By reading this scripture it tells me that Abram had to have a heart to move strictly for God's purpose.

One thing for sure is that when you step out and obey God, there has to be blessings in store.

I look at many of the churches today and most of them step out when it seem like it was no hope and no help from no one else. But they trusted in God. You are not going into any ministry unless you are trusting and having faith in God. People have started small ministries to mega ministries and the attack still goes on against the church. But the ministry continues in the power of His might.

I believe God sees the worship inside us and that worship belongs to Him. God sees the faith inside of us and that faith belongs to Him. God sees the glory that you have to give Him and you and I must give Him the glory. It is not yours, not one measure is yours or mine, and it belongs to our Lord and Redeemer of our souls.

Today, I want you to know that your obedience and faith in Christ Jesus is far better than any prophet or any other person in the bible. We need to have the hope in Jesus' return just like we have to believe in His resurrection from the dead. You see my friend Jesus moved by faith when He carried the cross on cavalry. He did so that we could one day see that His faith in His Father was stronger than even Abrams when He moves in accordance to the voice of the Lord.

I remember the days of warfare, fighting a fight that was not mine. Have you ever fought a fight that was not yours? I stepped between two brothers because they were blood brothers and got hit in an effort to stop the fight before blood was shed between those two brothers. But whatever happened between those two brother were relational and within the family. So even thou blood was shed, pain was inflicted and feelings were hurt, there was still reconciliation between the two. Why was that so? They still had faith and the love inside of each other because they were blood brother. They knew that they came from the same seed, same father and same mother and at home is where security exists. Jesus reminds us that He is the one who shed the blood that covers us that brings us into the family of Christ Jesus. We are the family that have salvation and will reign with Him in eternity. If It had not been for the blood of Jesus, where would be. He makes us blood brother and sister and brother in Christ. So we must live the life of love, joy and peace in pure holiness.

There are other warfare moments like serving in Iraq or Afghanistan where the bullets are all around your head. They will kill you without hesitation as sure as the midst and an open target. It is important that every soldier know that God loves them more than they could ever imagine no matter where you are. He loves you in battle and out of battle, at home and wherever soldiers are located. Your life is not over and it will not be over because you are a child of God

Jesus is showing us a land that we can possess. He is pointing out things that we need to do to glorify Him. Has God shown you anything yet? Has He shown you that He will order your steps if you just step out on faith. The same Jesus will bless you just like He blessed Peter for stepping out of the boat to walk on water to Him. You have got to believe just like Peter did for that moment in time. He knew it was Jesus! Can you feel Jesus in your life? If you step out and feel like you're sinking sometimes, Jesus will reach His hand out and pull you up so you will not drown. Blessed be His Righteous and Holy name.

PRAYERS

Father, at times I need help to move when you say move. I pray for the Holy Spirit to move in my life that I may be obedient to your plan and purpose.

JUDGES 6

GET THROUGH THE MAIN GATE

MATTHEW 7: 13 Enter by the narrow gate; for wide is the gate and broad is the way that leads to destruction, and there are many who go in by it. Because narrow is the gate and difficult is the way which leads to life, and there are few who find it.

One of the most critical skills to have in the military is having the ability to maneuver and negotiate obstacles and challenges on the battlefield. Therefore it is absolutely of the highest importance to have the Land Navigation skills to complete every course. Before you are tested, you get trained on what to do in order to know your direction on a map. A map has several gridlines, several north translations and features that you must know in order to get through and pass the test. If you want to be successful in finding your way home, you must be able to read a map. Then you must have the confidence to know the path home. It reminds me of entering the right gate or the wrong gate. If you enter the wrong gates, you could easily end up in the devils court.

Night Land navigation is much more difficult that day time especially when there are other tasks involved. It adds more stress because you have to more thought and execution movement to complete it at 100%. Routes are so extremely dark that you may not be able to see the hand of your leader not to mention your own hand. We like to think that you could see God's hand directing you. Our God has different way to direct us while we are on the path.

It is sometimes at the gate where you get some directions to which location and path to take. The gate also represents the place we call heaven, a place of thanksgiving, a place of worship and a place of deep adoration and exaltation, a place where we travel in spiritual style to get there. The gate represents a place of entry. Psalms 100:4 states "enter into His gates with Thanksgiving, and into His courts with Praise." What a blessing to be able to do so every single day of your life. We should always enter the presence of God with thanksgiving because of what He has already done. Another scripture says that "the gates of Hades shall not prevail against it". Matthew 16. Satan, hell and all of its demons can never stop the church because Jesus already defeated him. Jesus is eternal and has all power in His hand. His glory is forever and ever.

As a believer of Jesus Christ residing in your heart, evil will be unable to stop you for whatever purpose God sets out for you. The enemy may delay you and try to imitate denied you, but it is all a façade and all false imitation. You need to know that you are a child of the most High God. You need to understand it clearly in your heart, mind and spirit.

Our God allows us to see something in this wide gate so we can get an understanding of reality. The wide gate is the gate that can lead you to hell. It is a real place, but not for the believer to visit, not for the believer to worry about, only those who do not believe in Jesus Christ will end up in that place. Tell all of your friends today that they need to accept Jesus as Lord and Savior. We denounce and rebuke every measure of Hell and every evil spirit that presents itself against the Saints of God and the blessings of the Lord. We confess and profess the name of Jesus to rebuke and destroy all attacks of the enemy. Hell is a permanent place of residence to those who do not believe. We pray that they change their mindsets to believe in Jesus Christ as Lord and Redeemer.

The narrow Gate is the gate that leads to heaven, eternal life. Anyone who puts forth the best effort can remain on this path of the narrow gate. The just need to have faith **and "trust the Lord with all thine heart and lean not to your own understanding, but acknowledge Him in all your ways and He will direct your path."** Most people never try to stay on the narrow road because they experience a road block that might deter them. They experience pot holes and deep ruts that they find themselves in after taking wrong turns and traveling on the wrong paths and routes. God wants you to get on the best highway so you can enter into the best gate.

The military is located throughout the world. Large populations enter daily to get to a required destination. Every soldier that is currently serving and those that have retired for various reasons travel daily to get to military installations as well. Most travel to the military base because that is the place of duty. Some, on the other hand travel because it provides a sense of security for jobs and shopping centers. What is so important about the installation along with its high security is the fact that you have to have an identification card to enter the main gate and all military gates because they have the same level of security and restriction for access to enter. If your identification card is not stamped and approved and authorized by the proper agency, guards at the gate will not allow you inside. This gate is the proper gate for military soldiers to enter to get equipped for battle and to plan engagement against the enemy. In this gate you stay on the right track to defeat all the arrows that the enemy throws at you. In this gate, you have the capability to put armor on and fight back. In this gate, you get prepared for war that is happening on the outside. Here you have all the resources needed to be successful. When you function out of your atmosphere and environment, it may not be to your benefit. That is why it is important to remain on the right path and entering into the right gate. You would not enter into the enemy's gate unless you had been prepared to do battle. You would not enter the enemy's gate unless you were totally equipped to destroy the enemy and his foes.

They may even have some wrong ambition that will deter them. I want you to know today that Jesus moved every barrier, road block, and experience that got in His way to die on the cross. We do not have time to let something little or imaginary impede our visions and purpose of Jesus Christ our Lord.

The wide gate is symbolic of the path leading to hell. Stop and take an assessment of where you are in life. What are you doing every day to progress in the Kingdom? Who are you serving every day? We all need to know that we serve our risen Savior. Do you even know and care about where you are destined to go after this life is over? Sure you are, everyone dreams of a fantasy place. That place we often dream of is Paradise. I never hear people saying that they want to go to hell. It is because God designed us to want Him and to want to live with Him forever. Today, ask God to remove the scales from your eyes so that you can get back on the narrow path that leads to heaven.

The key to getting through the main gate of Jesus Christ is repentance, obedience, sacrifice, and believing by faith that He is the Son of God. He is the only true and wise God that delivered us from God's wrath. It is high time to tell friends and family about entering into the narrow gate. It is the gate where Jesus will bless you before you enter and while you are entering.

PRAYERS

Father, send your angels when I need help at various obstacles in my life. It is your power that gets me on the right path and through all barriers.

ACT 3

HE REMOVES ALL BLINDNESS

JOHN 9:13-15 They brought him who formerly was blind to the Pharisees. Now it was a Sabbath when Jesus made the clay and opened his eyes. Then the Pharisees also asked him again how he had received his sight. He said to them, "He put clay on my eyes, and I washed, and I see."

You heard that expression before, take off the blinders so you can see. Every Christian and every person needs to take off the blinders in all areas of their live, especially the spiritual. The question is where do you have blinders? You will feel better and live better when the blinders are removed. You see when those spiritual blinders come off; the truth is revealed and acknowledged. The word is illuminated and the truth comes forward. When the blinders come off, you are now in a spiritual zone that God has placed you to see. Can you see the things you have been missing all of this time? We as Christians have to continue the walking and speaking the word to help others.

Today is the day to take your blinders off! They can be removed whenever you are ready on this day. Jesus is waiting to enter your heart right now. That is exactly what happened to the Apostle Paul when he experienced Jesus during his wicked runs to murder. A conversion was waiting on him. So get ready! You will know that you are ready to run for Him in service as soon as you accept Jesus as Lord in your life. In fact the only way you are truly ready is when you accept Jesus as Lord and Savor in your life. He will be the one to give you permanent vision. Your eyesight and your vision will be restored for the remainder of your life and nothing can change it. Barriers and all kinds of obstacles will be removed. Start trusting in the power of the Holy Spirit.

I know living with the natural body you can see things and they seem so clear. But when you operate in the spiritual realm, God is showing you things that defy the order of the natural realm. He is the God of both supernatural and even the natural because He made us. I, like so many other people have difficulty explaining it all. It is just no way to tell it all. One thing for sure is that God is in charge of the supernatural things that occur in our lives. He is the God of miracles. Things that we cannot control nor understand He is there to show Himself strong. He defies natural order because He is the creator of all things.

A blind man was brought to the Pharisees because they were disturbed at the fact that Jesus had healed a man who was blind all of his life until He met Jesus. The Pharisees did not misunderstand the miracle Jesus had done. They were jealous and felt betrayed by the people because Jesus had gained so much fame for His ministry of healing and delivering people. Jesus had proved Himself to be the son of God. All of the evidence needed was present. However, the Pharisees ignored it because of their interpretation of the law. They ignored it because of the reputation Jesus had gained from the people. Sometimes in life when you are doing the work of God and you do it well, jealousy strikes the heart of people you know or may not know. Jealousy strikes at the core of nerves and individual pride surfaces because the enemy is busy. All this jealousy and thinking that they were suppose to enforce the law over the miracle working power of Jesus had no substance and no way of glorifying God.

Jesus tells us in Mark 2:27-28, that the "Sabbath was made for man, and not man for the Sabbath. Therefore the Son of Man is Lord of the Sabbath." Do not worship the Sabbath day but worship on that day and other days. God is telling us not allow religious beliefs to keep us from helping someone in need on the Sabbath or any day. The Lord has need of your service. If a brother falls in a pit on the Sabbath move with a heart to help him get out that pit. The only true and wise God is not about to allow someone suffer because of the opinions or false ideas and traditions. He does not allow a day go by that His healing touch is not involved in. He is our healer and protector. If you go to hospitals on the Sabbath Day, you will find that the Holy Spirit is there healing people. If you go by the nursing home where people are lonely and in need of companionship, the Holy Spirit is there. If you go by homes where people are not able to get out of bed, Jesus is visiting that person on the Sabbath day and any other day. He will heal on the Sabbath and every day.

In Mark 3: 1-5 **And He entered the synagogue again, and a man was there who had a withered hand. So they watched Him closely, whether He would heal him on the Sabbath, so that they might accuse Him. And He said to the man who had the withered hand, "Step forward." Then He said to them, "Is it lawful on the Sabbath to do good or to do evil, to save life or to kill?" But they kept silent. And when He had looked around at them with anger, being grieved by the hardness of their hearts, He said to the man,**

"Stretch out your hand." And he stretched *it* out, and his hand was restored as whole as the other.

Jesus heals again. This time He entered the synagogue and a man was there who had a withered hand. Jesus was under watch at this time by the Pharisees to see what He would do. And it is just like Jesus not to abandon anyone. He will not let you go broken when you call on Him. Jesus ask the man to step forward with His withered hand. He told the man to stretch out his hand. And he stretched it out and it was healed even better than the other.

The bible says that He never sleeps nor slumbers. He is always on watch, looking for someone who needs a miracle. You see it was on the Sabbath when Jesus opened the eyes of the blind man. He will open your eyes anytime you need Him to. He will remove the scales of darkness from those that have the Pharisee mentality. He will remove the spiritual scales that work to keep you in darkness, working sin. Millions of people today need a touch to see again. They are missing abundant blessings.

You heard the story of the mule stuck in the pit. The owner never thought for a moment to leave his mule so He stayed all night, digging the hole wider and trying to pull the mule free. He knew if he left that mule in the hole, he would just die. He also knew that the mule had a special place in him. You see when we fall into a ditch or a pit God has a special place for us in His heart. He is there no matter what the situation is.

PRAYERS

Father, speak your word and increase my faith that I may be able to see in the spirit. Your power is what I need in my life. I will trust in you Jesus in all things.

MATTHEW 15

RECEIVE YOUR SIGHT

Acts 9:9-14 And he was three days without sight, and neither ate nor drank. Now there was a certain disciple at Damascus named Ananias; and to him the Lord said in a vision, "Ananias" And he said, "Here I am Lord." So the Lord said to him, Arise and go to the street called Straight, and inquire at the house of Judas for one called Saul of Tarsus, for behold, he is praying. And in a vision he has seen a man named Ananias coming in and putting his hand on him, so that he might receive his sight. Then Ananias answered, Lord, I have heard from many about this man, how much harm he has done to your saints in Jerusalem. And here he has authority from the chief priests to bind all who call on your name.

Ananias spoke to God saying that this man Saul could never become a Christian because he was murdering Christians. In his mind this was absolutely impossible for a conversion to have happened with this man Saul. How could a murderer be changed so instantly and be proven in God's eye? Only God has such answer. The living God can do anything. He reminded Him that Saul was a chosen vessel. God's power worked on Saul inside and on the outside. He was transformed by Jesus Christ on the road to Damascus. I am convinced that one experience with Jesus can convert any man, woman and child. He has the only true transforming power.

Ananias was surprised that God would select someone who was once an enemy of our Lord and God's Saints. Saul had been a man who killed habitually because of Christianity. He hunted Christians down like dirty dogs to the death. Thank God that He still used Ananias to bless Saul through the Lord. This man whom God selected continued the remaining of his life in the powerful anointing, grace and mercy of God to write two thirds of the Gospel. He went on several missionary journeys to witness to unbelievers and believers and later ended up establishing churches in along the way in his missions. God can change anybody for His glory. God can change the worst of human life and dignity that the enemy tried to still. His compassion fails not. His power and authority can never fail. His power is all eternal and everlasting. He is flawless, infinite, perfect, infallible and all mighty. His mercy endures forever.

There is always someone in life that God leads us to for the working of His ministry. When the Lord sends you to that person to receive you, let them receive you because it could be of the Lord. However, always be aware that it is God who chose you before the foundations of the world. He already gave you sight before you came into the earth. Soon or a later more people will have gain their sight by removing the scales and using the power of Christ to witness. God is able to use anybody whether spiritual or non spiritual. I believe that you can never be limited by your past, any mistakes, any hurts, or any handicap, or thing that seems like it may be blocking your from prospering and being successful. Do not let anything hinder you because you are a child of the Most High God.

    When I was a young child, my mother use to say put the record on for me baby. She was referring to the old 45s size records that they used in the 1950's and 1960s. She would want me to put on artist like Mr. B.B. King, the Temptations, Stevie Wonder, and Mr. Charles, the old school. They all had amazing talent. But it was something unusual about Charles who was legally blind. I must admit that when I saw the actor, Jamie fox playing the role of Ray Charles it brought back memories of this legendary artist who captured the minds and hearts of people throughout several generations and around the world. What set Mr. Charles apart from other artist is his amazing talent demonstrated under disabled/blind conditions that most people would have given up on life and hope. Certainly many people would have allowed their condition to overcome them.

    Mr. Charles captured the heart of millions of people with his singing and piano playing talents while having a disability. He could even pat his feet at the organ and sing like no other. But I believe even today the majority of his fans never really saw him as blind because he never performed like he was blind. To some, blind means the inability to see from the lens of your eyes. Blind means unable to see the break of day. Blind means lacking the ability to see when you're walking from point A to point B. Blind is a condition that disables a person and sets limitations. I never knew Ray Charles' spiritual condition, whether he knew the Lord or not but the attitude he portrayed would make one believe that He knew about the blessings of the Lord. Because he demonstrated a zeal and thirst to sing and play skillfully for millions of people weekly and yearly, he demonstrated that there is no limitation. Christians should have that ability to sing praises to the Lord with a zeal that demonstrated a witness unlimited and unparallel to any other. Christians should sing with a heart of melody that will reflect the light of Christ and impact millions influencing them to surrender to the Lord.

Music touches the soul as so many of you already know. We get excited about so many songs. Life is good when you're dancing and having so much fun. Christians can reach out to help in touching souls and impacting to the point where people will say Lord please anchor me, please come into my heart. Please forgive me for backsliding and all of my sins. In order to be effective in the Christian life and the community in this world, people who need to know the Savior, we must allow our scales to fall off from our eyes. When Ray Charles sang, one would think that scales had fallen off because it appeared that nothing was ever blocking his view from performing his art. Because he moved to new levels in his career of singing. We as Christian should do the same. We should move to new level in Christ Jesus our lord. Whatever your scale of hindrance is ask the Lord to help you in allowing it to fall like the Apostle Paul's experience. The scale can fall and you can see again and be active in the Lord by serving Him alone.

PRAYERS

Father, I pray that you to keep my eyes open to the reality of spiritual and natural life. Help me to walk as a Christian ready to serve. I call on the Holy Spirit to help me on my blind sides. Remove the scales from those areas so that I can walk better and increase in faith.

LUKE 18

OPENED TO A SECOND CHANCE

Acts 9 Saul! Saul! Why are you persecuting me?

Thank God that He allowed me to have a second chance at life. When I was a young boy growing up, there were opportunities to do things too easily that could have easily caused harm and danger resulting taking my life. I am grateful that God heard my cry and He saw my frailties and weakness that could have been for the worst. The enemy can't wait to steal the life out of any person and their family members. There were times that I had bullets flying over my head in a neighborhood that had no intention to have peace in the community. Certainly they were not looking for peace in the future.

Some neighborhoods are just that rough. It was my choice to visit that place called the "Bottoms." It was my choice to visit "cross town" where violent gangs hang out and cause disruption and havoc on the lives of some innocent people. God is waiting on gang members to turn their life over to him as well. God is ready to change lives for anyone who comes to Him. He has no respect of persons. When you think you are about get stabbed or engage in stabbing someone or even anticipate in a shooting of any kind, stop and think on the goodness of God in your life and your family. God is real and God does exist. Don't listen to anyone who says opposite. God wants your life to give you and me a second chance regardless of what situation we are facing. Trust in the Lord with all your heart and lean not to your understanding. Acknowledge Him. He will direct your path. Acknowledge to Him that you need Him for this second chance. He will come to you.

There are second chances for everything that God allows for His glorious purpose. It does not change just because you come into the ministry and call yourself a minister or servant of the Most High God. Trouble still comes our way. No exemptions exist! So open your eyes and seek God for a second chance at life. Life is not over! Your life has a new start! Take this new lease on life and move for God's Kingdom purpose. Thank God for restoration. Thank God for renewal. Thank God for changing a destructive and evil mindset. The Apostle had all those conditions. We he met Jesus is when he allowed himself to die to sin and be born again. You must have a conversion. In John, it says, you must be born again.

What do you think the Apostle Paul said when he heard the voice of Jesus? He said who are you Lord? Although he did not have a relationship at that time, he still acknowledged Him as Lord. I believe Saul knew something divine and so spectacular was about to happen to his life that would transform him for the rest of his life. At that very moment, Saul had been given a second chance on life. Jesus could have taken him but He decided to use him in the Kingdom to win souls into the Kingdom under the influence of the Holy Spirit. He has been given a second chance to set the record straight. Jesus gave Him a second chance to follow Him under obedience. Jesus gave Him a lifetime of ministry to substitute the pain and suffering he has caused Christians. He was a murderer, a man filled with hate for Christians, But God intervened and no longer could he hate and murder Christians. Jesus had converted Saul on the spot. Jesus made Him over for the purpose of the Kingdom of God. He made Him to be a witness to the transforming power of Jesus Christ. He made Saul and changed his name to Paul and sent Him on the missionary field to express the love of God.

The Apostle Paul was positioned by Jesus Christ Himself to shake nations throughout the world that God might be glorified. God ordained the Apostle Paul to be fearless and truly committed to preaching the gospel throughout the world. This Gospel is to be preached that all captives are set free. God opened the door to a second chance for all that calls on the name of Jesus. It's time to go to your prayer closet and start seeking Him for yourself, time for a second chance as an individual to impress God. God is waiting for you to make a move so He can bless you. Do not wait on man or else you will be waiting too long and you may miss the timing of God in your life. Listen to His voice when He says move. No matter what happened in your life, God can change it for His purpose and for your good. You have a second chance to preach this gospel and help deliver the lost. You have a second chance to be successful in the community and be a positive role model. You have a second chance at your marriage. You can shake the devil off of your marriage. It's yours because God fixed it and ordained it for you to live a good life, long and joyous with your love one. You have a second chance at serving the right God. Who is your God? Are you caught up on religion and do not understand that you have been blinded by Satan and his demons.

Cast them out of your life right at this moment. Call the Lord and be move in the power of deliverance. You have a second chance at accepting Christ as Lord and Savior. Do not wait another day! Read

Romans 10:9-10hat if you confess with your mouth the Lord Jesus and believe in your heart that God has raised Him from the dead, you will be saved. For with the heart one believes unto righteousness, and with the mouth confession is made unto salvation. Say this! Lord Jesus, I repent of my sin. Lord, come into my heart and save me. I believe that you Are the Son of God and that you bled and died for my sin and rose from the dead.

Lord, Thank you for a second chance in life. You sent someone to give me a word and pray for me. You used Jesus example to let me know that I must be born again. You reminded me that my life is not over and that can win by accepting you as Lord.

JOHN 3, ROMANS 4

GOD IS ABLE

Jude 1:24-25 Now to Him who is able to keep you from stumbling, And to present you faultless Before the presence of His glory with exceeding joy, To God our Savior, Who alone is wise, Be glory and majesty, Dominion and power, Both now and forever. Amen.

God is able to keep us from falling. Have you ever fallen down hard? Have you ever failed a test in your life that was important? Have you ever failed a mission that you knew had to be completed? Have you ever fallen accidently and it was difficult to get back up on your feet? Some of us have fallen and everyone around us have seen us physically fall. It always seems like a sense of embarrassment because you did not keep your balance, instead your appeared to be clumsy and unbalanced. Even through the embarrassment we still get back up. Have you ever fell to the bottom of life because of an addiction to a certain drug, drink, or a type of medication or just anything in general? Have you ever fell spiritually from a relationship with Jesus Christ? Have you ever chosen anything or anyone above Jesus Christ? Ephesians 6:12-16 tells us that there are principalities and rulers of darkness. The Apostle Paul says, **"For we do not wrestle against flesh and blood, but against principalities, against powers, against the rulers of the darkness of this age, against spiritual *hosts* of wickedness in the heavenly *places.* Therefore take up the whole armor of God, that you may be able to withstand in the evil day, and having done all, to stand." "Stand therefore, having girded your waist with truth, having put on the breastplate of righteousness, [15] and having shod your feet with the preparation of the gospel of peace; [16] above all, taking the shield of faith with which you will be able to quench all the fiery darts of the wicked one.**

Many people have problems in their lives with drug habits and alcohol consumption which leads to so many improper actions and a wrong lifestyle. All in fact need help in those struggles. Many people have fallen to adultery and fornication and just all sorts of sexual relations. Some people fall from their self made empire that seemed strong and invincible. Some people have desires that take them to places that can lead to a fallen state of life in general. There are so many good things in life to live for. This life is worth living. God gave us this free life and now He is offering salvation free. Salvation is free living eternally. God looks to bless rather than be bothered with the evil one. He removes that issue of life. God already knows that the enemy is on a personal rampage to destroy His people. We are told to be watchful in our lives but we need the Savior to watch over us. We will mess it up every time unless we trust in Him. God is on your side to bless you in ways unimaginable. The continuation of Ephesians in chapter 6:17-20 says, **And take the helmet of salvation, and the sword of the Spirit, which is the word of God; ˉ praying always with all prayer and supplication in the Spirit, being watchful to this end with all perseverance and supplication for all the saints and for me, that utterance may be given to me, that I may open my mouth boldly to make known the mystery of the gospel, ˉ for which I am an ambassador in chains; that in it I may speak boldly, as I ought to speak."**

In the movie "Fallen" by Mr. Denzel Washington, it was portrayed that an evil spirit was loosed and was on the attack against any and all people everywhere. The enemy sought to kill, steal and destroy the lives of people in every business it could reach. The enemy was on duty to take away life. In his movie, it was revealed that the enemy desired to go to one place revealing to us that the enemy was always looking for a host, the entire body, mind, soul and spirit of a person. Many people were falling into the enemy's trap of deception. It appeared to me that the enemy was like a roaring lion seeking who he may devour. It also appeared, in large part, that the enemy was searching for empty vessels, those that did not have Jesus Christ on the inside of their heart. At the same time, the enemy was looking for saints as well. He wants every Saint to fall. Jesus will not allow it because of His love. It is important to know that in the enemy's mind, if you do not have Christ inside your heart, you are an open target and set apart for a fall of the enemy. Jesus Christ can keep you from falling.

We need to know today that Jesus can keep us from falling. When the enemy comes in like a flood, God is there to take hold of the situation. He has a standard that stops the enemy in its tracks and rebukes and sends it back to the pits of hell. You have an advocate strong and mighty, who is our Lord God. You see, the bible reminds us **in Jude 24 "Now to Him who is able to keep you from stumbling, And to present you faultless Before the presence of His glory with exceeding joy, To God our Savior, Who alone is wise, Be glory and majesty, Dominion and power, Both now and forever.** You see He has been keeping you your entire life. He has kept many people for 20,

40, 60, 100 and some over 100 years of life on this earth. His grace and mercy is from everlasting to everlasting. God with His own infinite wisdom and blessings will present you faultless before His very presence. Accept Him in your heart today and have a trusting relationship with Him that will last in eternity with Him.

What was the Lord saying when He said, keep you from falling? He was simply saying that any danger in your life, I will keep you from it if you trust me. If the attack is so massive and has the potential to overpower you, God will still keep you under the shadow of His loving care. When the attacks get so heavy on your back, I will be there to remove the enemy attacks. You see God controls all things. You remember what happened to Job. God allowed the enemy to attack him to almost a breaking point. The enemy was allowed to strike him with sores and pain and take away his family members in death. God allowed it! God always knows exactly what He is doing. He never allowed Job to fall and die. God specifically commanded the enemy to "do not touch his life." When God speaks and give orders, power is released beyond measure. The enemy did not take Job's life. He touched things that mattered to Him most; however Job still lived because of God's power. God blessed him more abundantly that his previous riches and possession. God kept Job alive for the blessings that He had stored for him.

God can keep you from falling into deep hurt. It is more than just falling and getting scratched up knees. It is more than falling and getting a hurt ego and pride, it is more than falling and getting your reputation stained and getting a bad name. God keeps you from many kinds of falls in life. Trust God. It is a fall you take that changes your life to a new destiny because now you know Jesus saved you from hell. You have to accept Him as Lord and Savior. He already redeemed me and you with His precious blood. But you still need to get on the right side of the track.

Listen, the Lord will hold you up more than friends will. You still need to have some friends but no one on earth can do you like Jesus. He is a comforter when you need Him. He is love when you feel unloved. He is the one who keeps you in perfect peace. He is the one who visits you in the midnight hour. You see when you are lonely He is there. When you are suicidal, He will change your mind so that you can think and know how to live life abundantly. He will remove the thought your heart and mind. You need Jesus just like me and everybody else.   You are not an exception to the rule.

Today, make a decision in your prayer request to Him that He would keep you and your family from falling away from Him and not in the hands of the adversary. Live a new lifestyle in the Kingdom of God from this point on. You will not regret it because you will reign with Him in eternity. He loves you right now and forever. Blessed be the name of the Lord.

PRAYER

Father, thank you for keeping me from falling in such evil ways of life. Thank you for your love and kindness. I pray that your Holy Spirit help me through my faults and my weakness. Give me strength in your word to walk this life.

PSALM 27, MATTHEW 5

HE WORKS ON THE INSIDE

EPHESIAN 3:20 Now to Him who is able to do exceedingly abundantly above all that we ask or think, according to the power that works in us, to Him be glory in the church by Christ Jesus to all generations, forever and ever. Amen.

    God is able to do exceedingly abundantly above all that we ask or think, according to His power that works in us. He is able to do things that are impossible to us. But we need to understand that His power works on the inside of us and that He can do anything inside and outside. His power works at all times. We need to realize that we are speaking of the God who created all things from nothing. His power is at work on the inside of the believer right now. He is working out every plan by allowing you to move under His authority and power today. He is working on your mind and mine at this very moment. If we could even imagine what He has put inside our minds, the capability to expand to levels beyond human comprehension. God's power is not limited in any stretch of imagination nor at any time, or in any way. Whatever the situation is, He has already worked it out in the life of the believer. He works out those that are called in His righteous name. You are the one who is blocking those particular blessings in your life and that particular mission He has set you apart to go on. He will send you whether you like it or not because it is for His purpose. Everything that God wants done, He will complete it through you or who He has chosen. You want God to do it all for you! He has already done what is needed to be done for you. You just need to start claiming what He has already delivered to you. Start giving Him all the glory due Him because He has already blessed you in abundance. What about you give Him the glory?
    There certain things that He wants you to do. One of them is move when He says so. One of the books I am working on now is called "You can't stop the move of God" It will target all the people who are feeling down and lost and confused. It will move those who know it's time to make a move. It will tell those who are supposed to be blessed that you are to start receiving your blessing and stop holding yourself back based on people's attitudes and opinions. You need to start telling yourself, they don't count, especially if they are not blessing you in the Lord. I was just speaking with a leader in the church who has a ministry and several ministers under him that it's time to be fruitful.

You can have 22 ministers or 52 or even 100 plus under your watch, but the fact remains to determine whether they are being truly mentored to or just stagnant. Are they just checking a box to appear holy and righteous or they key players in the ministry. A strong ministry will develop people and start sending them out beyond the four walls. It is time to take what God has taught them and become fruitful disciples in God's Kingdom.

Another one is that you are responsible for activating your faith. Do not let your faith die. Do not let your faith depend on someone pumping you up in church. Do not let your faith be dependent on false gods and images. Do not allow yourself to get caught up on things that are in darkness. Do not allow yourself to get placed into a pit and not get out. Do not allow your faith to be approved by someone else. God is your approving authority in faith, truth, spirit and word. The flesh is the flesh. The scripture reminds us that there is no good thing in the flesh. Your faith is the same kind of faith that God was looking at when He saw Abraham's faith. So start walking in the faith God destined for you. It is approved by God and you will not neglect it if you have a relationship with Jesus Christ.

Another one is that you need to believe in God when He ordains something because it will come to past. If you truly believe, you will push and press your way to the victory that He has set before you. Living in victory is part of the abundant life. You will start receiving the benefits of victory. Those benefits are the abundance that God is pouring out in your life. You just need to reach up, reach out and get it. Then giving Him glory will be easy for you. Stop holding back on God. He has filled you in abundance. I always find myself holding back. The God of creation, the ruler who sits on the throne in heaven has already blessed a brother to bless another brother.

At one particular time in ministry, I found myself stuck and at a standstill in ministry. I start seeing people play the same tired, wicked ministry games in the church. I started seeing people in different areas of my life acting in ways not pleasing to God and it was a turn off. In my mind, I was saying, I don't want to be involved in mess. I started believing that I can get ministered to at home watching evangelist preach the gospel. The Word is the Word and no one can change the Word of God. At last, I was at a distance. But the fact of the matter is we all need Jesus to straighten out those matters of the heart. We need Him to help us to be obedient. I need Him to help me be obedient to the call of ministry and family.

You and I both have the power to change our own situations as they occur. We can change as fast as God moves in our lives. We just need to allow the Spirit of the Lord to work a good work on the inside. If you do not enjoy being down and depressed, call on the Lord and change it. You have Him on the inside of your heart! You should not be walking depressed anyway. There is enough of God for everyone to have. You just need to count on Him. Depend on Him. You need to know Him for yourself.

It is time to stop limiting God in what He can do. You may have had a situation of drugs and relationships ups and downs, but it is not too much for God. People may have run out on you. You thought they were going to love you the rest of your life. You better get it together and stop waiting on folks to love you like they are God. No one can fill you with abundant love and His pure love like He can. The same God we are talking about is the one who called the world into existence and created Adam and Eve and all human existence. He gave life in abundance. He formed societies. He formed states and cities. His power was working then in us and on us. His power is still working for the change of our lifestyles.

I am telling you that if you want to see God work, use your faith and believe that the Holy Ghost will work it out. What do you think is impossible for Him? The scripture says that nothing is impossible for Him. If you think that a disease is more powerful than the Lord, think again! He cleansed men who had Leprosy. He restored sight to the blind. He even raised Lazarus from the dead. He raised a little girl from the dead. God has the power to give life again. He can restore and bless you in ways unimaginable.

People in the music industry use what they have to produce record labels year end and out. They trust that the power of singing in them exists and that it will never fade away. Why can't you as a believer and you who are lost believe that God can put His power in you and that His power will never fade away? His power can and will produce something great and spectacular in you that you will glorify Him and witness to the world that Jesus is Lord.

The Apostle went on journey after journey to please God. He encountered the worst case scenarios. He was even snake bitten. But the power that works on the inside kept Him alive to overcome that snake bite and all the people who came against the work and testimony of Jesus Christ through His servant Paul. When things get so bad, you need to trust that God's power is working. Remember, He sent His Holy Spirit to work in our lives. There is nothing more powerful than God's Holy Spirit working on behalf of the believer to give God all the glory through us. We should give God the glory for His many blessings. Bless His righteous name.

PRAYERS

Father, I call on the name of Jesus to bind anything and all things that come against those who serve and witness for your Kingdom. I pray binding power over all enemies for those that are lost.

MARK 8

AUTHORITY TO BIND

Act 9:14-18 And here he has authority from the chief priests to bind all who call on Your name. But the Lord said to him, "Go, for he is a chosen vessel of Mine to bear my name before Gentiles, kings, and the children of Israel. For I will show him how many things he must suffer for My name's sake. And Ananias went his way and entered the house; and laying his hands on him he said, Brother Saul, the Lord Jesus who appeared to you on the road as you came, has sent me that you may receive your sight and be filled with the Holy Spirit." Immediately there fell from his eyes something like scales, and he received his sight at once; and he arose and was baptized.

Something like scales fell from the eyes of Saul so that he could receive his spiritual sight for the ministry of Jesus Christ, our Lord. Now his life had begun a new course. God blessed the Apostle Paul to be a Chosen vessel. He chose him to bear His name before Gentiles, Kings, and the children of Israel. This means that He would be faced with ministering to many people of authority and those that were lost, those looking down on, those calling him names lower than dogs, and those rich in their own eyes, even those that claimed to be righteous in Christ, those who did not regard God as being the only true God, those that kept people in bondage, and of course His chosen people of Israel. So then, the Apostle Paul would have many missionary journeys to bear the name of Jesus. Yet be reminded that bearing Jesus name on mission has a cost. The cost is to suffer and be persecuted when least expected for His name sake. The cost is persecution. But above all be ready for His return to bless you when He pulls you in the air to forever be with Him.

It takes God to change things in our lives. It takes God to move us from sin to righteousness. It takes God to move us from sin to servant hood. It takes God to restore a man to be on God's side rather than evil's side. God can use anybody He desires to use for His Kingdom.

When God sees you in any way you are, even in your worst condition, He can still choose you because He alone can and will restore you. All you have to do is ask and receive His blessings in your life. Some people have been destructive or deceitful, but God still chose them and He is waiting for the next person to ask for deliverance. Believe this, He can change you from destructive to witness for His name sake. He can change you and me from our worst heart and mind state to become one in the five fold ministry. He is no respecter of persons. When God wants you, He will get you. He can change your daily habits to serve Him. He can remove your bad habits and make you live with the best good habits. Think about it, you do things to please everyone else, but do you please God? He will not hold it against you. He will just choose you then you will choose Him. He has the power to do anything regardless of what man says.

The Apostle Paul had bad habits. His habit was to kill Christians. But God, stepped in and changed his evil habits and life. Then God made the Apostle one of His chosen men. Do you want to be one of God's chosen men? Ask God and expect an experience to happen to change you right now for the glorious purpose of God. Ask Him to remove the scales from your eyes so that you can see like He did for the old man Saul who was transformed to the Apostle Paul. Then you will become a light to the world as a witness to the one and only living God to bear His name. Later it would be Jesus who said in

Matthew 16:18-20 "And I say also unto thee, that thou art Peter, and upon this rock I will build my church; and the gates of hell shall not prevail against it. And I will give unto the keys of the kingdom of heaven: and whatsoever thou shall bind on earth shall be bound in heaven; and whatsoever thou shall loose on earth shall be loosed in heaven." Jesus also reminds us "For where two or three are gathered together in My name, I am there in the midst of them."

PRAYERS

Father, I call on the name of Jesus to bind anything and all things that come against those that serve and witness for your Kingdom. I pray binding power over all enemies for those that are lost.

MATTHEW 16

YOUR CALLING AND ELECTION

2 PETER 1:10-11 Therefore, brethren, be all the more eager to make your calling and election sure. For if you do these things you will never fall, and you will receive a rich welcome into the eternal kingdom of our Lord and Savior Jesus Christ.

Peter wanted to let people know that your salvation is not based on a good life. He also wants them to understand not to become complacent in the ministry to the point that they might listen to false doctrine. Peter is saying, do not allow yourselves to get complacent and just accept anything and any type of doctrine. God wants us to receive and accept the doctrine of Jesus Christ our Lord and Redeemer and no one else.

You have to work to develop yourself in the Lord when it comes to His doctrine or any service. The word will work on you and through you. But you must remain in the doctrine of Jesus our Lord especially if you received your calling. The Holy Spirit will guide you into truth and keep you on the path of righteousness. The Holy Spirit will help you to be diligent in your calling. He will help you through the hard times and even strengthen your calling and election for service in the Lord. An entrance will be supplied for those who hold on to their calling and election. Child of God keep on standing on the word of God. He will never let you go. You can count on it with Jesus! He loves His people. He loves those that are called according to His purpose. Hold on to your calling. Remember what the word tells us. The enemy comes to kill, steal, and destroy. If you have a calling, you need to understand that you are God's child. You do not belong to the enemy, but the enemy will come at every angle to destroy you. He will try to kill, steal, and destroy your calling. Jesus came to give us life and give it more abundantly. Your mission is to be ministered to by the Holy Spirit to do what you are called to do. If God called you, certainly the Holy Spirit will equip you and protect you in that calling. You have to use your mouth and tongue and speak things into existence by using the power of the word. That is why God put the Holy Spirit here. He is our guide for life. He is your protector. He is our rescuer. He helps you speak the word with power, authority and boldness. God is still the Most High God and is able to do what He has already predestined for your life.

The Holy Spirit is here to help us when we feel like we are drowning. He serves as our lifeguard all through the year. He rescues us over and over even when we do not know it. When life feels too heavy, He is here for us to strengthen us. When the mission seems too difficult, the Holy Spirit is here to help make through the mission. He gives us more strength and holds us up.

So you received your calling! How do you know? Was it a burning desire on the inside of your heart? If so, don't let anything stop you from your calling. God is the one calling! Rest assured if He is calling you, you are in for blessings of a lifetime. Remember how Jesus called the Disciples. He chose one by one and taught them about the ministry. He did not turn them away to be lost. He did not look down on them to hurt them. Jesus wanted men to build the Kingdom of God. He has already chosen more disciples than men can even imagine. Yes, you are correct; you are one of His disciples yourself. You can find out by asking yourself, have I been serving God? If you are a servant, you are one of His disciples. You do not have to try so hard to become a disciple. You just need to know that Jesus called you to missions and be obedient and faithful to the call. Remember, there are so many callings in service for our Lord. So you do not have to get bogged down on just what you think. Continue in your daily walk to seek the Lord for counsel. You need the Holy Spirit to teach and guide you to become an effective witness. The word mission means that you have service to do in God's will for your life. There is a place for you. It is the expressed blessings in the ultimate sense of serving the Most High God.

The Apostle Paul lived one of the most dangerous lives on earth. He was a murderer who went about killing the people of God. Then it became his time to have the "script flipped." He became a Servant for the Lord because the Lord chose Him. He was a mission minded servant. He was a man on a mission regardless of what you said or anybody else said about his calling and service for the Lord. It was the Lord's anointing that rested on the Apostle Paul while traveling to Damascus. It was His anointing that kept him as he served all of his years. His life was never the same. God changed his life just like He can change yours and mine even more.

One of the things I think about is the military mind set and the service. In the military, we always maintained a high level of mission minded attitude. If you reject it or allow it to diminish, or go, then the ball would drop, meaning that important mission and tasks would not be accomplished. People would suffer because of that. Then someone will start the blame game. But in Christianity, serving God no one can point the finger at anybody else. You have to be a man or woman of

God for yourself. It is your relationship. The Apostle knew because it was him that God confronted while on the road to Damascus. God changed his heart and mind in that one moment. It takes a heart change to become a mission minded servant. Remember this visitation was the beginning of the scales falling from the eyes of Saul's conversion to the Apostle Paul.

Another important point is the fact that the Apostle Paul was led by the Holy Spirit to make his election sure. God said that he was a chosen vessel. So then God was the one who elected him. It was not a man who elected him. God wanted Ananias and anyone else to know that it was His choice. That is powerful because we know that God wants us to make the choice to surrender our lives to Him, to serve Him, and worship and praise His righteous name. We need to understand that our election is also by God. He knows who wants to be one of His before they even attempt it. When the people elect a President or a new government Representative, they know if that person wants it bad enough. They know because of the debates and the constant campaigning and advertising to win. They know because of the constant theme or slogan that are consistently being used such as "choose me," I will be the best president or representative because I will do this for you. I will represent you and get the best results.

God wants us to have that kind of attitude. Christians should aim to get the best results in God's kingdom. When you get born again and have the type of experience where the scales have fallen from your eyes and your heart; you will also start campaigning and advertising for God. You will put off the old you in your mind and set your sights on things above because in you are the blessings of God.

Today, make our Lord you new focus in life. Make Him the center of your life. Make your faith walk the center of life in Christ Jesus. Once you make Him the center of your life, blessings start flowing in abundance. You will start seeing things different in your life and all around you. You will start to love people better than you use to love. You will start to put your marriage into a better perspective and focus in your heart. Life is just better all around in Jesus Christ. Open your heart right now in your private room and in your secret place and give your life to Jesus! You do not have to wait on anyone, just do it today so you will have eternal life. Eternal life means living with Jesus forever. It is a free gift and opportunity. Nothing can beat it! Blessed be the name of the Lord who reigns forever and ever.

PRAYERS

Father, thank you for helping me in the call to serve you. Guide me in your Holy Spirit. Make me more committed in to you by faith.

2 PETER 2

A COVENANT RELATIONSHIP

GEN 17:1-8 When Abram was ninety-nine years old, the LORD appeared to him and said, "I am God Almighty; walk before me and be blameless. I will confirm my covenant between me and you and will greatly increase your numbers." Abram fell facedown, and God said to him, "As for me, this is my covenant with you: You will be the father of many nations. No longer will you be called Abram; your name will be Abraham, for I have made you a father of many nations. I will make you very fruitful; I will make nations of you, and kings will come from you. I will establish my covenant as an everlasting covenant between me and you and your descendants after you for the generations to come, to be your God and the God of your descendants after you. The whole land of Canaan, where you are now an alien, I will give as an everlasting possession to you and your descendants after you; and I will be their God."

Abraham was one of God's chosen men of faith. In fact, Abraham was a friend of God. He was known as the Father of many nations. He was known as a man of faith in God. He was known to have conversations with God and receive the blessings directly from God. The Lord put blessings in the life of Abraham that He had set apart for him. God promised to bless His seed through generation after generation. Abraham had one of the most blessed experiences in the Bible. He was in covenant relationship with God. A covenant is a binding agreement between two or more parties. It is a promise that will not be broken.

God blessed Abraham after his departure with Lot, his nephew. Lot stands for veil. It was Lot who was blocking the vision of Abraham. After the separation, God show Abraham all the kingdoms from east to west and north to south and told him that He will bless Him. Then God told Abraham that kings would come from his seed. The point here is that God always reveal things to you when the veil is removed. So many people have veils over their eyes and over their lives that hinder them from blessings that are in immeasurable. When they realize that God is the one that gives blessings and the remover of the veil, it is then when they will see the power of abundant blessings shower them. God loved Abraham's obedience to walk in faith to the point that He blessed Him abundantly.

God also recognized Moses as a man who He blessed because of obedience and faith. Moses' veil was lifted to see God's blessings. This is important because so many people today are walking in their own power and not the power of Christ. They see with their own vision but not the vision that the Lord has equipped them with. I tell you once you look beyond your own vision and your own self made veil and begin to see the vision that God has given you, you will step out on faith and get what God has for you. God has blessings laid up everywhere for you. Wherever you place your feet, God can bless you there. He told Joshua wherever his feet touch, that he would be blessed. Joshua 1:3.

Lot made his choice; He chose Sodom and Gomorrah, the worst place on the planet. He chose sin city. He was still blinded by riches and led by his own spiritual sight. I tell you if you allow your own spiritual sight to guide you, you will remain broken and misguided by the enemy. He wants you to lack spiritual sight and humility at heart. With all that sin in Sodom and Gomorra, it eventually caught up to Lot. You know the story of the angels visiting the city and those in sexual immorality wanted to go into them. You know the story of Abraham asking God if He would save that city of Sodom and Gomorrah if 50 righteous people where in the city. God replied that he would spare the city for fifty righteous people. He could not find fifty righteous people. Abraham continued by asking God if he would spare it for ten righteous people. God's answer was yes. Nevertheless, God could not find ten nor one righteous person in the city. Well it did not work out Lot and his family had to get out so God could destroy it. God rained brimstone and fire completely destroying Sodom and Gomorrah. What is the point? You need to look beyond the veil in your city and your life. Know what is happening in your city so you can pray for deliverance. If they had prayed for deliverance in that city, things could have changed, lives could have changed. Depart from sin and do not look back like lots wife, who became a pillar of salt. God already had a covenant with Abraham. It takes people with faith also to accept deliverance. Genesis 18:16-19:29

In your life today, ask God to remove the veil from your eyes. He will remove it and then you will see the manifestation of God in your life. You need to have faith in Him. You need believe that God can do what He said He can do. He already blessed all nations through Abraham. You are blessed through Abraham. Now you have received the greatest blessing. You are blessed through Jesus Christ, the Son of the living God. It was Jesus' death on the cross that removed the veil of sin in our lives. The scripture reveals that the veil was split in the temple when He died for us. That means we are no longer separated from the Father and sin has been conquered and defeated through Christ Jesus, our Lord and Redeemer. Before that Jesus ensured that the middle walls were no longer in existence. There was no separation between the Jews and Gentiles. Hebrews 8,9,10

PRAYER

Father, thank you for a covenant relationship and building my faith. I will trust you and walk in covenant to please you. Keep my faith strong each day I serve you.

HEBREWS 1

EXPERIENCE YOUR CALLING TO THE END

Matthew 10:1-4 And when He had called His twelve disciples to Him, He gave them power over unclean spirits, to cast them out, and to heal all kinds of sickness and all kinds of disease. Now the names of the twelve apostles are these: first, Simon, who is called Peter, and Andrew his brother; James the son of Zebedee, and John his brother; Philip and Bartholomew; Thomas and Matthew the tax collector; James the son of Alphaeus, and Lebbaeus, whose surname was Thaddaeus; Simon the Cananite, and Judas Iscariot, who also betrayed Him.

When the disciples were called, they were about their daily business. Jesus selected these men for missions that would impact the world to this day. They did not know that He was coming to choose them to become His followers. They did not know that they were destined to be some of the greatest Christian men that ever lived. They did not know that their lives were about to change and they would be known in later generations to come. They did not know that their ministry and calling would be extended until the end of time. They did not know that over 2000 years later men would be preaching the Gospel that they wrote inspired by the power of Jesus Christ Himself. Men today might as well get ready because you will be called out by the Lord to serve just like these men. The Holy Spirit will help you serve God and to be pleasing in His sight. There is a call for men and women to serve. God knows who is His and He alone opens the ministry for His glory to be revealed. Men put limits, God opens doors for you.

These men became the disciples of Jesus of Nazareth. Jesus specifically called them and did not need someone on earth to call them. It was not that they were self proclaimed. They had to be obedient to the call. That is what it took on their behalf and that is what it takes on yours and on my behalf. It was because of Jesus and the power of the Holy Spirit in their lives that they accepted the call. You have got to be ready for such an experience, but if you are not ready, He will equip you for it. He is the only one who can truly prepare you for the ministry. It may be difficult to know your complete calling in your life but Jesus knows exactly why He called you. In your calling to serve Jesus, you need to know what He is saying to you daily. In order to do so, you need to get a prayer life and start fasting and submitting under His authority. If you do not believe that He is speaking to you, then it's time for you to get on your knees and pray some more until you get a breakthrough. Pray like Daniel prayed if you have to but pray. God can hear you. If fact it will be a good habit if you start praying three times a day or more. In being a servant for the Most High God, or Father, you need to stay in constant communication. Prayer is one of the primary means. His word is another mean. Worship and praise is another means of communicating with God.

Too many people are beating themselves up about what their calling is or whether or not they have been called. You know if you should be a preacher, a deacon, usher, missionary or any areas of service for the Lord's house. Other people may have some insight through demonstration of your calling and ministry, but God and you are the central focus. Use the gift if you want to please God. Jesus called twelve and no one knew that He was about to call that twelve. Nothing is standing between you and the call on your life, but you and the enemy. Those are easy obstacles. Just rebuke the enemy and trust God. Trust Him more than you trust anything else. In fact, the best way to look at it is to trust God more than you trust you. That does not mean that you should not use your brain. It means that God is more powerful than you and your flesh. The Apostle speaks of the flesh always getting in the way. Romans 7:14-19 Whenever you try to do right, you end up doing something wrong because the flesh keeps on getting in the way. No matter what the problem appears to be, you stand the test of time. You hold on to your calling and the keys to the kingdom. Matthew 16 If it is one thing you know that you have, it is your calling unto the Most High God. Blessed be His righteous and holy name.

PRAYERS

Father, thank you for the call on my life. I rely on the power of your Holy Spirit to lead me on missions and witnessing. I praise your name for your power and blessings.

LUKE 5

MINISTERING GOD'S PROMISES

HEBREWS 6:10-12 For God *is* not unjust to forget your work and labor of love which you have shown toward His name, *in that* you have ministered to the saints, and do minister. And we desire that each one of you show the same diligence to the full assurance of hope until the end, that you do not become sluggish, but imitate those who through faith and patience inherit the promises.

God sees that you are willing and able to minister and He will reward you. The Lord sees your obedience to the call to serve Him. He has your rewards and inheritance laid up for you in heaven. He will bless you anywhere because you chose to be one of His. What a thought! One of His! That means you are no one else's property. No one else controls you. No one else can bless you like Jesus. You have Jesus, the son of the living God on your side. He is the one who holds all power in His hand.

Jesus will not forget your obedience to the faith and to His call to serve. He wants His Saints to maintain hope in their lives in the spirit. Hope will bring you through it all. You have to know that God is with you during your service. Listen to what the Apostle is saying, you have ministered to the saints, and do minister. Too many people believe that the church is the only place to minister. God has news for you! It is not the only place to minister.

God wants you to know that it is easy to allow yourself to get discouraged. God has not forgotten about you, me or our families. God sees every good work that we perform under His anointing.

In the early years of Christianity, people thought that good works was the final solution to salvation, getting to heaven. But God did not design it that way. The path to heaven is simple yet there are things that try to prevent you from getting there. Repent of your sin with a sincere heart to our Lord Jesus Christ. That is the way to get to the Lord our God. Confess with your mouth the Lord Jesus and believe in your heart that He is the Son of God and you will be saved (**Romans 10:9).** Some days are harder the others in this life. Thank God , we know that days are hard because the adversary seeks to destroy those that follow Jesus. We know that this flesh also has it days when it will not submit to the voice and the move of Jesus. Sometimes the flesh gets over emotional and misled with false inner wisdom.

There are thousands of movies that were made with extremely

creative minds behind them. Some weekends are advertised on television as movie marathons. Movies are poured out left and right, hour after hour, day after day. New titles are birthed and show rapidly faster than ever before. What strikes so many people is the ability to imitate a developed script by themselves or someone else. It takes skill to put yourself into another character and project it as you being so real and persuasive. It takes skill to be so diverse and flexible with script adlibbing and maintaining posture and different identities. The other important piece to it is the level of commitment and diligence toward the performance in entertainment. Please understand there is nothing wrong with possessing those great skills because I believe so many movies do make extremely valuable points in life. Some make you cry, some make you laugh and some even make you frown and wonder.

The point is that there are thousands of imitators in those movies that impact and influence society in ways that God can use them. For the Christian community, we must be imitators of the faith of the Gospel of Christ. We need to be committed to Him even more than actors are committed to their work on screen. I think it is time that followers of Jesus started launching out into the deep to catch fish like actors do. In Hebrew 11, God illustrated through the Apostle Paul, the heroes of faith that touched God's heart in the work of the ministry as good imitators and the list goes on throughout the Bible and even today with His Saints. Glory to His Righteous name.

Today is your day to have an out pouring of life into the ministry. Let your light shine through your life in the ministry that was assigned to you. Ministry comes in different ways. Everyone just needs to understand that it is under the operation of the Holy Spirit.

Who comes close to being the imitator of the faith? You and I are the imitators. We witness throughout the world, in our communities, and right where we are at the moment. God is everywhere and His eyes see all things. When you need help, He is there.

PRAYERS

Father, I count on your promises. I believe you will strengthen me for your service. Guide me to imitate you and follow the example of those who through faith pleased you. I can do all things through Jesus Christ my Lord who strengthens me. I praise your name.

GALATIANS 6

PEOPLE ON FIRE FOR GOD

ACTS 2:36-47 "Therefore let all the house of Israel know assuredly that God has made this Jesus, whom you crucified, both Lord and Christ." Now when they heard *this*, they were cut to the heart, and said to Peter and the rest of the apostles, "Men *and* brethren, what shall we do?" Then Peter said to them, "Repent, and let every one of you be baptized in the name of Jesus Christ for the remission of sins; and you shall receive the gift of the Holy Spirit. For the promise is to you and to your children, and to all who are afar off, as many as the Lord our God will call." And with many other words he testified and exhorted them, saying, "Be saved from this perverse generation." Then those who gladly received his word were baptized; and that day about three thousand souls were added *to them.* And they continued steadfastly in the apostles' doctrine and fellowship, in the breaking of bread, and in prayers. Then fear came upon every soul, and many wonders and signs were done through the apostles. Now all who believed were together, and had all things in common, and sold their possessions and goods, and divided them among all, as anyone had need. So continuing daily with one accord in the temple, and breaking bread from house to house, they ate their food with gladness and simplicity of heart, praising God and having favor with all the people. And the Lord added to the church daily those who were being saved.

My Korean experience was a positive one that I could never forget. In one instance, there was a wild fire sparked by weapon fire. At first it looked like a few people were going to try and put the fire out, but the entire city came out to fight the flame before it could spread and do major damage. I never seen anything like it before in my life. There are literally thousands of people that are on fire for the Lord, ready to serve just like the Apostles were once they knew that the Lord Jesus was sent by God and they received his teachings. Once they witnessed His miracles in the lives of people. They knew He was and is the true deliverer. People are used by God in different types of ministries and the Holy Spirit is there as a guide to help them stay on the right path. It's amazing that God would choose men to serve in so many different capacities. When I think about someone being on fire for the Lord, I think of the men that have fixed in their minds that they will not be moved by carnality and those that block ministry and those that place obstacles in the road. When God puts the fire in you, no man can put it out. You might as well start telling everybody you know that you have the fire inside your heart from God and for God to witness to the world through you.

In **Acts 2 when the Day of Pentecost had fully come, they were all with one accord in one place. And suddenly there came a sound from heaven, as of a rushing mighty wind, and it filled the whole house where they were sitting. Then there appeared to them divided tongues, as of fire, and *one* sat upon each of them. And they were all filled with the Holy Spirit and began to speak with other tongues, as the Spirit gave them utterance.** For people to be on fire for the Lord, they need to be filled with the Holy Spirit. God is the one behind the infilling of the Holy Spirit. None of this takes place without Him directing it. Our Father in heaven has full control of distributing power under the Holy Spirit. He alone sets His anointing on the life of the believer. He awaits those newly transformed that He might do a good work in them.

When you set your heart to be on fire for the Lord, God will make room for your gift. You do not have to worry about not being used. There is a ministry everywhere! There are all kinds of ministries as well. You just have to step out of your comfort zone and your rigid way of thinking. It is time for new ideas to be blended with old ideas and of course new ideas in its original meaning as well the word never changes is what you always have to remember. Millions of books are written to persuade you or encourage you and that find as long as it's directing to the word of God. The word of God stands forever.

One of the primary reasons that this book is written is to reveal that the eyes of people can be opened and will be open so that they can be on fire for the Lord. Open your eyes to see what God wants for you as a servant. Ask the Father in your personal closet to open your eyes that you may see what He desires for you. The intent is to get you to act on it now so that spiritual scales can fall away from the eyes, heart and mind so that you will be filled with the Holy Spirit like the Apostle who waited for promise of the Holy Spirit. Your fire comes from Him. Your commitment and sacrifices of service comes from Him. Your acts of obedience are helped by Him. Your power to heal and witness to the glory of the Father comes from the Holy Spirit.

It is vitally important that you do not allow your dreams to be stripped from you by the enemy. You hold on to your dreams and visions just like Joseph, son of Jacob. He never let His dreams go until the Lord revealed to him and as a result Jacob's name was changed to Israel. Joseph never let go and as a result he became second in command of all of Egypt. He was highly favored because He stayed on fire for the Lord. He walked in the Spirit of the Lord and everyone noticed him. What you do for the Lord is what God sees. You just stay on fire in whatever you do for the Lord. He will be pleased with you. Make it personal.

    I love the story of the Hebrews boys. They would not give in to anything. The King could not strike fear into their hearts in any way. They knew who they stood for and whom they worship. These men were on fire to the point that they were willing to go into the fire and die for the Lord. They put their lives on the line for their belief in the one and only true God. The bible tells us that they were put into the fiery furnace and it was turned up to the highest point but God showed up as the forth man in the fire. Daniel 3:1-30 God is always there to rescue us. No harm or danger was done to these men. I tell you when you are on the Lord side, He knows what to do to help you.

    In this chapter, Peter demonstrated a boldness that revealed the fire burning on the inside to preach the gospel and as a result of the Holy Spirit infilling Him and the other who waited, blessed in salvation hundreds of people. Peter's preaching under the power of the Holy Spirit and helped to deliver 300 people on that day and moment. It was the fire of God burning on the inside to perform the purpose and will of God. **In His sermon He said, "Repent, and let every one of you be baptized in the name of Jesus Christ for the remission of sins; and you shall receive the gift of the Holy Spirit.** When you make a decision to repent and turn your life around, then will you know that God is working in your life. Once you experience the blessings and know for yourself that God is your ever present help in time of need and power source, you can do all things through Jesus as the Apostle Paul put it, "I can do all things through Christ who strengthens me." That means you can preach the gospel, you can teach the gospel, you love through the power of Jesus, you can accomplish any mission you put your heart to with the help of the Holy Spirit.

    Get on fire Saints that we might be pleasing to Him who sits on the throne in heaven. Get on fire families all around the globe to give God all the glory due His name. Your fire might be different from my fire. Nevertheless, it is still the fire of God burning on the inside of you to let loose and surrender to help someone turn their life around. Get on fire God's witness because you will turn the world upside down. You are chosen and appointed to do the will of God. It is His manifold wisdom that will carry you while you help to deliver a person out of darkness to this marvelous light. Your light will shine as you demonstrate the fire within you.

Saints, the fire we possess by the Holy Spirit is more powerful than wild fires. We have more power to speak the word and prayers of deliverance for those that are captive. No wonder those Hebrews confess that their God is God and they do not bow nor serve any other god. We need to speak that kind of faith with fire from our tongues and heart.

Today, make sure that you have repented of your sin, been baptized, and received the gift of the Holy Spirit. He will help your with your zeal, readiness, ambition and vision for the Lord in your heart for the glory of the Lord. God has set His promise in His word for you and me to take hold of all the promises. God's blessings are reasons why we must give Him the glory and thanksgiving in all things.

PRAYERS

Father, forgive me of my sin. I accept you Lord as my Lord and Savior. Baptize me by your Holy Spirit. I desire to serve you after all of these years of serving other things. Help me to become a witness.

ACTS 2

PROMISES OF GOD

HEBREWS 6:13-20 For when God made a promise to Abraham, because He could swear by no one greater, He swore by Himself, saying, "Surely blessing I will bless you, and multiplying I will multiply you." And so, after he had patiently endured, he obtained the Promise. For men indeed swear by the greater, and an oath for confirmation is for them an end of all disputes.

Thus God, determining to show more abundantly to the heirs of promise the immutability of His counsel, confirmed it by an oath, that by two immutable things, in which it is impossible for God to lie, we might have strong consolation, who have fled for refuge to lay hold of the hope set before us. This hope we have as an anchor of the soul, both sure and steadfast, and which enters the Presence behind the veil, where the forerunner has entered for us, even Jesus, having become High Priest forever according to the order of Melchizedek.

When God makes a promise no one and nothing can make Him go against His word. God made it extremely clear that His promise of blessing Abraham is a sealed promise. He swore by Himself. He sees the promise before anyone. He reveals what He desires for His people.

You have to allow the Holy Spirit to open your eyes to see what God has done in the spiritual realm and His manifested glory on earth in your life. When He opens your eyes is when you will begin to see the promise of God manifested before you. Even when you think that you do not see God's promises they have already come to past. God can not lie. God is in control of His personal will and He also knows the natural will of men.

The Lord God's promises are similar to a contract agreement between two or more people. But God's agreement is more binding and perfect in every possible way. In the contract agreement, you make specific agreements and by no means do you break it. Many people have an agreement with a car dealership. You may have purchased a 2009 BMW which means you signed a contract to pay up each month a specific car payment. If you are late, creditors could come after you and not to mention the mounds of late fees. If you are late more than once, you could be facing repossession. If you go through some or all of that, then you are breaching the contract. God will not and He cannot go against His own word. He will never breach His covenant and promises for your life and well being. He is the God who provides. His promises are guaranteed. His promise is more than a guarantee of having money in the bank.

God wants us also to be patient. Patience can test character and the entire person. You do not have to rush anything. When the Lord tells you something, no matter how many years go by, how many months go by or even how many weeks and days go by, He will live up to His word. It is time to be patient in the things of your house and watch blessings start to overflow in your house.

God has two immutable things that He deals with is Hebrews 6:18. God declares His oath and His promises, meaning He is unchanging. God is truth and He cannot lie. You can be secure about God's promises. He seals it with the fact that we are anchored in His hope. We are anchored in His promises. We are anchors with more power than the anchors on the largest sea vessels. . So when He speaks there is absolute assurance that He will accomplish what He set out to do. He will not go back on His plan for our future. Once He set blessings in order expect to receive them in multiples.

The Lord God wants us to know that our souls are anchored by the High Priest Jesus. That is one of actions in securing the promises of God. We do not need priest to go before God for us any longer. Jesus paid it all. The veil that separates the Holy and the Most Holy Place is no longer needed. Jesus died and rose and now is seated at the right hand of the Father. Jesus is in the presence and will of the Father continuous. This is good news for everyone to know. Jesus did it once and for all. He saved a sinner soul like mine. We can live knowing that God's promises for our lives are real and cannot be broken.

PRAYERS

Father, thank you for your counsel and the faith you put in my spirit to count on you. Thank you for making me over into a child of God and a Priest to serve you. Lead me to witness on this earth that I might be pleasing to you.

HEBREW 6,7

PROPHECY IN POWER SAINTS

1 CORINTHIANS 14:1-4 Pursue love, and desire spiritual gifts, but especially that you may prophesy. For he who speaks in a tongue does not speak to men but to God, for no one understands *him;* however, in the spirit he speaks mysteries. But he who prophesies speaks edification and exhortation and comfort to men. He who speaks in a tongue edifies himself, but he who prophesies edifies the church.

Our goal as Christian believers is to give God all the glory and honor. We must edify Him in all we do each moment of our lives. We may not be able to give all that is due to His name, but we can try in this lifetime through expression and acts of faith with our ability to serve. We need to use gifts that God gave us. When God gives you the ability to prophesy, then prophesy! If He gave you the gift to preach, then preach, likewise teach as well in the spirit. God is looking for Christians that are in the pursuit of their gifts, ready to activate what God has given you. God wants all of His people to understand what it is that He has for them. He continues to pour out His word for more understanding and blessings in your life. You must know what God is saying to you to activate His destiny for your life.

Prophecy means having the ability to predict future events. It could be for your life or someone else's. When we speak of to prophesy, it refers to men and women of God divinely inspired to speak the word of God and revelation, to communicate God's message providing correction now and insight to future events, warning and correcting us by the power of the Holy Spirit. We operate in a supernatural proclamation and a known language. We are understood by the people.

Kind David had a prophet to advise Him. Each time Nathaniel the Prophet visited David and revealed to him things that the Lord desired Him to know. He even revealed to King David of his sin that caused him to send Uriah to the front line. It is important to understand that God was looking for a man who's heart would be an honorable heart. So then the prophet was to help King David to learn to walk in the path pleasing to the almighty God. God wanted him to be a Godly King. One of the things that was important is that God used these prophets to express edification, exhortation, and comfort. They did this through their messages from God. Before that Samuel had revealed to him that he would be King by the power of God.

King Saul had a prophet; Samuel was his advisor during his kingship. The Prophet Samuel warned him of his disobedience toward the Lord when he did not destroy the entire camp. Saul had one of the poorest excuses that he seems to stick with. It is almost always the people made me do it. If we say the people pressured me and made me do it, we might as well look forward to being delivered to hell as well.

The Apostle Paul makes it clear that prophesy (preaching) is necessary because it benefits the church in ways that we can't even imagine. But only God can give such gifts.

We all are looking for someone to encourage us in areas of life. Our first priority of encouragement should come from the Lord.

In Ezekiel 37:4 Again He said to me, "Prophesy to these bones, and say to them, 'O dry bones, hear the word of the LORD. God reveals Ezekiel's spiritual gift. He had to go into a valley and speak to dead bones. When he speaks to these dead bones, they were supposed to rise up from the dead and be covered up back into their life form. This is army is risen to be strong and mighty army that God has made. Only God can make strong armies. It pointed out several important factors. One is that if God gives you the gift, to prophesy.

Please read 1 Corinthians 14:1-40. It blesses us to know that God wants to let a dying world know of His saving grace and what it takes to demonstrate and convey understanding in his gifts and power.

PRAYER

Father, thank you for giving power to speak. I pray to edify you Lord. I pray to prophesy with the gift you have given me. Lead me in speaking your word that someone might be saved and delivered.

1 CORINTHIANS 14

GOD OPENS EYES

2 KINGS 6:16-17 And Elisha prayed, and said, "LORD, I pray, open his eyes that he may see." Then the LORD opened the eyes of the young man, and he saw. And behold, the mountain was full of horses and chariots of fire all around Elisha. So when the Syrians came down to him, Elisha prayed to the LORD, and said, "Strike this people, I pray, with blindness." And He struck them with blindness according to the word of Elisha.

God has something for you and you need to receive it. God has a vision for you. He wants you to open your eyes and see the blessings set forth for you. Victory is for you in ways unimaginable. Start seeing your Blessings from God. Do you see anyone else trying to give you a blessing? Open your eyes, God has something special for you and you will never be the same again. When you need help opening your eyes as we all have need of, ask God to open them for you. It is a blessed experience to see things in the spirit realm. God will equip you.

The promises of the Lord are for you. God has blessings waiting on you to grab them. He has blessings laid up in heaven for you. You no longer have to wait on anyone to make you feel complete. You just need to do what Elisha did. He prayed to the Lord to open the eyes of the young man. When you pray, the Lord will show you things that you can only see in the spirit realm. He showed the young man His Armies for His support. God can open eyes in all kinds of situations. Start asking Him to reveal things to you by sight, heart, spirit and mind.

Elisha did something else remarkable in his combat strategy. He asked the Lord to strike the enemy with blindness and the Lord blinded his enemy. Almost moment by moment people allow the enemy to strike them with blindness and disease and hurt and shame and guilt and so many things that keep them in bondage. If they could learn to call on the name of Jesus and ask Jesus to strike the enemy and believe that God can and will, then their belief would increase and confidence in God would manifest in their lives even greater. Ask God to strike Him with a bolt of lightning just like he was kicked out of heaven to hell. Ask God, Lord if you could just strike the enemy enough to get off of the back of your people, they can start witnessing to the lost. Ask; Lord if you could just strike the enemy with blindness to keep him away from my family and my wife and my children, I will serve you. Keep my faith determined and true to you Lord.

God wants us to speak to the situation. Tell everything and everyone around you to move for a moment because your God is about to do a new thing in your life. Tell them that you are about to express your faith in God over every situation that tries to keep me in bondage. You need to say in your mind, excuse me, and move for a moment, I have business to take care of in the Lord. I claim my blessings by faith in Jesus Christ. You have been in my way long enough. If you want to walk with me and get your blessing, let start moving into the presence of God right now at this very moment. I walk with Jesus now. My life is filled with the light of the Lord Himself. I am more than a conqueror in Jesus Christ. Favor is in my life. Nothing can separate me from the love of God.

It is important that you know that God is on your side. The bible says that the battle is not your, but it is the Lords. No wonder so many Christians lose at warfare with the enemy. There are many who should never even go to battle because of their lack of knowledge and strategy and tactics. All tactics should be employed by the Lord. A wise King will win. A foolish king or servant will lose each time. Find out what a wise King is. What you need to understand is that God already has you covered. Look what God did for Elisha when he prayed unto the Lord. He was supported and covered with chariots of fire all around him. God had placed His Heavenly Army around the protection of His children. God has a way of fighting your battle for you.

PRAYERS

Father , I pray that you open my eyes daily to see the things you desire of me. Open my eyes for the ministry and mission you set out for me.

MALACHI 3:6-10

THE VEIL SPLIT

John 19:1-24 So then Pilate took Jesus and scourged *Him*. And the soldiers twisted a crown of thorns and put *it* on His head, and they put on Him a purple robe. Then they said, "Hail, King of the Jews!" And they struck Him with their hands. Pilate then went out again, and said to them, "Behold, I am bringing Him out to you, that you may know that I find no fault in Him." Then Jesus came out, wearing the crown of thorns and the purple robe. And *Pilate* said to them, "Behold the Man!" Therefore, when the chief priests and officers saw Him, they cried out, saying, "Crucify *Him*, crucify *Him!*" Pilate said to them, "You take Him and crucify *Him*, for I find no fault in Him." The Jews answered him, "We have a law, and according to our law He ought to die, because He made Himself the Son of God."

When Jesus died on the cross, the veil in temple split from top to bottom to fulfill prophecy written in Isaiah 53 and Mark 15:37-38. We were no longer separated from the Father, our God. We are now restored to Him because of Jesus' death on the cross. What the enemy meant for bad, God came through with good. God can never fail because He ordained the mission and victory over all enemies.

The veil splitting in the temple signifies that the gap was now bridged to God. Restoration is present right now in the life of the believer. Simply put, we have been restored. The opportunity to accept Jesus as Lord is here and available now because of what He did for you and me. Our relationship with God is now restored because of the precious blood of the lamb. It symbolizes that each person can approach God through the precious name of Jesus Christ. You can cross over the bridge now. He bridged the gap. He completed the mission to bring you home to God. I thank God that He made my understanding clear. I see the death of Jesus as a way to reveal to all people that Jesus defeated death and made Himself available for all men.

In Corinthians 15, the scripture tell us that He took the sting out of death. It reveals that Jesus lifted the veils of all people who accept Him. He also lifted the veil of those who have not acknowledged because His power is infinite. They of course just have not acknowledged Him as their personal Savior. He is available for all people. I believe not only was the veil split for salvation, He removed the veil from the eyes of those who walk in darkness and blindness. Now you can call on the name of Jesus. He removed the veil from the eyes of everyone so that they could have the opportunity to have salvation. The veil was split because everyone needed and still need to know that Jesus is Lord of all creation throughout eternity. He defeated the enemy and at the same time gave us life everlasting to reign with Him.

What was so significant about the veil? A veil can be used for so many things. One of the most common uses of a veil is in marriages when a bride is presented to her groom; she is covered up to be presented as a gift from God. She is supposed to be treated preciously and honored by her husband. The relationship should be a mutual one in marriage. Your marriage can be absolutely made in heaven. She was ready to take on the meaning of becoming a bride. In the wedding the man always lifts up the veil to kiss her acknowledging publicly and intimately that He has accepted her as his gift and wife from God. Not only did the veil get lifted to signify their unity, it is a symbolic meaning of unity with God in their marriage. Jesus makes this so significant to believers because all believers are transformed into His image and likeness. We possess the love and tender kindness that Jesus has. Jesus wants us to know that we are His bride, the church.

The veil was so significant because it is known to have been a curtain hung in front of the temple room called the Most Holy place, a place reserved by God. This veil separated the Holy God from sinful people. This place was only entered by the Priest once a year on the Day of Atonement. The High Priest had to enter in on the behalf of the other people for sin. He needed to always take a sacrifice. Jesus came along and died for us as the perfect Sacrifice for God. There is no requirement for the old system anymore. When Jesus died on the cross and the veil split, He reconciled us to bring us back into relationship with God as His children. Hebrews 9

What is so key and central about these four gospels is that they involve the resurrection. They all prove that the resurrection happened and bare witness to it. The veil lifted from the resurrection simply means that all people can see with their eyes and heart that Jesus rose from dead with all power and authority. The veil was an indication that the world had been united to Jesus. No more division from God. Sin was lifted from people transferred to the body of Jesus and crucified on the cross. Everyone was made free instantaneously by the power in the blood of Jesus.

What touches so many people the most is when they see the crucifixion. You can hear the effects such as "why did He love me so much?" In the carrying the cross, He demonstrated love unconditional and eternal. In carrying the cross, He knew it took someone to carry so many others living in sin. To destroy the works of the devil and at the same time give life back to a dying world. We hunger to know Him today because of what He has done for us and our families.

I can't help but to think of His love pouring out in incredible amounts daily that nothing else can equate to. The Lord's love is so powerful; He forgave even those that crucified Him. He forgives those who have rejected Him today. His love is so perfect it changes you instantly. He loves never changes. I always like to associate something with the rain that God gives us. It is His love that gives the perfect picture. In His perfect timing He sends the exact person to the exact moment through the exact circumstance that He might get the glory.

My mind takes me to a story that happened with a friend a few years ago. James had been a unique soldier with various hardships. James was also that stellar soldier who was on the fast track. He would volunteer for any mission and get it complete. One of James' favorite stories in the bible is the one of the crucifixion of Jesus Christ in John 19. James had dealt with all the missions that he went on in Iraq and found out that he would finally come home. Well, when he came home, he found out that he had a tumor in the back of his head and he had developed some type of gain green in his knees. Not only did he have those things to deal with, he was evaluated with PTSD and anxiety. But James through the comfort of his beautiful wife and family received more tragic news. His mother had died by having a mass stroke and a long time suffering with heart problem. Whenever death and pain enters the life of a believer and a nonbeliever, God is always there to comfort.

When I discover or hear about stories where a soldier or anyone served the Armed Forces and came home to discover different problems not only does my heart and prayers go out, I believe that it is when the outpouring of His love is revealed at a level even our minds are unable to comprehend. James felt like he had been crucified and he did not understand anything about his suffering. The Lord God never stops loving us and our families. He is the one who helps you through the tough times even when the enemy comes to shatter your hopes and dreams. We have the Holy Spirit on our side that protects and saves us over and over again.

Today, look at the love of Jesus on the cross and imagine that love being poured on you right this minute. Ask God to soak you and bath you in His love. Ask the Lord to get intimate with you regarding His love. You need His touch of life to move on in life. He will not limit you. He will truly balance your life in the storm and deliver you from the elements of evil. God's love is more than all the water that rain on us in a life time. Just like God waters the planet, He blesses us in with more blessings.

James' friend Mark had an amputated leg and right arm due to an IED explosion. He was surprised to see his best friend because the last thing James had heard is that Mark was missing in action in Iraq. Thank God that He sits on the throne in heaven showering us in His love and compassion on a daily basis even when we do not ask. God is in the midst of things that we do not see. God is love and His love and mercy last forever.

James is now a stronger believer because of his experience with God touching and restoring his life. He is now a full bonefide believer. James through all of the pain and agony in his life now witnesses in the local community, around town and in his local church. James realized that there are some places in his life that God wanted to access and help him dream a dream he had been waiting and desiring in his heart.

He lives forever and He lives in my heart. When Jesus carried the cross while wearing twisted thorns in His head and bleeding in abundance, He thought about me. He thought about every city, state, home, church, the lost, priest, pastor teacher, love one, family and His remnant.

The crucifixion represents suffering by suffocation. No one can never forget the boldness and the humility that Jesus had given to every soldier to make sacrifice. We need to spread the word even if it overflows in the lives of people.

PRAYERS

Father, thank you for cross that Jesus carried for my sin. He paid the penalty for me and I know that I could never bear. Your love Father is all I thirst for.

PSALMS 22, MARK 20

UNVEILED RESSURECTION

MARK 16:1-20 Now when the Sabbath was past, Mary Magdalene, Mary *the mother* **of James, and Salome bought spices, that they might come and anoint Him. Very early in the morning, on the first** *day* **of the week, they came to the tomb when the sun had risen. And they said among themselves, "Who will roll away the stone from the door of the tomb for us?" But when they looked up, they saw that the stone had been rolled away—for it was very large. And entering the tomb, they saw a young man clothed in a long white robe sitting on the right side; and they were alarmed. But he said to them, "Do not be alarmed. You seek Jesus of Nazareth, who was crucified. He is risen! He is not here. See the place where they laid Him. But go, tell His disciples—and Peter—that He is going before you into Galilee; there you will see Him, as He said to you." So they went out quickly and fled from the tomb, for they trembled and were amazed. And they said nothing to anyone, for they were afraid. Later He appeared to the eleven as they sat at the table; and He rebuked their unbelief and hardness of heart, because they did not believe those who had seen Him after He had risen. And He said to them, "Go into all the world and preach the gospel to every creature. He who believes and is baptized will be saved; but he who does not believe will be condemned.**
And these signs will follow those who believe: In My name they will cast out demons; they will speak with new tongues; they will take up serpents; and if they drink anything deadly, it will by no means hurt them; they will lay hands on the sick, and they will recover." So then, after the Lord had spoken to them, He was received up into heaven, and sat down at the right hand of God. And they went out and preached everywhere, the Lord working with *them* **and confirming the word through the accompanying signs. Amen.**

Can you imagine being in the tomb and witnessing the resurrection? It is beyond our comprehension and what we can imagine. It is so sacred that we are constantly amazed at what is revealed to the naked eye and spiritual eye. I believe that the power of the Holy Spirit has unveiled this Holy, miraculous event to all men so they we will believe and form the relationship available to us. The Holy Spirit has removed scales and blinders from my eyes to see what He and only He reveals to the mind what happened in the tomb by God's power and authority. I need His revealing power. In my mind, I call it the "unveiled resurrection" because no one can truly explain this blessed, Holy and powerful operation of our Father in Heaven. Nothing can compare to His power to execute operations and reveal it to the human and spiritual eye. Hebrews 9, 10

    We can see Jesus being raised from the dead by God the Father. If you can see it in your mind, then you have an unveiled mind to see other things in the spirit. True, we may have not been physically there but God allows us gifted abilities under His power alone to see in the Spirit the things that affect our lives by God, the Father, God the Son, God, the Holy Spirit. He allows us to approach Him now because sin has been terminated by the blood of the Lamb. All of the entanglements today and yesterday and the future have been wiped clean. Your life has been restored. We no longer have to go to a human priest to confess our sins on this earth. We have to go to Jesus who is our High Priest forever. When we go to Him in thanksgiving and praise, He recognizes our hearts then blesses us. We can go to Him and worship at all times. Even when sin tries to erupt and deliver corruption in your eyes, heart, and mind, His power helps us to overcome.

    When Thomas saw Jesus in person after He had risen from the dead, he then believed in the power of the resurrection. He saw Jesus with his own eyes. Can you imagine the visual thoughts that went into Thomas' mind? Being a follower of Jesus Christ, his eyes had to become opened. Scales had to have fallen off of his eyes as well. There are some people who do not believe that God had raised His son Jesus from the dead. They will argue you until you turn different colors, some until they die. You do not have to argue with anyone. God is God and nobody can change Him. God is the center of all life and power. No one and nothing is above Him. He gives out the mission to us. Our mission is to witness by the power of the Holy Spirit to win souls to the Kingdom. Our mission is help people to see and remove the scales from their eyes.

    We need to be able to tell people that in the resurrection, the stone was rolled away from the tomb after Jesus had risen from the dead and He left that grave site to show Himself to more than500 people. We need to tell people that Jesus is alive. He is at the right hand of the

Father. The grave could not hold Him. He got up! God had resurrected Him and left His garments. Jesus rose from the grave with all power. He is our Lord and Redeemer. His love never failed and never will. God unveiled His Son Jesus to prove His love to the world so that the world would be restored and that His people would return to Him and worship Him only. God revealed to us that Jesus is the conqueror and the restorer of Life to all men. God unveiled His Son to be the one who would draw all men unto Him.

The resurrection was always right before our eyes. It is time that every Saint walk with a new attitude knowing that it was He who gave us life everlasting and not wrath that we so deserved. The resurrection is the most powerful piece in man's life. We must be resurrected ourselves to serve Him whole-heartedly.

I believe the next unveiling of Jesus' resurrection was when the tomb was open, the stone was rolled away. It was open for all to see. Today, it is still open for all to see. Get up and go and see if you do not believe. He is not there in the tomb where they laid Him. It was important to Mary to find Him because in heart He was so precious and she knew He was the Son of God. She wanted to take care of His body. Mary still had worship on her heart for the Lord. You know Jesus showed her and blessed her. When you go looking for Jesus, He will see you, remember you and bless you. Jesus rose and was given all power in His hand. His Father entrusted all the power over everything, all existence, all creation, every mind, every heart, every soul, every spirit, everything that had breath, all the animals, plants, oceans, stars, planets, galaxies, famous people, water, rain, snow, the sea world, fish, oceans, rivers flowing, ponds, gold, silver, coal, mercury, and diamonds, stores, humanity sports, football, basketball, soccer, baseball, and the American dream and governments and kingdoms. If you can think of it, God owns it and placed it in the possession and authority of His Son Jesus. Get this, we do not own anything. When we die, it goes away also. He is the same God who gave everything to Adam, all dominion and all power.

We Thank God and praise His Holy name for unveiling the resurrection. The resurrection is what redeemed us from the wrath and the sin that beset us. The blood in the death of Jesus Christ is what redeemed us from sin and the wrath of God. His love is transcendent. His love can be seen by us because His love is in us. What God wants is a person to be resurrected from the pride of life, the sin of Life because He has already destroyed it so that we can live the abundant life by seeing the blessings in the spirit. All Glory to His Holy name.

PRAYER

Father, thank you for the power of the resurrection. I live because you rose from the dead. Thank you for loving me so much.

MARK 20

THE GOD OF IMAGERY

PHILIPPIANS 4:6-11 Be anxious for nothing, but in everything by prayer and supplication, with thanksgiving, let your requests be made known to God; and the peace of God, which surpasses all understanding, will guard your hearts and minds through Christ Jesus. Finally, brethren, whatever things are true, whatever things *are* noble, whatever things *are* just, whatever things *are* pure, whatever things *are* lovely, whatever things *are* of good report, if *there is* any virtue and if *there is* anything praiseworthy—meditate on these things. The things which you learned and received and heard and saw in me, these do, and the God of peace will be with you. But I rejoiced in the Lord greatly that now at last your care for me has flourished again; though you surely did care, but you lacked opportunity. Not that I speak in regard to need, for I have learned in whatever state I am, to be content:

Think on Godly things and observe the blessings of God in your life. He alone is the image that we must keep in our minds. Allow Him today to take over your mind more in areas like technology, substance and life in general. It is important to have Jesus Christ at the center of your mind because everything is being taken to the big screen, internet, radio, Ipods, I-reports, Youtube, Facebooks, and methods of email, Twitter, AKO, Hotmail, Yahoo and advancing technology. Nothing is wrong with having these excellent tools of necessity and convenience for communication and enjoyment. Do not allow any of it to separate you from God. Instead use it to glorify Him and receive more blessings.

More ideas and images are moving at an alarming and extremely fast pace. What is so fascinating about the big screen-movie theater and technology itself is that almost anything goes on television and in some of the other areas. Communities in America and all across the world need to improve on censoring programs for young adults and small children. We still need to keep our future generations protected from contaminated programs with evil entrapments. Children are impressionable and will fall for the enemy's trap if we do not help them. We do not need to wait until it is too late.

Do not forget about prayer and supplication. It is the fastest of all communication tools and the most effective for life's benefits in the spirit.

Some of America's favorite past times are going to the movie theaters, and viewing DVD's at home by big screen or computer. All kinds of movies are being developed. You might love to watch sports, drama, action thriller, horror or some comedy type of show. I enjoy good drama and comedy. One thing is for sure, the association with evil does not mix with good, spiritually minded folks. Avoid the kind that will tears you down. Horror is the worst thing to watch in my opinion because what you watch is received inside of your mind and can remain there. If you do not believe me ask all the people who watched the exorcist years ago and observe their response. Better yet ask the question how did it make you feel then and today? For me, without even knowing God as my personal Savior, it made me know that evil exist then and today. Your spirit will pick it up.

It is vitally important that all people be informed that what you watch affects your spirit man and your life. If you watch horror, then you start feeling the effects of horror. Yea, you might not think so now. But if you remember horror over the last 10 years or so, then you can identify with what is being said here. What you take in be careful because it may try to take over you. Do not entertain evil. Teach your young children in a way that they should go. Proverbs 22:6 Teach them about what Jesus requires of them. Think pure thoughts. I want to make it perfectly clear that Jesus has all power to denounce any spirit on your behalf. Trust Him today.

I just wanted to tell people that images of what you see on the big screen can be etched into your mind and your heart for life. So why pay for something that will cause you nightmares and a troubled spirit just because you decided to watch a 2-3 hour movie. Please understand that movies have impact and what you view has impact.

Philippians' writer says to think on these things. Let all your thinking be absorbed with the thoughts of entering into God's court with thanksgiving and giving Him the fullness of praise.

How do we get ahead in the movie industry? We exalt God with making movies to reflect His image and His glory. We want Him to have all the glory in what we do. God, our Father is pleased when we put forth the effort to please Him. Train more actors to demonstrate the Lord and His time of blessing people. Reveal to them the image of God.

Here are four areas in our lives that we should apply the use of imagery. Jesus saw Himself for who He really was and is, the Lord of Lords and King of Kings; Next is the word, see the word for the power and authority and truth that exist within it and the mystery. Next is worship, see yourself worshiping God before His throne; in marriage, meditate on the love in the marriage and keep your vows before God, anything else outside should have no bearing. In praising Him , visualize yourself lifting up your hands toward heaven with a completely open heart, mind and spirit unto our Lord. Finally, be fruitful and a blessing to others, remember God's kingdom belongs to Him and He alone gets the glory and honor and power forever and ever. So bless someone even when you think it hurts. You will get blessed in return. Start seeing yourself planted in the right place to please God. Why have images of Jesus? It is who He is that fascinates and turns our spirits on with His word and mystery.

The word talks about His marvelous way of touching and healing and loving people with an everlasting love. To know Him and the power of His resurrection is enough to want more images of His glory inside our lives. His resurrection says it all. He got up from the grave and was victorious and defeated all enemies. Today, you can be assured the Jesus is Lord over all creation.

The word is another type of imagery. Imagery is like presenting a picture, painting a picture in your mind. Every time you watch a television program, some images stick with you, they never leave. That is why it is so important that you get the word. Keep Hebrews in mind, it states that the word of God is powerful like a two-edged sword. The word of God is seen in John the Baptist who was also known as a forerunner. He knew that Jesus was coming and He worked the work that God had prepared for him. He announces that Jesus would be coming to save His people.

One of the most important parts of life is to know when you have pleased God. When you know that you have pleased God then you can be content. The Apostle Paul speaks that he was content in whatever state. Of course that state is the mind of Christ without having the wants of society. He was fully aware that Christ Jesus, the same one who delivered Him from evil ways would take care all of his needs. If your life has peace and you know that God has filled you with the His Holy Spirit and you are aware and fully conscience of the fact that He is your God, then you should have a certain level of contentment about your life in Christ. The Apostle also reflects on a full trusted relationship in Christ. There is no guessing game about who Jesus is and what He means to the Apostle Paul and all the Saints. Lock Jesus in your everyday thoughts. Use the method of imagery to reflect on Jesus and His word in your life. Use imagery to walk with Him daily.

PRAYERS

Father, thank you for transforming me into your kingdom of righteousness. You made my life better. Thank you for making me over into a child of God and a Priest to serve you. Lead me to witness on this earth that I might be pleasing to you.

PHILIPPIANS 3

DON'T GIVE THE ENEMY A PIECE OF YOU

MATTHEW 22:36 Teacher, which is the great commandment in the law? Jesus said to him, you shall love the Lord your God with all your heart, with all your soul, and with all your mind. This is the first and great commandment

Give all of yourself to God today. Give the praise to Jesus. If the enemy keeps on your track, God will be there to rescue you. Talk to some Saints who know the power of prayer.

In His commandment, in Matthew 22:37 "Jesus said to the lawyer, you shall Love the Lord your God with all your heart, with all your soul, and with all your mind. This is the first and great commandment." Imagine surrendering to a God who holds all the power. You can stop worrying; you know the scripture, "Be careful for nothing." You can start an obedient walk with Christ Jesus, walking in the Spirit like it says in Galatians 5:16 I say then Walk in the Spirit and you shall not fulfill the lust of the flesh. What a combination! Love your God with all your heart and Walk in the Spirit. Walk with God and do not give the enemy a piece of you. When you give of yourself to God, you impress Him and Glorify Him alone.

People give of themselves often to others they do not even know. It's good to give to the needy, poor, and those that are suffering, God ordained the power to give to them. People give money to orphanages and some never even say a word. People give to local churches to build for the Kingdom and what God placed on their heart for it. People give because it's their gift to do so. I believe giving is of God's highest priority. John 3:16 says, for God so loved the world that He gave His only begotten Son. For whosoever believeth in Him shall not perish but have everlasting life. Look what Jesus gave. He gave His life for a ransom. He gave His life that we could be free. He gave the blood that covers us from the wicked sin.

Jesus already did what He told us to do. He did much more than we could for Him.

To express our love for Him is good but we need our guide the Holy Spirit to be able to walk in His commandments. Trust the Lord with all thine heart and lean not to your understanding and He will direct your path. Start worshiping the Living God and you will be blessed in salvation and repentance.

Most soldiers are familiar with commands. Military Commanding

General and Command Sergeants Majors send commands throughout the Armed Forces daily and expect them to be obeyed. These authority figures can call soldiers to attention with authority and Soldiers listen and respond. These commanders have the ability to write orders and all soldiers must obey these orders. If soldiers do not obey, they will receive some form of judicial punishment for disobeying orders.
When our Heavenly Father gives out the command, "Love Him with all your heart, mind, and Soul," He definitely means give Him more than a piece of you. Give Him the best of you because He has already blessed you and the enemy can't take it away.

If you have to give the enemy anything, you speak the word of God so that it will flee back to Hell with all of its demons. You do not have time to mess around. You have a mission to do.
God is faithful to deliver you. God is faithful to take care of you.

But if you just cannot stop yourself from giving of you, then speak the word and the enemy will flee. If you can not contain yourself from certain action, start praying in the spirit to Break the bondage of it. Keep good habits and break negative habits, not just spiritual but in spirit because some have deeply rooted themselves to your deepest part of mind and heart. You must have the help of the Holy Spirit. Give all of yourself to Jesus Christ the son of God.

PRAYERS

Father, keep my mind on you. Keep my heart on you. Keep my love centered on you as the priority of life. You made my life better because of your love. I need your Holy Spirit to help me walk in accordance to your commands.

MATTHEW 21

PRESS FOR THE PRIZE

Philippians 3:13-14 Brethren, I do not count myself to have apprehended; But one thing I do, forgetting those things which are behind, and reaching forward to those things which are ahead.

What is your goal in life? Are your pressing for a particular prize in life? Jesus was the first person that I can see clearly pressing for a mark. His mark was different. His goal was different. His goal was to give life. It was simply to save a dying world of sin on the verge of defeat. Jesus started reconciling us in the very beginning of His ministry. He saw our sinful ways and came from heaven to fix the sin situation, to bridge the gap that had separated us from the Father. Thank God that Jesus pressed His way with the cross, death, burial and rose from the dead.

What past thing haunts you? You do not have to keep on going down the same path. For some
reason you want to see what you can't change and you wonder how things could have been better at the same time you are recalling that past and dwelling in it daily. You wonder what that
relationship could have been like with that person but must have the courage to get over it.

You say things like, we could have had beautiful family! She loved me so much! Now you are at a place of repetitive voices speaking to you about old love versus new love vs. lost love. But then you realize the amount of hurt you went through. Then you realize how God delivered you through the pain. That is reason enough in itself to magnify His righteous name. We glorify Him because of His tender mercies, power and love.

We always have memories and past issues that rise up and make us meditate on that stage of life. Don't give it a second thought. After all are they thinking of you? Your life needs to go on and face Christ's loving gift in your life. Getting a grip on your life is the biggest step you can take. If you do not have it, someone else will certainly try to take your life. The enemy comes to kill, steal, and destroy. Jesus said I came to give you life and give it more abundantly.

If we think those positive thoughts, we can make it through those difficult storms that rage all night long that sometime seep into the next day of life. Yes, most people have those raging storms at night even when rain is nowhere in sight. One thing I love about Jesus is when He calmed the storm while in the boat with disciples. Jesus simply said "Peace, be still" and all creation stood still. We know that the storm ceased and His disciples were amazed.

It is a blessing to know that you have Jesus who can stop storms in its tracks. So since we know that He can stop storms in its tracks, we ought to know that he can heal past hurt, new hurts, and direct us and place us on a firm path. Then He guides us all day long so we do not fall completely. So do not feel apprehended, captive to the past because you have a King to rely on.

You have God almighty who rules all of Heaven and earth. You need to look toward the future pressing your way by the power of the Holy Spirit. When anything arises against your spirit,tell it Jesus Is Lord. I am standing on His word and His promise. He will never leave me nor forsake me. Bless His holy and righteous name.

PRAYERS

Lord, help me to determine the goal in my life that will please you. Father help me to prosper in those goals of life. Lord I pray that my goals will reflect Jesus Spirit in me.

PHILIPPIANS 2

PLANTED BY RIVERS OF WATER

Psalm 1:1-3 Blessed is the man who walks not in the counsel of the ungodly, Nor stands in the path of sinners, Nor sits in the seat of the scornful; But his delight is in the law of the Lord, And in His law he meditates day and night. He shall be like a tree planted by the rivers of water, That brings forth its fruit in its season, Whose leaf shall also not wither; And whatever he does shall prosper.

The Lord is the one who blesses in planting causing fruit according to His perfect will. Obeying His word is one of His Highest orders because it proves to Him that you are obedient in His word and The word is planted in you. You are walking with God's seed inside you. When He blesses, He makes the rivers flow in people lives. Rivers of water that flow in your life will continue in abundance because God wants to bless you in abundance.

God is looking for men that will receive the blessing and stay the course in planting His word and His love all around the world. When He gave the command to the Apostle in Matthew 28, it was a commission, a charge to spread the word and bless people throughout the world. His intent was to execute every word in Matthew 28. Jesus wanted His Apostles then and His witnesses today to plant and watch the fruit multiply from you preaching and teaching and baptism in the name of the Father, Son and Holy Spirit. He wants men that will stay on the path of obedience and servant hood. He wants us to stay the course even when it gets difficult. Stand firm in the power of God's word when challenges and difficulties occur. We need to maintain a positive and steadfast attitude in this walk.

We need to hang in there regardless of what things look like. Deception comes in all forms to trick saints and those that are lost. The enemy strives to deceive. He is a loser, a liar, and has no authority over you. You are blessed and highly favored of God. You are fruitful. You bear fruit in the name of Jesus Christ. You reign in Christ. You walk in the fullness of blessings and have inheritance laid up in heaven. Believers stand for Jesus and righteousness. Believers are blessed and they stand against destructive paths and rebellious attitudes in the home and in our lives. We bless people in our homes and all over the world. We bless people on the job and in hospitals, in prisons, on the street and brothers and sisters in church. We bless people outside. Our blessing is not based on judgment. We do not judge the world. Jesus said that he did not come to judge the world. He came to save the lost. We are on a mission for Christ to bless others. We stand against all evil by the power of prayer and faith in Jesus Christ. We are fervent prayer warriors. We are under the influence of the Holy Spirit to express fervent and effectual prayers. We pray because as God sent an angel to Daniel during His prayer, so can He send for our prayers. We plant when we pray because he hears us. We can also get a break through when we prayer as people of God's . We stand on the word of God and His promises to answer prayer and send the power of breakthrough and fruitfulness.

Adam was blessed but lost focus to disobedience and the world became as you see it now filled with all kinds of issues and concerns. Thank to God that He would help us. People could only be restore by God's only Son who would set us free. Once you have truly become obedient, you will line up with God's word because you will experience the power to know Him as Lord. Your scales will have fallen from your eyes then you will begin life again. You need to hurry and began to see things as they really exist. Reality in the spiritual realm is important because your life depends on it and eternity is for you child of God.

Have you ever seen a river flow and the speed of it? He makes them flow with power and force. Anything in its path will be crush, move and destroyed. God knows the exact force and timing. Rivers flow for several reasons. They are designed to carry things at the bottom of the river to another place. They are designed to clean out certain places by taking the unclean to the ocean so it could be eliminated. It shapes and molds, it builds and designs, rivers are in the Garden of Eden. Genesis 2:10 They carry blessings in the life of the believer. God made it so. God shows us rivers to show us blessings. The river can flow in your life. God is behind causing your river to flow. He wants to bless someone. There are more rivers to flow than we can imagine. God controls more rivers than what we see. You can get wet in the natural river of water. But you will get blessed. Do you know about rivers flowing in your life? When the scales fall off, then you will see the rivers flow.

A strong current has power to move things out of its path and cause devastating destruction. God shows us the power of His flow and that He can cease it as well in moments. His Holy Spirit flows in our lives day after day. Therefore , we meditate day and night.The power of the Holy Spirit is far greater than the imagination and surely far greater than water on earth, including Tsunami storms. He controls the waters, the rivers, and seas and oceans by His power.

PRAYER

Lord, I thank you for the blessings that come my way as I walk in tune with you. You planted me exactly where you wanted me to be. Lead me to witness on this earth that I might be pleasing to you. For you have blessed me to be in good company and not to receive the counsel of this world.

Psalm 1

SPEAK BLESSINGS

James 3:8-10 But no man can tame the tongue. It is an unruly evil, full of deadly poison. With it we bless our God and Father, and with it we curse men. Who have been made in the similitude of God. Out of the same mouth proceed blessings and cursings. My brethren these things ought not be so.

God spoke blessings and when He had finished making all things they were pleasing in His sight. God spoke and life began. Our lives were filled with all kinds of blessings. Heaven and earth was created. Everything that came out of God's mouth was pleasing to Him and For His glorious purpose. God revealed His identity to us through His work of salvation and the words He spoke. He reminds us of our destiny to walk in His image. We were made to speak blessings and not curses. He gave us these tongues for the proper use. The tongue is an instrument to be used for God's glory and edification. The tongue is powerful and carries the word of God and the word of God is more powerful than a two edged sword that pierces even the very asunder of the soul. The word speaks life and death to us (Proverbs 18:21).

Acts 2: 4 speaks of tongues of fire during the day of Pentecost, it says, "And they were all filled with the Holy Spirit and began to speak with other tongues, as the spirit gave them utterance." God wants us to know that He was revealing Himself to show us what He did in the book of Acts by allowing the power of tongues to rest on His people, God has no respect of person. No one is above Him. He will empower all His people for the uplifting of His Kingdom. He poured out the Holy Spirit on people then and is doing it today as well. The Holy Spirit will work on behalf of the Father in all circumstances.

When the tongues of fire rested on them, they spoke with power. They did not speak damages and hate; they spoke edification to the Lord. They spoke different languages but all languages in the form of edifying God. It was the Holy Spirit that was the guiding power enabling these people to get their blessing. He is the controller on God's behalf.

The Holy Spirit will help us learn self control in our lives and with that little member in our mouth. The tongue is powerful. Every time we say things negative and harsh, we give in to the enemy's delight. The Holy Spirit desires to help all who need to change in this are to glorify and lift up Jesus. He gives us power to fight against the works of the enemy. The Holy Spirit will help us to use a tongue that blesses people and not curse them. Try saying something positive about someone. There is power in that little member in the body called the tongue. If we allow the Holy Spirit to work in and throughout us, we will avoid lashing out to hurt someone, gossiping about situations or even speaking hatred. The Holy Spirit will help end backbiting and all the negative words that were once a habit. It is the Holy Spirit who will help us with our faith as we call on Him for help.

God can do anything with the tongue. He can use it for His glory. Speak the word using the tongue and gifts(the Greek word for gifts is Charisma) which points us to grace and revealing the word. 1 Corinthians 12:10 and 14:1-22 Speak Prayers with that tongue. Bless people with your tongue and gifts. God will purify your hearts to help us to speak according to our identity in Christ Jesus. People will know us by the way we speak. God is not asking us to be flawless because He already knows that we are sinful at times. He provided His never ending love to be imitated and expressed to His people. Our Father delights in people speaking blessings in the lives of others. Today speak blessings into the lives of others. God will be pleased with you. Praise to our Lord who gives power to speak blessings.

PRAYERS

Father, I present myself to you as a sacrifice. I submit to you Lord to tame my tongue. Every negative and profane word, I cease it today. I will bless others by speaking blessings.

JAMES 4,5

HONOR THE LORD

Proverbs 3:9 Honor the Lord with your possessions, And with the first fruits of all your increase.

    Everything we own already belongs to God. All the increase is from God. Cattle on every hill belongs to the Lord. God made all these wonderful things for His pleasure and gave them to man. We must honor the Lord with our possessions because everything belongs to Him anyway. God blessed us just like He said He would under Abraham. It is a blessing to know that God keeps His promises from His word. His blessings continue to overflow in our lives. It is so important that those who are blind and skeptical seek the Lord's face and get into His presence and become believers in Him. The word of God will help all believers to honor God. The word of God fills the heart and makes it right with God. The word of God will help everyone through the toughest of test. When we are tested with our possessions, He helps us to realize that all blessings come from Him. The word helps you see your heart and the blessings in your possessions. The word helps us really understand some things about the heart of giving and honoring God. Do you honor God or not? That is a personal decision for everyone. Make sure you know you honor God. Give yourself first and the remainder will follow. Your possessions could cause you to get blessed even more if you act under obedience.
    The God we serve owns the abundance of everything. There is nothing anywhere that He does not own. So in our abundant life, He wants us to give first fruit. What is this first fruit. The first fruit is the best of all you have. The first fruit is giving Jesus your best or ten percent from the top of your earning. This scripture refers to giving God your first and best. It is one way of showing God has first place in a person's life. Giving of the first fruit acknowledges obedience to His will and commands. God blesses those that are obedient in giving.
    There was a rich man who had issues with his money. Jesus Told him to give the money away, immediately his it was troubled. You can't turn money into being your Lord. But you can make you heart turn away by thinking that it is more powerful and needed more than God is needed in your life. Set aside the first fruit and present it to the Lord and then watch the increase in multiple blessings in your life. God is able to help you break that bondage, that stronghold that constantly tries to ride you. You are not broken. The circumstances

that you are in may have you appearing and acting like you are broken. The enemy will not have a laugh today! This time you speak the word with blessing authority. We know that the enemy delights in seeing saints suffer especially when he believes he has crippled your faith.

There are many people that are rich right now. Watch what happens to those that are rich when they receive spiritual sight. They will feel far blessed than the possession they have on hand. When you get blessed, you owe it to God. If you get blessed with a million dollars, that is a fruit blessing from the Lord to you. He always gives to us. In fact, He never stops giving. All we really have to do is look around and see what He has done in each of our lives and even in the lives of others. His blessing come directly from heaven. Malachi 3
He deserves the first fruit of our earnings. Think on your blessing because He is the reason why we get blessed in the first place.

The Lord worked on me to make me understand that all I have belongs to Him anyway. If we leave this earth tomorrow, it still belongs to Him. Everything to everyone is on loan status. God freely gives and God looks to see the heart of man and his giving attitude.

PRAYERS

Father, I ask for help in obedience to honor you with my first fruit continuously. Help me to be a seed sower. Help me to give my portion of tithes and offering according to your word. All things in creation already belong to you. I praise your Righteous name, Lord Jesus.

2 CORINTHIANS 9:6-7

GRACE SAVED ALL HUMAN RACE

Ephesians 2:8 For by grace you have been saved through faith, and that not of yourselves, it is the gift of God.

Faith and Grace are two of God's holy blessings. Grace is a gift from God. They are the key sources of strength for salvation. Most people are still unaware of the power in grace. It was grace that kept you from committing spiritual suicide, not to mention suicide in the natural realm. Grace is unmerited favor given by God. No one can earn grace. It is not a power source that you turn on and off. No one can work for grace. There are no countries that can work for grace. No society and no community efforts can earn grace. It is freely given. Jesus gave us grace. Grace is given freely at no expense of people. Jesus came with grace and truth that all men might believe and be saved into His Kingdom. We never had a right to see this blessed gift of grace from our Lord. Our penalty was simply death. We were destined to the wrath of God. But He washed us as white as snow in the power of His love.

When someone is truly saved, they have the ability to see these holy blessings called grace. They see the evidence of it in their lives. Since you are a new creature in Christ, you see basically all good things in life associated with His grace. Your scales have fallen off. It is by the grace of God that we live day to day, breath moment to moment, love time again and again. He did not have to give us any time nor any chances. But He is the God who never changes.

We deserved His wrath because of our sin nature. Nevertheless, in grace, He took away sin that we may live according to His perfect will and love among one another. You see in grace, you get favor that no man could ever give you. Grace never turns its back on you. Grace never ceases
in blessing your life. Grace has the perfect mixer of God's love to sustain you and help you to grow all together. We are speaking of God who is all powerful and sovereign. God has perfecting ingredients in his grace. We do not know it all but we do know that the power of love is in His grace. We do know that His glory is in His grace. We do know that His healing power is in His grace. We do know that salvation is in His grace. We do know that eternity
is in His grace. We do know that restoration is in His grace. We know that He is Sovereign, and omnipresent. Grace is in it all. His blood

released grace on us. His love and grace both exist to will us into His loving hands. Those perfect ingredients are love and faith that we continue to experience.

There will be some times in life when the enemy will make your mind think that there is no grace. It will seem that way because all of hell appears to have entered your life. At the same time the enemy is playing tricks in your mind. Many people have felt that way before.

When you get anointed the enemy has someone to go after. Even those in Christ sometimes feel heavy burdened. But they should not allow heavy burdens nor does the trick of the enemy fool them, especially if your mind is stayed on Him. Remember, grace did not come because we called on it. Grace was given because the Love of God sheds abroad and He first loved us. So it is by Grace that we are saved and not of ourselves, it is the gift of God and not man-made. Praise and glory to His holy name.

PRAYER

Thank you Father for supplying never ending grace. You deserve all the praise and worship. If I had ten thousand tongues, I could not praise you enough.

EPHESIANS 3

GOD COMMANDS LIGHT

2 Corinthians 4: 6-7 For God, who said, "Let light shine out of darkness," made his light shine in our hearts to give us the light of the knowledge of God's glory displayed in the face of Christ. But we have this treasure in jars of clay to show that this all-surpassing power is from God and not from us.

   God commanded the light in the beginning of creation. He has the power to put light in man's heart. God knows the darkness that is in each man's life. He knows exactly what we need. He knows that glory will be given to Him through people.

  He commanded light to bless us. There are many illustrations that can be used when it comes to the light of God in our lives. He made light in the world when it was darkness throughout. He even made the day and night. He made light in man's body to represent Him as the life giver. He put the very thought in man's mind to invent the light bulb currently used in every home, business and building throughout this world. It was His power that gave the intellect and ingenious ability to think of such a product and invention. Light is in this world all around us. When we see the sun and the moon, we see the evidence of light that only God can create in the sun and the moon. He is the God who made those elements of this world. In your home, each time you walk in a dark room, you hit the light switch and a beam of light penetrates the darkness in that room. We see again the power of His light breaking through the darkness. Would it be something if everyone called Christians could let this light shine and penetrate through us to be effective witnesses in this world. It is the light that penetrates so powerful that it forces evil spirits away.

   When we walk in the light, He wants us to share His holy word to a dying world. We may be clay vessels but the power of Christ rest upon us to do the will of our Father. This light that He has granted us is a blessing and remarkable faith that goes along with it to humbly serve Him. Many people may have been blinded by other lights. It may have been a light from a distant place that keeps on putting you in bondage .Our primary purpose is to let people see Christ Jesus through us by walking in the light. Jesus made that statement that no one can shake it, He said, "Let your light shine that they may see your good works." Once you become a new born Christian, there is a walk that you must take.

PRAYERS

Father, thank you for transforming me into your kingdom of righteousness. You made my life better. Thank you for making me over into a child of God and a Priest to serve you. Lead me to witness on this earth that I might be pleasing to you.

MATTHEW 5

KNEEL BEFORE GOD ON THE THRONE

ISAIAH 40:15-17 Behold, the nations are as a drop in a bucket, And are counted as the small dust on the scales; Look, He lifts up the isles as a very little thing.

Most of us have heard that phrase "drop in the bucket" before. It is one of those common phrases in our lives that have a specific meaning. It has that connotation that the value is less not what you think it is. It also refers to the effort that goes into something. In this case, it's too easy! So do not put it above or exalt above the Most High God and creator of all existence. When we exalt Him, He lifts us up as the isles and to Him it is easy and pleasing. He can do it again and again, just like the blessings He bestows daily. Don't you just love His name and all of His goodness and mercy that extends in our lives by Him and through Him?

Do you really want to see the throne of God? Well, if you want to you can. Did you know the word will reveal the throne to you? The word will give you a glimpse of the throne. Everyone loves to have the ability to see. Use your inner spiritual sight to see Him on His throne and bow before Him. There is a great white throne according to the scripture. Everyone will appear before the throne whether they did good or bad. It is better to be humble, obedient and faithful, filled with the attitude of worship and praise to His righteous and Holy name. He already knows our heart toward Him and everything about us. See Revelations 4, 8 for a picture of God in heaven on the throne.

It is amazing that once we get there, He who sits on the throne has already decided where we will spend eternity. You will never meet someone who is really not concerned about where they will spend eternity. Yes, you are correct even those skeptics, atheist, and false god worshippers, and even cults and you name it, they are concerned at least a fraction. As long as you wearing this dirt suit and equipped with what God made you, you have a conscience about things. It does not matter if someone thinks that his or her belief system is the only one that is valid. He already knows the beginning to the end of every thought. So surely what someone believes in has an impact with God Almighty.

God makes it very clear that every nation is as a drop in the bucket. That is important because the scripture clearly says that He is not a respecter of persons. So if a person is lifted above God in his own eyes, he is an enemy of God. Even if a nation or many nations exalt themselves above God, they are enemies of God. There are consequence and even more important, you still will have to go to the Throne and answer to your actions. He makes it perfectly clear that we are counted as small dust. We are as a drop in the bucket. God can let us go and if He wanted to He could have started all over again. No one controls the Lord our God. He knows our destiny and our faith walk. He already knows who stands with Him.

God knows what it takes to humble a man. He knows that it will take good humility for a man to consider accepting Him as Lord. It was humility that took Jesus to the cross and experience a death for all mankind. Certainly everyone should bow down in exaltation and honor and bless His name forever and ever. He could have allowed us to be a drop in the bucket. We could have looked at us with as the lowest on earth, but He did not. Instead he looks on us with love. We deserved as sinners His wrath. But God's love is so great that even through our worst sin, He forgave us. We need the Holy Spirit to help us to love people when they sin in a spiteful manner.

In the book of Revelation Chapter 4, the Apostle John had a vision of being in heaven. While he was in heaven, there appeared to him a throne and one sat on that throne. God's throne belongs to Him alone and will never end. I believe the Apostle John wondered why God allowed him to have this vision of heaven to be transported into Jesus' presence. The answer is that Jesus loves us so much that He makes it a priority to make Himself available so we can get into His presence. He wants us to know that He is alive and on His throne. We must all bow before Him with all honor and glory. Praise to the Lord our God.

PRAYER

Father, you know all things and all people. I thank you that when you see me, you see the best in me. You make it so that I am important to you in your kingdom. I exalt your Holy name. I thank you for not disposing me. You allowed me to live another day and I am blessed and thankful.

MARK 1

SEED EXPERIENCE

LUKE 8:10-12 And He said, to you it has been given to know the mysteries of the kingdom of God, but to the rest it is given in parables, that seeing they may not see, And hearing they may not understand. Now the parable is this: The seed is the word of God. Those by the wayside are the ones who hear; then the devil comes and takes away the word out of their hearts, lest they should believe and be saved.

Farmers do not know the very secret of God when it comes to the growth of his crops. No one knows the secret recipe that comes from His power. The farmer knows fertilizer and seed have much to do with the process of production and fruitfulness. But no one knows the exact power of God when He takes the harvest and produces the abundance from that harvest. They may not understand God taking a seed and producing the abundance in likeness from that particular seed. God teaches us the law of sowing seed. When you become a seed sower, you might as well get ready for the enemy to put forth his best tactics to steal the word from your heart. You are a threat to the enemy. He does not want you to have the seed God gave you. He will come after you with all his might to take that seed from you. You are now a target because of the word of God inside your heart. Once the enemy thinks that he took it from your heart then he wants your mind and your confession to be destroyed as well. The enemy will try to hinder, block, steal and conceal your blessings from God every time. Please understand that the enemy is concerned about taking everything you own including your family. You are like fertile ground that receives new seed. The enemy does not want the word (seed) in your heart, your mind and in your spirit man. Once you get the word rooted inside you, then you can walk in the fruit of the spirit and be filled in faith. You can walk under the anointing and nothing can stop you.

The enemy's mission is to take the seed from you, stunt the seed in you, burn it up, choke it out of you, and destroy the seed in you. The enemy wants to break you and me in every possible manner. Do you think the enemies in war respect you? The enemy does not respect any Christian, any believer regardless of who you are. Every Christian must embrace the power of the Holy Spirit's protection. Start recognizing the actions of the Holy Spirit to protect your life. In Psalm 91, God gives His angels charge over us to protect us.

When you have the power to call on Jesus, you are dangerous to the enemy. When you have the authority of the world, use it because it matters to have Jesus on your side in all things. Christians are destined to suffer persecution. So we all need Jesus. Sometimes persecution comes when you least expect it and it will come. When you get the word which is the seed in you, the enemy hates it and will try to demand you to step down in serving and worshiping God. Stay in the word; meditate on it day and night as Psalm 1 says.

I never understood those that thought everything was okay when the enemy comes your way.

I am so excited about the power of His word. I remember working on a farm, doing dirty and hard work with livestock, chickens, cows, horses, and all kinds of vegetables and plants. The farm life was adventurous. One of my adventures was riding horses. It quickly became an instant passion. I rode horse and that was one of my main missions. I did get bucked off several times. On the farm, I learned how to be disciplined in working in so many areas. My father was responsible for placing me and my brothers on the farm to work.

One of the most important things I learned on that farm working in extreme summer heat was plowing the ground at the right time to put seed in it was a tough labor intensive job. Nevertheless, I did that job because it was time to learn how to work hard and earn my keeps. When you plow the ground, you will always need a strong mule, dependable plow, and or a good tractor. During those years, tools were available, but Mr. Brown was old school and depended on that mule he talked to day and night. That mule seemed like it respected old Brown. Sometimes as a human being or little youngster, I would watch him and be amazed how that mule responded to him even after a long day of plowing. I watched Mr. Brown talk to that mule in the backyard many times. The point is Mr. Brown was a man who knew the power of planting seed and the cost associated with planting seed. Although, he left us to be with the Father in heaven, he was a remarkable example on how to plow to plant seed, ensuring the best outcome. Because he was wealthy in his ability to plow and plant seed, others would be wealthy along with the farm owner. I believe that we need some new ground to plow and plant. We need hearts that will receive the power of God's word penetrating on the inside and manifesting inside out.

That farm has a special meaning in my life because it always left the power of the seed in my mind. The seed in one watermelon creates the abundance of seed to be planted. The seed that will multiply comes from the original source. In many cases, it is the seed that had been planted years ago or just yesterday, that produces many of its kind. Christians fall in that category. God has a way dealing with the enemy on our behalf so that we can sow seed to glorify Him. Child of God do not give the enemy an inch! Do not give the enemy an opening of any kind at any time. I never forget eating all of those watermelons and hoping not to swallow those seeds. It was God who taught us and saw us through those summer times of working the fields in hard labor. When I was eating those watermelons, I always tried not to swallow the seed because we were not alike. I need to swallow the Lord's word, the seed we all Christians need daily. We are empowered and sustained with God's seed.

Believers have to have the Lord's power in their Christian walk. It helps to be cautious in their walk. Don't give in to foolish demands of others. Do not be persuaded to do worldly things unpleasant to God. God sees all things. He wants us to walk in obedience. He even plants His seed in us to get us to prove His power and ignite the faith in us to serve Him. Give your life to Jesus Christ today. You have waited long enough. Today you may be able to help someone who has fallen to the wayside. .

PRAYERS

Father, thank you revealing mystery to me. Help me to see in the areas of my life that need changed so that I will serve you. I prayer to be a seed sower for your Kingdom. In Jesus name, Amen

MARK 4

GIVE GOD ALL PRAISE!

PSALM 150:1-6 Praise the LORD!

Praise God in His sanctuary;
   Praise Him in His mighty firmament!
Praise Him for His mighty acts;
   Praise Him according to His excellent greatness!
Praise Him with the sound of the trumpet;
   Praise Him with the lute and harp!
Praise Him with the timbrel and dance;
   Praise Him with stringed instruments and flutes!
Praise Him with loud cymbals;
   Praise Him with clashing cymbals!
Let everything that has breath praise the LORD.
   Praise the LORD!

David tells us that the saints of the Lord must give God glory and experience joy in doing so. God deserves all glory and praise! This has to be one of the most simple Psalms to obey. But if we allow the enemy to defeat us, then we would be letting God down. In this Psalm, Saints have a specific position in praising God. We are to have that heart of praise like a warrior going to battle. Our praise to the Lord is that of one whom is confident in defeating the enemy on every front. Praise destroys those strong holds in the lives of people. Praise works faster to destroy enemy attacks. Praise defeats the enemy in a moment's notice. The enemy may not even know what hit him.

We can be assured it was the Lord who is on our side. Remember, If God be for us, who can be against us? God will fight your battles. You and I just need to stand and trust the Lord. God is on the throne and He loves for His children to praise Him. Do you want victory in life over all the defeat you were up against? Yes, you do want victory just like millions of people around desire. We'll, it is time you start doing what Paul and Silas did in the prison. You know what happen when they praised the Lord together. The Lord showed up in power and both of their chains were broken as they were locked in the prison. The next thing that happened was that the doors were open for them to be set free. Then the prison guard received a change of heart after witnessing God moving in the prison. When praise goes up, blessings come down. Our God in heaven is acknowledged as the only God who has the power to save and break prison holds.

We get God's attention and He is ready to pour out blessings that we have no knowledge of.

Start thinking about praising God with all of your heart, mind, soul and spirit. Give yourself to the Lord. Let yourself go into the presence of God with full praise filled in the Holy Spirit. Just call His name with adoration and absolute reverence. It is time to be set free. Do you know what Jesus said when Lazarus was in the grave? He said, "Loose Him and let Him go." I am sure you want to have the experience of a lifetime in your heart. Start bowing before His throne and know that He is real in your life each and every day. Praise Him and watch the enemy flee from you. If the enemy persist in coming after you, continue in your praise, and put all of your heart and soul in it. Worship Him and speak His word and expect peace. Give God all the glory.

PRAYERS

Father, thank you for all the things you have done in my life. Thank you for changing my lifestyle. Thank you for allowing me to see things better. I will praise you from now on because of your goodness. In Jesus name, amen.

JOHN 3

JESUS SITS ON THE THRONE

ISAIAH 40: 21-22 Have you not known? Have you not heard? Has it not been told to you from the beginning? Have you not understood from the foundation of the earth? It is He who sits above the circle of the earth, and its inhabitants are like grasshoppers, Who stretches out the heavens like a curtain, and spread them out like a tent to dwell in.

No matter where you are in life, what troubles you are facing, the pain that is unbearable, the situation you are currently in, even the judge have to face tomorrow, and no matter what position you hold or what you think or do, God is still on the throne in Heaven. He sits high and looks low, always expressing who He is with everlasting love joy, and power. He will not be moved from His throne. His throne is forever and ever. No matter how hard or difficult something may be He will not be moved. No matter How your heart may feel when it is stepped on, God is still on the throne. No matter how friends may put you down, and you feel hated, God is still on the throne. No matter how sadness may creep into your life, God is still on the throne. No matter what attacks you have been under, God is still on the throne. No matter how much you've been cheated on and lied on, God is still on the throne.

No matter how death may have impacted your life and dealt you a blow, God is still on the throne. He is looking at you right now with wide open arms of compassion. He is on the throne orchestrating your life for His marvelous plan for you and me.

God is so powerful that He sends us signs and wonders and always a message. He has a message through Revelations that history itself is coming to a close. History and all of time is God. No wonder the writer asked the question, Have you not known? If you have never worshipped God in your life, then you need to get with it because life will happen. Eternal life will happen. God sits on the throne and every true believer desires to see His face, bow before Him with complete individual exaltation. The word tells us that He sits above the circle of the earth. God shows us that whatever and whoever, I put in place will come to pass. When God sent soldiers to visit Iraq, He already knew that the dictator would be captured and put away for his evil deeds. God already knew that top position would become vacant because those put in places have no praise for the provider of the blessings. You can be a well known CEO

And not give God the glory. The same God that people neglect giving glory is the same God who can remove the CEO from that position and promote someone else. He still sits on the Throne. God is telling people that He is the one to worship and glorify.

In the eyes of the man who thinks he has it all but neglects the will of God in his life, he has the opportunity to make God his Lord. You see God can touch Africa, God can touch the United States, God can touch England, the British, God can touch Australia. God can touch every kingdom on Earth. God can touch every hiding place. God can touch every facet of society and every class of people, every man, everything in existence. God's eyes are everywhere. Nothing is unseen by Him. He sits on the throne and sees us as His children and at the same time like little grasshoppers. God knows exactly what we need and where our minds and hearts are. He can make a way out of no way. He cools the mountains. He orchestrates the running rivers. He designed the sun and stars and all galaxies. He even positioned them that they will be perfectly aligned. He made life and gave us the perfect design in the body.

God who sits on the throne made the heavens. He designed it just as though He was a home designer. He has more skill than HGTV. He has more decorative ideas that any homemaker.

God still sits on the throne and can never be moved from His place.

PRAYERS

Father, I thank you that your throne is the highest throne and the only place my heart should focus on. Because of you, I denounce all idols and sin that tries to trap me. Lord, I praise and magnify your name.

ISAIAH 40

JESUS OPENS EYES

GEN 3:5 For God knows that in the day you eat of it, your eyes will be opened, and You will be like God knowing good and evil.

Adam had the power in his mouth to stop the devil in his tracks. In fact, Adam had the power to send the devil back down to hell. He had the power to protect his wife from any involvement especially a conversation with the devil in the garden, the perfect place to live. Be on guard man of God, woman of God in your house and at work and everywhere you go. It was sin in the Garden of Eden that caused our eyes to be wide open. Adam had all dominion and all authority and did not know what to do with it. He lost it because of his disobedience. The man was in charge of the garden like he covers his own house. Eve could not see beyond the manipulation and deceit of the enemy at that very moment. It was her husband Adam who could see and who could use the power to deal with that old Serpent on the spot. Because of one disobedient act all of our eyes are wide open to sin. Our eyes are not opened to be like God as the enemy tried to manipulate. They were opened to sin. It would be later when Jesus came, our eyes would be open to righteousness, in good standing. This would happen only by the blood of the lamb.

Instead they became open in a sin nature. Man will never hold the sight of what God sees and does. Man is not God and will never be God. Man is the substance of what God is made to live in. The harmony of what God designed for him. One mistake that the enemy did make is that the Lord God through His Holy Spirit did create us to have our eyes wide open for multiple reasons. He wanted us prepared for all things to come. He wants us to have the best life and experience blessings poured out in our lives by our Father in heaven.

GEN 3: 7 Then the eyes of both of them were opened, and they knew that they were naked; and they sewed fig leaves together and made themselves coverings.

The moment both of them knew they were naked, they were ashamed and felt that they needed to cover up their bodies. They went from freedom to darkness in an instant. You see God had made their bodies beautiful and handsome with no worries. Everything was in perfect harmony. Our eyes do not have to be wide open to sin like in the garden any more. But it can be open to recognize the tricks and maneuvers of the enemy. Our eyes can be used to our advantage in giving God glory throughout eternity. Our eyes are to be watchful for His holy and glorious return to earth. Thanks to Jesus who washed us clean. Now our eyes can be wide open to recognize what God wants for our lives and for His purpose. Be encouraged to live by these words that the Apostle Paul stated "We walk by faith, not by sight." Even with our eyes wide open, we still need to walk by faith. Faith in God will carry you all the way through this life. Your eyes might see something but do you really have faith for it to be manifested in the spirit. Your eyes have the power to see what God has for you and your family for the edifying of the ministry.

One of the most important things in life along with your eyes is the ability to listen. Everyone must learn to listen to God's voice only. The enemy is filled with lies, tricks, manipulation, and devices that can easily cause you to turn. Do not listen to anything that the enemy says to you. You take all of your commands and the word of God directly and strictly from God. That is one the reasons why the Lord wants us to be in direct relationship with Him. Because if you get into a relationship with someone else that wants you to be on their course of life, then you no longer listen to God. The Lord wants you to listen and keep your eyes wide open. It is time to walk in the spirit and see in the spirit.

It is time for people to start having their eyes wide open to their environment. There are many things happening all around us and you need to be on watch and in touch with reality. Be watchful in that Jesus Christ will return from the heavens to claim His own. Be watchful as the elect of God rebuking the snares of life by the enemy and the will of the flesh. The will of the flesh is powerful if you do not put it into subjection by fasting and praying.

You must also be watchful because the enemy constantly seeks to kill, steal and destroy lives in the ministry and those that are babes in Christ. Hold on to God's unchanging hand for your life. Be careful for the enemy specializes in trying to manipulate everything he possibly can. As soon as you see it happening start praying because praying puts the devil on the run. Prayer is our direct connection to the one who sits on the throne forever and ever. Call on the name of Jesus because His name makes the enemy flee because there is power in the name. Start counting on Jesus to be the one who helps you in all circumstances. He will make a way out of no way. When you think that you are unable to see the things around you, ask God to open your eyes and make it visible and plain with understanding. When you start to prosper in your ministry, with money, with friends, with material blessings, with the abundance of life, the enemy will start raising its ugly head in your life, trying to destroy a happy home.

No matter what it is start praying in the Spirit and call on the name of the Lord, Jesus Christ so that the enemy will flee. Rebuke Him entirely. When you know that the enemy has started his attacks, you can start singing praise to clear the atmosphere. The presence of God will overtake the enemy if you trust Him during your worship and praise sessions.

What do you really want to see? My heart's desire is to see Jesus glorified and serve Him entirely. Your eyes can be opened to so many things in life good or evil.

We want to see a hard move of God in the lives of His people. We want the word to be revealed to those who have not accepted Jesus according to Romans 10:9; John 1:1-12. Come back to Jesus. You have lived out there long enough. Start pressing your way back in. Ask God to open your eyes by removing the spiritual scales.

PRAYERS

Father, thank you for teaching me to be obedient in your word. I need your Holy Spirit to guide me through temptations of life. Lord first, spiritually open my eyes to see challenges that come before me and give me a discerning spirit. In Jesus name, Amen.

GENESIS 4

VISIONARY MAN

Habakkuk 2:2-3 Then the LORD answered me and said: "Write the vision and make *it* plain on tablets, that he may run who reads it. For the vision *is* yet for an appointed time; But at the end it will speak, and it will not lie. Though it tarries, wait for it; because it will surely come, it will not tarry.

    Write the vision and make it plain. You see things that God grants for you as clear as day. Stop refusing the blessing that God has for you. Start speaking it in your spirit that your will be obedient to our Father in heaven. Start confessing with your lips the promises that God has for you. You do not have to rely on someone else to announce it. Just call on Jesus, the Son of the living God. God will bless your vision especially if it is for His kingdom. If you want it, get it. Blessings are for the taking from the Lord. Blessings will overflow in what you do for the Lord as long as you glorify Him.

    There are many men who built churches for the uplifting of God's kingdom. They are built for worship and praise. King David had a vision to build a temple for God to place the Ark of the Covenant inside. But God wanted a place where He always dwelt. King David could not build the temple because he had blood on his hands. The Temple had to be built by his son Solomon. You see God has the vision over man. God is looking for those who will be obedient and act on the vision He alone set out for them.

    When Moses saw the burning bush, his heart was ignited to move toward God. Nevertheless, He moved toward the mountain and discovers it was the voice and the presence of the Lord with a mission for Him. God blessed Moses that day and for days to come. He empowered Moses so that he could tell Pharaoh to let His people go. You see God had a plan for His people. They were to be set free from bondage and prosperous all their days.

    Jesus had the vision and made it plan. His vision was to lay down His life for the world. His vision was to take away the sin of the world. Jesus made it plain that He was the savior of the world. His vision was to cover everyone in His precious blood. For God so love the world that He gave His only begotten Son for whosoever believeth in Him shall not perish but have everlasting life. This vision that God has for us is for an appointed time. Jesus' death, burial, and resurrection were for an appointed time. All praise to His holy and righteous name.

    You may have to give up something to make your vision happen.

You may have to work hard at some things so be strong in the Lord and in the power of His might. Remember, if the Lord is in it, then it will be successful. Your visions come from God. He is the maker of your inner being and your entire mind. Seek Him for clearer visions. Make your request known to God. You have some visions and dreams inside that must be awakened and manifested to give Him glory.

    I watched the picture X-Men origin and the original. It was a movie with extraordinary powers. They were known to be mutants who had a bodily defect. However, they had powers beyond their comprehension for a while. Then when developed, they realize the force and the vision within. One thing was for sure, they needed a leader with vision of their capabilities.

PRAYER

Father, thank you for the vision you placed in my heart and mind. I desire to serve you and give you glory. You made my life better. Thank you for making me over into a child of God and a Priest to serve you. Lead me in vision and to witness on this earth that I might be pleasing to you. All glory to your righteous name.

MATTHEW 10, 12

LOVE CONQUERS A DIVIDED HOUSE

Matthew 12:25 But Jesus knew their thoughts, and said to them: Every kingdom Divided against itself is brought to desolation, and every city or house divided against itself will not stand.

Love can conquer all things because of the power of God is love. Love conquers a divided house in any condition. The love that I speak of comes directly from the Holy Spirit. In Matthew 12, it says, "Every kingdom divided against itself will not stand." You must keep your house in order if you want it to survive. Kingdoms must be ruled properly if they are to remain undivided.

Families depend on love to conquer all the obstacles in the house. The man of the house and his companion must walk in agreement to keep the house together because once divided, it will fall completely. Your focus is on a God house. Joshua said it, "for me and my house we will serve the Lord." You are the priest of the house. You are the head of the house. No one else has your authority. No one can take your specific place unless God intervenes. Your prayers keep your house together. Your love keeps the house together. Your worship to the only wise God keeps your house together. Put God an altar in your house so that you can kneel before Him day and night. It is your responsibility to seek the Lord to remove the immediate attacks of the enemy that desperately wants you to fall to the bottom of the pit. But you keep clinging on to God who is Master over all. Jesus keeps your house together. You do not need to destroy your own house nor allow anyone else to do it. You set the course in your house under God's mighty hand. You keep the worship flowing in your house. Ask God to bless and sanctify your home each day and give Him thanksgiving from the heart.

One of the most famous homes on the market today is a split home. Its design is attractive. It has everything you may desire. The design is unique and it is an eye catcher. The problem is not the purchase of the home. However, it is those who live in the home with an unwelcome spirit. We have to pray unwelcome spirits out of the home in Jesus name and believe. You want to manifest the Lord in the house. It is how everyone demonstrates peace and respect and love and compassion in their own house. You never have to show your home life to someone who lives outside your house, you just have to show it to those who live in your house. If your life reflects holy living, people will know you and approach you for answers or even help. They will also know it by your fruit. Remember whose you are, and who you are. You are a child of the Most High God and you will reign with Him in His Kingdom forever. So stop allowing defeat in your house today. Pray now!

What causes a split house or divided house is the failure to love Christ Jesus. It is the failure to communicate, the fear of sound counsel, the lack of trust, and not having the mind of Christ which allows the enemy to come in and shake up your house. In many cases, the enemy comes in and destroys the house. If you allow Jesus to come in, you will have everlasting peace and joy in the home. You have to walk in all of the authority of God when you have the Lord on your side, nothing can stop you. Stop playing with the devil. He already seeks to kill, steal and destroy. In the enemy's eyes, you and I are good prey to him. So when you let your guard down, he loves to come in and wreck your life and home in which Jesus put together for you. The enemy wants the Lord to look bad before you and I. That is not going to happen. We know that God is all powerful and controls the enemy.

A happy home filled with love is what you desire. Don't settle for less. You can make love shine in your home regardless of the obstacles before you. Every time the enemy puts trip wire in front of you in your house and each room, you will have the ability to walk through and diffuse the situation with the peace of God that surpasses all understanding in your heart and mind. You have an earthen vessel that is filled with power. Also your house is filled with blessings beyond the imagination of all creation including angels and even the enemy. Put your whole armor on and fight back by speaking the word. Tell everyone in your house that you love them. Tell them that Jesus is Lord over this family, over this house.

In Isaiah, we are told that Jesus is our counselor. In Psalm 32 He said to trust Him. In Romans 12, "Be ye transformed by the renewing of your mind." In John 14, He said, "In my house are many Mansions, I go to prepare a place for you." It is a blessed thing that the enemy can not disturb our house in heaven with Jesus. He has blessed us mightily. Keep your house on earth intact, ready for the great day of our Lord. Today, allow the Holy Spirit to run your house. Division is for the enemy. Order and God's love is for your house. Shake the enemy off in every area of life. Father, you are the peace keeper. You are the reason for living. You are the shelter in storm. You are the one who blesses my house. You are the Priest of my house.

After Solomon, the united monarchy falls apart. Jerusalem is the capital of Judah, the southern kingdom, which is led by Rehoboam. Its inhabitants are the tribes of Judah, Benjamin, and Simeon (and some Levi). Simeon and Judah later merge. Jeroboam leads a revolt of the northern tribes to form the Kingdom of Israel. The 9 tribes that make up Israel are Zebulun, Issachar, Asher, Naphtali, Dan, Manasseh, Ephraim, Reuben and Gad (and some Levi). The capital of Israel is Samaria.

After the death of Solomon (some time between the years 930 and 925 BC), his sons were unable to reach an agreement which would keep the kingdom united. His one son, Rehoboam informed people in the north that he would be even harsher with them than his father had, causing them to seek support from a rebel named Jeroboam.

Jeroboam was supported by Egypt and leaders, who probably thought it would be useful to encourage political and religious divisions among the people on his northern border. Because of this, the ten tribes in the north broke away from the rule of Rehoboam, who was left to rule just the two tribes of Judah and Benjamin. The southern kingdom's name would be taken from the name of the former tribe, Judah, while the northern would be known as Israel.

Jeroboam even erected two golden bulls in shrines where idol worship was encouraged, thus firmly establishing his break from Hebrew traditions and rule. After he died 20 years later, his son took over but was in turn removed in a military coup. Eventually Omri, an officer in the army, took control and established a new period of political stability in Israel. He moved his capital to the new city of Samaria and conquered the neighboring Moabites. Indeed, Assyrian records refer not to Israel but instead to the "House of Omri."

PRAYERS

Father, thank you for teaching us to remain in Jesus Christ and not divided. Help us to walk in love, one body, unified in faith in Jesus Christ.

1 CORINTHIANS 13

THE LORD SEES ALL THINGS

Psalm 34:14-20

Depart from evil and do good;
   Seek peace and pursue it.

The eyes of the LORD *are* on the righteous,
   And His ears *are open* to their cry.
The face of the LORD *is* against those who do evil,
   To cut off the remembrance of them from the earth.

The righteous cry out, and the LORD hears,
   And delivers them out of all their troubles.
The LORD *is* near to those who have a broken heart,
   And saves such as have a contrite spirit.

Many *are* the afflictions of the righteous,
   But the LORD delivers him out of them all.
He guards all his bones;
   Not one of them is broken.

   The sight of one bird can amaze us especially when it is going after something it desires as prey. The fact that the eagle can see so far from a distance in the sky to a little mouse or some prey is just remarkable. It seems like he can see from miles and when he comes in he moves with a unique attack mode while zeroing in on it. Why a bird? God chose them to be unique. We did not have any say so about it. He knew exactly what He was doing and designed His way.
He has a specific tasks for them. They helped to revolve this ecosystem just like so many other creatures have a purpose in this cycle of life.
   The scripture says in Isaiah 40:31, "they that wait upon the Lord shall renew their strength; they shall mount up with wings as eagles, they shall run and not be weary, they shall walk, and not faint.

Eagles demonstrate patience and precision. They also show a zeal to get what they desire; food for the eaglets. This captured my mind because God is always watching us. The Lord our God sees everything straight from heaven. Nothing is able to hide from His presence. He sees all things.

God sees from heaven when tragedy strikes and just family situations and concern occur. He is always on His throne. He never has to leave it. God is present and even faster than the light. God sends angels when He wants to for specific missions. He sends angels faster than we can think. God gave them a better wing span and power in it. Heput more power in His angel than all the eagles and birds combined. The reminds His saints that His eyes are all on the righteous. **Psalm 34:15 The eyes of the LORD *are* on the righteous, And His ears *are open* to their cry.** For the righteous, we will be able to see Him like never before.

PRAYERS

Lord, I thank you that your eyes are on the righteous and that you guard my bones. You watch over me and protect me from my enemies. In Jesus name, Amen.

PSALM 34

IN THE TWINKLING OF AN EYE

I COR 15:52 in a moment, in the twinkling of an eye, at the last trumpet. For the trumpet will sound, and the dead will be raised incorruptible, and we shall be changed.

Imagine yourself in a time machine with a lever to pull to any destination at a blink of an eye. This passage refers to 1 Thessalonians 4:16 which signals the end of the present age. It will happen as fast as you can blink your eyes. There are two groups mention in this passage. The Apostle Paul tells us that those who are dead will be with Jesus Christ. When he mentions we, he is referring to those who are still alive and will go through the rapture. one blink or twinkle of the eye and your life and the world will be changed. Make a decision today to accept Jesus as Lord in your life.

Have you ever had something in your life that affected you so fast that you did not know it was coming. Lightning is one of those occurrences that happens in the blink of an eye. On the other hand there are things that you do not expect to happen especially in the spirit realm. We don't worry about it because some things cannot be explained by humans. In the case of Jesus, we just trust that He will return and pull the believer up in the air with Him. We should trust that God will do what He says just like we trust our hearts to beat daily. We do not often asked questions about our hearts beating daily, nor do we doubt that it will keep beating today. We just know that it will beat and we will keep living with no questions asked. This is important because there are people who do not understand that their heart is beating because God allows it to beat. If He took a way one beat we would be fatalities.

I thought about that one beat of the heart so important to us for life. Then I thought about that "In the twinkling of an eye" moment when Jesus returns for those that accept Him.
In that one twinkling, Jesus will not miss the pick-up and transformation of one person that loves Him. This one moment is necessary for you to be pulled up into the air, just as your heart need not skip or miss a beat. It is fast and noticeable yet you need it to happen to live. We need the last trumpet to sound so that the dead in Christ will rise incorruptible and be changed as the Lord has planned. We are the people of the Lord and He will not go back on His word.

Listen to what the Lord is saying. A change is coming and everyone needs to get ready for the blessed return of the Lord. Don't miss this ride of a lifetime. It is the final ride for all that call on the name of Jesus. Call on Him today to help every area of your life. Jesus is Lord.

PRAYERS

Father, I believe in your promises in your word. Help me to be ready when the trumpet sounds. On that day, we who are your saints will hear a glorious sound and await the change of our bodies to live with you forever.

1 CORINTHIANS 15

HIS MANIFESTED GLORY

EXODUS 33:18-20 And he said, please show me your glory. Then He said I will make all My goodness pass before you, and I will proclaim the name of the Lord before you. I will be gracious to whom I will be gracious, I will have compassion on whom I will have compassion. But He said, you cannot see my face; For no man shall see Me, and live. Read vs. 22-23.

This is one of the manifested glory moments that fills the heart with joy, praise, and exaltation, unspeakable and unlimited joy in the Lord. I strained to hold back tears to the best of my ability because of what this scripture spoke to me. Then the tears rushed out uncontrollably with joy. Moses was the only man to see this manifested glory of God as the Lord reveals in this passage. We are talking about the same God who spoke the universe into existence. Imagine the God of all creation took out time to come on earth and walked in His own glory to reveal Himself to Moses, the man of God. He did not have to do it. He did it because of His love and because of His plan and purpose of Israel, Jewish People and Gentiles. Then there has to be another reason. He built His man Moses up to show Him that He is Moses' God. You have not worked in vain for me. God made a statement that no other God could do. There is nothing to compare the glory of God with. He expressed His love and compassion.

Listen to what God says, "I will make my goodness pass before you." Has anyone ever told you that they had a good side that they could use to pass by you? Has anyone ever said they had a goodness that would bless me and be gracious to you? No, absolutely not! The only one who ever pass before you and show His glory is God.

I believe that God is showing us that He passes before us on so many occasions and we miss His presence. He passes before us in the midnight hour when no one else is there to see Him but you and Him and His holy angels. He passes before us when we are in hurting situations and it seems like there is no one to cry on. He wipes the tears away. He passes before us when trouble comes our way and it seems like the enemy may have the victory. But God passes by and steps right in the situation and turns it around. He is good. His mercy endureth forever. I believe when God shows His presence to you there must be something on His mind. He desires to bless you, mold you, strengthen you for a journey that seems to be endless. He puts some of his on glory on you and makes everything alright. He will never pass by and not bless you. God is always up to something. Moses knew it that is why Moses said, show me your glory.

I believe there are people who don't mind saying show me your glory in the midnight hour when I need you to touch me. Show me your glory when life seems too hard to deal with. God, I need you to talk to me. Speak you word through your manifested glory.

PRAYER

Father, I thank you for making your goodness pass before me. Every day manifest your goodness before you people. Thank for removing those spiritual scales so I can see your goodness in my life.

1 CORINTHIANS 15

ABIDE IN JESUS

JOHN 15:7 "If you abide in Me, and My words abide in you, you will ask what you desire, and it shall be done for you.

Jesus teaches us affects of being fruitful. He wants us to be connected to Him as the source of life just as a fruit is to a fruit tree. He reveals to us His promise to bless those who abide in Him. He will answer petition and fulfilled desires of the heart to those who abide in Him. if we abide in Him instead of abiding in skeptics, false doctrine, false religions, evil practices, unhealthy habits, unbelieving spirits then His awesome promises are fulfilled. He made it simple to all believers. **"If you abide in Me, and My words abide in you, you will ask what you desire, and it shall be done for you."**

He wants to give us desires of our hearts. He wants us to know Him with all of our hearts. Jesus wants us to know that if we trust Him totally with His word, He will bless us more than we can imagine. Abiding in Jesus means opening doors that were closed. Abiding in Jesus means getting breakthroughs and experiencing new things in your life like never before. When you abide in Jesus, hell can't hold you. No weapon formed against you will prosper. It will not work against God's chosen ones. His blessings reign in our lives. He reigns and lives forever in heaven. We need to understand that our God owns everything in this world and the worlds to come. Psalms 37:4 said, "Delight thyself in the Lord, and he shall give thee the desires of thine heart." He is the creator and can make anything possible that seems impossible. He is the God of the invisible who makes things come to be. So when you are looking at the impossibilities, God is up to something in your life to turn it around. God is up to something to show you. You might want to take a look right now at your surroundings and your life itself. Our Father in Heaven is capable of supplying all of our needs. According to Philippians 4:19, "And My God shall supply all your needs according to His riches and glory by Christ Jesus." We have the word that gives us the answer to all of God's solutions and blessings We have His supernatural power.

The Lord shows supernatural results. He can give you the healing you want. Abide in Him, and allow His word to abide you, then ask Him. He can visit any hospital and demonstrate His power in miracles. He can raise someone from the sick bed when death approaches. He is the God of resurrection and miracles. There are witnesses to His power. You can read 1 Corinthians 15. People witnessed others people walking the street because of his resurrection power. I am telling you today that if you want the promises of God, abide in Him and let His word abide in you, then ask what you desire. He is the God of resurrection power.

God is the answer to all of our hope, dreams and desires. He can and will fulfill what is necessary in our lives according to His word and purpose. We can count on God to bless us in so many ways. He is blessing us right this very minute. If you are alive, He is blessing us. The same God in Heaven sent us the Holy Spirit to guide us for the purpose of glorifying Him in living our lives. We need a consistent prayer life to keep our lines of communication open to God and to maintain our obedience and humility toward Him. That is exactly why He gave us the Holy Spirit. In Romans 8:26-28, God sent the Holy Spirit to make intersession for us especially in our weakness. He knows exactly what you and I am in need of.

Believers know that God has the power to control everything from His throne in Heaven. I like the attitude that Peter and John had in Acts 3, when they saw the lame man at the gate of Beautiful. There was at a specific moment three attitudes with a specific person on their mind. It happened when Peter said in Acts 3:6 "Silver and gold I do not have, But what I do have I give you, In the name of Jesus Christ of Nazareth, rise up and walk." That instance, according to scripture that lame man got up and leap and walked and rejoice. This man had been there for a while expecting something to happen soon or later and it did. God blessed Him. Today you can get up and walk out of your lame condition.

PRAYERS

Lord, I pray to hide your word in my heart to avoid any sinful acts. Help me keep the faith that connects me to you daily.

JOHN 15

DON'T LET RICHES BLIND YOU

LUKE 12:15 And He said to them, Take heed and beware of covetousness, for one's life does not consist in the abundance of the things he possesses.

Covetousness means excessively and culpably desirous of the possessions of another. People literally want to have what someone else has. When I drove by the yacht lot in Florida, I thought of the expenses that go along with that yacht. We saw every possible type of classic yachts at the river front auction show last week. They had yachts every size and color, every model on had expenses. As I looked at the yachts as a spectator, I begin to realize that you almost had to be a filthy rich person for these type of yachts. I think yachts are wonderful and private vessels for enjoyment and entertainment.

For a moment I was in fantasy world thinking what if I had a yacht? The answer is I would learn to cruise the waters and have fun. I would probably have a party on the yacht, Of course it would be a different kind of party. I guess I was in fantasy world because I always wanted to take my wife on a cruise in a private yacht in a sense. The problem with that was that you have to make the commitments on providing funding early. In Luke 12, this man was holding on to money and using it as a crutch. Because of this man's actions, his life was in danger of destruction. When Jesus found out, this man was categorized as a fool. This is not the kind of thought that our Lord wants to have of anyone.

You might be asking the question today, what does Jesus want from me? Jesus requires your soul. He wants all of our being. Jesus does not want half of us. He wants total surrender. He wants us so that He can do a good work in us and through us for His purpose. He is capable of making us over again as many people expect. We already know deep in our hearts that we need a makeover. We need God in every area of our lives. There are too many things that can blind a person and certainly riches are at the top of the list. Today, what is needed is confession to God. We need to confess to God that we have been blinded and we need to be fixed. We need the Lord to know that our possessions are not more important than He is in our lives.

PRAYERS

Lord, thank you for an eye opening experience on managing my finances, protecting me against it manifesting as my master. Keep my mind so that I do not commit covetousness. Guide me in obedience in my giving to you as well.

LUKE 12, MALACHI 3

BE AN EYE WITNESS

1 CORINTHIANS 15:3-6 For I delivered to you first of all that which I also received: That Christ died for our sins according to the scripture, and that He was buried and that He rose again on the third day according to the scripture, and that He was seen by Cephas, then by the twelve. After that He was seen by five hundred brethren at once, of whom the greater part remain to the present, but some have fallen asleep.

Are you an eye witness to the blessings that Jesus poured out in your life? Be an eye witness So you can tell the world of the glorious life God gave you. Testify of how He saved you in combat operations in Iraq or Afghanistan. I am not sure what kind of warfare you encountered but you made it through. Someone asked a question at work one day about whether or not Jesus returned to see Pilate after He rose from the dead. He rose from the dead and Pilate and nobody had to validate it for Him, it happened. Pilate was not on Jesus' radar to visit Him. If you recall in John 1:1-8, He had to come to His own and they received Him not and that was in the beginning. Jesus already knew that people were going to reject Him. Pilate rejected the fact that He was the Messiah, which means the anointed one and Christ in the flesh. If you recall, Pilate did not want to dirty his hands but he still turned the Lord over to the mob.

I thank God that He allowed this vessel to use this scripture today with a brother who wants to get back into a relationship with the Lord. The Lord will always have witness. He will never run out no matter what happens. Somebody is going to have to tell of His resurrection. Somebody will have to tell of His saving grace. You can never get away with the most elementary facts of Jesus.

Christ died for our sins. Secondly, He was buried and He was raised from the dead on the third day. It is amazing in God's plan that He could strategically place people to see Him and turn over some of the blessings. Five hundred people had seen Jesus after His resurrection. Then there were 12 disciples that saw Him.

PRAYERS

Father, thank you for revealing evidence that Jesus was seen on earth as He was in your manifested glory. Help to remove thought

to those that are in the world and of the world. Use your servants to witness your glorious name and acts of deliverance.

1 CORINTHIANS **11**

CHRIST DWELLS IN YOUR HEART

Ephesians 3:17-19 that Christ may dwell in your hearts through faith; that you, being rooted and grounded in all love, may be able to comprehend with all the saints what is the width, the length and depth and height to know the love of Christ which passes knowledge; that you may be filled with all fullness of God.

Do you want Jesus Christ to dwell in your heart? Most people want Him inside their heart right now. Many do not understand the necessity of having Him live in their heart. All people need Him inside their heart. The bible reminds us that the heart is extremely wicked. Therefore, it is not an option to ask Jesus to come into the heart; it is an extreme emergency that He comes into the heart. What do you think the Apostle Paul was saying to the church? Surely he was encouraging them to know that the fullness of blessings is in the Lord, Jesus Christ. He was praying for the believers in the church at Ephesus that they would be strengthened in the inner man. He was encouraging them to hold on to Jesus who is the one who keeps us grounded and rooted in faith and the word of God. He helps us in our faith. The only way to make it is to have your steps ordered by the Holy Spirit.

There will be some hard and evil things that will approach your life in the natural and the spirit. But our Savior knows how to rescue us and comfort us all at the same time. He has that kind of power. We as Saints must walk with the fullness of God in our hearts. I am finding out every day that there are challenges that await us before we even wake up good and go about our business at work. We need the fullness of God to dwell in our heart even to forgive a co-worker or anyone who comes up against you with evil plots and schemes and outrageous and dysfunctional attitudes and behaviors. It takes the love of God in your heart and that means the fullness of Him to overcome and forgive on a daily basis.

The Apostle Paul said that we "may be able to comprehend with all the saints what is the width, the length and depth and height –to know the love of Christ which passes knowledge;
that you may be filled with all the fullness of God." He took my mind back to high school when we had to work out mathematics with similar type of equations. God is not an equation. He is not complicated. He is the God of multiple blessings and I believe that is why we can not comprehend the width, length, and depth of His unfailing love. His love is so powerful that it fills the very core of all

of our being to keep us in His perfect will.

If you are challenged by anything in your life, If you are lonely or have complications with medical issues, if you have problems with maintaining your faith, or if life just dealt you a blow that made you believe no one is there for you, please understand that there is nothing more powerful that His Love that is already extended to you right at this very moment. God is omnipresent. He is in your presence right now. He knows all about your decision to kick the drug habit, put down the alcohol, leave the world of sleeping around and violating yourself. You are better than anyone else.

Today is your day to clean up your act and cast off every bondage that has been trying destroy you. Today, you can ask God to come into your heart and cast down any other imagination and stronghold. Repeat this statement after me. Jesus, I believe and I confess that you are the Son of God and that you died for my sin on the cross and on the third day you rose from the dead with all power in your hand by the Father in heaven. May the praise the glory and the honor go to your name O' Lord.

PRAYERS

Lord, I pray that your Holy Spirit dwell in me and through me as I go about my job today and at home. When you dwell in me, people will see the love of Jesus Christ manifested.

HEBREWS 11

CRUCIFIED WITH CHRIST

ROMANS 6:6 knowing this, that our old man was crucified with Him, that the body of sin might be done away with, that we should no longer be slaves of sin.

We must know that all our sin was taken away in the death of Jesus on the cross. The crucifixion was one of the worst forms of death. Jesus was crucified for us. He hanged on a cross causing suffocation. He was nailed to the cross after they had beaten Him. He had thorns put in His head. He had a spear to pierce His side. Blood came out of His body. He died because He bared the sins of the world resulting in the defeat of sin. His crucifixion stood for eternal love. His blood washed our sin away.

We are asked to crucify our flesh that we can walk in the Spirit. We are not strong enough to walk alone. We will need the Holy Spirit to strengthen and guide us in our Christian walk. John 15,16 Our lives are not ours. We believe in Jesus and belong to Him. We were created for God's purpose. He wants us to crucify this flesh so that we will not put ourselves, the flesh before Him. The tendency in life is to worship ourselves or idols without realizing it. The reason why we need to cast off some things in our lives is because Jesus already destroyed sin. It is the enemy and our flesh that raises sin. Listen to what the Apostles said, we should no longer be slaves of sin. We do not need to get in comfort zones where we welcome sin and become slaves to it all over again. Break old habits.

To be crucified with Jesus means to put off the old you and cloth yourself in righteousness. You have to be reminded that you are a new creature in Christ; the old one has passed away. Old things like an old negative relationship has to be broken, old alcoholic issues have to be broken, drug addiction, cocaine and ecstasies habits, dirty needles and marijuana, adultery and fortification and a host of other drugs issues and habits. If you need to go on a diet, you can do it, ask the Lord to help you crucify the flesh. Know that Jesus will pull you through. The Apostle Paul said in **Philippians 3:10 "that I may know Him and the power of His resurrection, and the fellowship of His sufferings, being conformed to His death,"** Get your sights set on Him and know Him. Learn of Him. He is the only true and wise God. He is the redeemer of my soul and yours.

You can start anytime walking in as a Child of God. It is a good thing to acknowledge who you are in Jesus Christ. You will allow your

light to shine and your flesh to be crucified. Start walking in the ministry as a new creature and new man of God. Jesus will not let you go! There are blessings when you walk in Jesus name. That is what God wants you to do. Walk in boldness and power. Let everyone know that you are a child of the King of Kings and Lord of Lords!
Philippians 4

PRAYERS

Father, Guide me in crucifying the old man who loved sin so much. Baptize me according to your word. Fill me with Holy Spirit. In Jesus name, amen

JOHN 19

NEWNESS OF LIFE

ROMANS 6:4 Therefore we were buried with Him through baptism into death, that just as Christ was raised from the dead by the glory of the Father, even so we should also walk in the newness of life.

You can have a new life in Christ Jesus any time you want it. It is available twenty four seven. The good thing about it is that you do not have to beg for it, just surrender. You do not have to purchase it because He already paid the price. God already knows your heart's desire. He already knows whether you trust Him or not. If you trust Him, He will bless you. You need to confess that you receive Him then allow Jesus to come into your heart right now.

In baptism, when we see a person immersed into the water who has committed their lives to the Lord, we see a picture of that person being resurrected from the dead. In other words, the old person is left in the water and the new person rise to walk with Christ. He was born again in the water, but he acknowledged the fact that he believes in the death, burial, and resurrection of the Lord, Jesus Christ.

Grave sites have always sent an uneasy feeling to most people. Nevertheless sooner or later we have to appear at a grave site. We really should not be afraid because God requires us to leave this body sooner or later. He makes us realize who we are in Christ when it comes to death and life. I realize now that I am dead and now quicken in the Spirit of Christ. I am no longer who I use to be. I am a new creature in Christ Jesus. The grave yard not only symbolizes that time is up, it also symbolizes a new life must start, the past life is gone, and more importantly I reign in God's kingdom. I am a new creature in Christ Jesus. The old man has passed away and the new man is here to stay eternally. It is interesting that the Father raised Him up. Sometimes people do not want to hear that however, they need to hear it. They need to witness what God has for people.

PRAYERS

Father, Thank you for allowing me to be baptized according to Matthew 28. You accepted me Lord. I repented of all my sins and turn my life over to you.

HEBREWS 6

THE BEST FATHER IS GOD

LUKE 15:15-23 Then he went and joined himself to a citizen of that country, and he sent him into his fields to feed swine. And he would gladly have filled his stomach with the pods that the swine ate, and no one gave him anything. "But when he came to himself, he said, 'How many of my father's hired servants have bread enough and to spare, and I perish with hunger! I will arise and go to my father, and will say to him, "Father, I have sinned against heaven and before you, and I am no longer worthy to be called your son. Make me like one of your hired servants."' "And he arose and came to his father. But when he was still a great way off, his father saw him and had compassion, and ran and fell on his neck and kissed him. And the son said to him, 'Father, I have sinned against heaven and in your sight, and am no longer worthy to be called your son.' "But the father said to his servants, 'Bring out the best robe and put it on him, and put a ring on his hand and sandals on his feet. And bring the fatted calf here and kill it, and let us eat and be merry

Always call on the Father in Heaven during a time of uncertainty and family difficulty. Always call on the Father in Heaven when crisis arise in your life. Never hesitate to think that some other God is going to rescue you. Only one God will rescue you from any situation and His name is Jesus Christ. Did you hear that? One God is your rescuer. He is also the best father anyone could have. Make sure you turn to God for everything, including advice and wisdom and counsel.

I was thinking of the prodigal son's father who blessed his son upon returning home. The father in this story needed the help of God to be patient and loving in order to bless his son. The father did not look back at the past mistakes that his son made. He just welcomed him home with open arms. I find that Jesus wants all men to have the spirit of loving their sons and opening their arms wide open to welcome them home. No longer do men have to put up with the attacks and manipulation of the enemy trying to force Father against son and son against Father and same applies with mothers and daughters. Ask God, the Father to let His love overpower all the tricks and deception of the enemy. The enemy always gets involved when there is love involved. He raises up when there is inheritance involved, you might as well expect to fight the good fight when birthing something is involved. Whenever seed is at the front of the issue at hand, you can expect persecution and attacks. Thanks be to God who strengthens us in these weak moments of attacks. God will always deliver His people.

The Father has an inheritance for all of His children. When all issues are settled in inheritance, a new attitude is birthed. When they come to the light of understanding, there are things that are needed to know for survival. They need to know the Father's grace, love, and forgiveness.

Most sons are loaded with ambition, have strong training, and have the desire to achieve, but when they cry for help, it is a different sound. God makes it known to you of the blessing that waits. Man must be aware of when he needs to step in to nurture the son regardless of him being a blood son or step son. Men must be ready to step in and step up to the plate. I discovered that my son listens, hears sometimes, but not everything is received. In other words, nothing effective is happening. So then I must train continually, however, I turn it over to the Father in Heaven.

My Father was my hero in my life. He took care of seven children. Before, we were born, he took care of his brothers and sister. It was our Father in heaven giving him that kind of heart. It was the Holy Spirit who was leading and guiding him. I have never been so honored and proud to be his son. He took care of more than He was obligated to. He was just a young adult at the time, nevertheless, his heart led him to bless others. God fixed it where Fathers have to know when to love and when to keep things in high intensity. There are many men and young men much like the prodigal son who needed to learn the lesson that you cannot get over the Father in your house. Our Father in heaven is even strict and precise on exactly what He requires of His men. He simply wants service and to remain in His will.

Every young man and daughter needs to rely on the wisdom of their Father. If they ignore the wisdom, there all types of confusion and misleading in life that could result. In other words, God speaks to your Father and He speaks to you as well. Everyone in the house must understand who is the authority in the home.

One of the most powerful things that can happen in the house is when a Father forgives and grants a kiss. Old testament characters displayed that kind of attitude. He may not have to kiss as the prodigal son's Father, but if he forgives sincerely, God has smiled on him.

Today take hold of the word of God. Take hold of the God who has redeemed us from the devil's grip. Love your entire family regardless of past experiences and hurts and pains. Love them like never before. Jesus spoke of His Father in prayer. Let us pray like Jesus did. Let us admire our Fathers on earth as Jesus desires us to do. Jesus said, "Our father in heaven, Hallowed be your name, your Kingdom come, your will be done on Earth as it is in Heaven. Give us this day our daily bread. And forgive our debts, As we forgive our debtors. And do not lead us into temptation, But deliver us from the evil one. For yours is the kingdom and the power and the glory forever. Amen." Prayer brings home prodigal sons and daughters. May Jesus' name be exalted forever.

PRAYERS

Father, I thank you that you saw me at a distance, separated from you. Yet you still accepted me into your arms. Thank you for your tender touch. Today I stand firm in your kingdom because you first loved me when I did not love myself enough. Thank you for coming to my rescue due to by choices in life.

HEBREWS 6

HELP ME ROUGH HIM UP

HEBREWS 13:5-6 Let your conduct be without covetousness; be content with such things as you have. For He Himself has said, "I will never leave you nor forsake you." So we may boldly say: "The LORD is my helper; I will not fear. What can man do to me?[1]

There is always something going on in this world that needs some attention whether its tough
love or just plain old love. Nevertheless, keep a positive attitude regardless of those difficult trials you are faced with. One of the phrases my friend Willie use to use all the time, is "Scuff Him Up" when referring to Soldiers that needed discipline. We really had some laughs out of that one because it was much needed for a soldier who had no discipline. In those days, you tell a Private First Class to pack his wallet one way, and he packs an entirely different way. You tell the private to put the pillow case on this way, when you return the pillow case is on backwards or on the floor. Those were the times when soldiers needed to drop and knock out about 100 push-ups to work and condition their mind. When things got too out of order of discipline, Drills would have to get the Senior Drill Sergeant. The entire motto stamped in his mind was to rough them up within the standard.

Another problem is gang violence is on a rise in so many areas in our communities. It seems that it never ceases. Innocent people are always victims of unnecessary violence. You can visit almost any country and find out that someone has a need of help against predators. Sin is like a predator that keeps on seeking who it can take hold of and destroy. You need the word for your protection. This is what you need to do, speak the word and so you can rough that enemy up. Instead of you being on the end of receiving the blow, you shake the enemy up with the word. You do not have to be victimized any more. Tell the enemy that God's word has you covered and you are content in His word. The word of God is powerful and cuts through every attack.

You have the victory so start walking in it. That will affect him. Stop the enemy under your feet. Saints, it is time to get together and rough him up. Start praying saints. Make time to pray today, right now in Jesus name. Pray until you have a breakthrough. Pray until you hear from God. When you pray, please understand that the enemy is receiving a blow to the head each and every time. It is time for you to believe that the power of the Lord is at work in your life. When we pray, we pray expecting something to happen and honoring God at the same time. You do not have to worry about being afraid again. The Lord said that He will never leave you nor forsake you. I am content with the blessings of the Lord. Even though I am content with blessings flowing in my life, I still have a mission to witness and serve Him.

There is no need of counting me out of the picture. That is the attitude all of us need to gain. You see in my witness and my service, God is always there. He said I will never leave you nor forsake you. That is exactly how I know it's time to rough the devil up. It makes no sense if the enemy keeps attacking you and you do nothing but entertain Him over and over again. Some people walk around moping and crying about what the enemy did to them. All they have to do is to use the faith and power that God equipped them with.

It is time to live like you are ready to rough the enemy up. If you were in the combat zone, you would put full force and full ammunition to the targeted enemy. Use your prayers.
Give God all the glory.

PRAYERS

Father, I depend on your presence in my life. You remind me over and over that you will never abandon me. Praise to your Holy name.

PSALMS 27

BEFORE THE WOMB

JEREMIAH 1:5 "Before I formed you in the womb I knew you; Before you were born I sanctified you; I ordained you a prophet to the nations."

The Lord, God knew everything before you and I were born. He knew things before our parents even thought of being fruitful and multiplying. He said, I knew you before you were in your mother's womb. How can you know someone before the seed had even been developed? God is the one who decides what the seed will be because He made the seed in man. We existed in God's eyes even before our time could be manifested on earth. Shout because no one else can express such power and make creative miracles come into existence. The greek word for formed is plasso meaning shape or mold by an artist.

God wanted Jeremiah to be encouraged about the mission he would be faced with. He was appointed by God as His prophet to the nations. He wanted Jeremiah to know that all power is in His hand and that He would be with Him in delivering messages from God. So to express His power He wanted Jeremiah to know that He knew Jeremiah before He was conceived.

The Lord has already thought about us before we could even know ourselves, before we even came into the world. He knew everything about each person individually and accurately before we could know anything about ourselves. That is enough to shout about. God knew our hearts and minds and soul and strength before we knew anything about it. What a reason to praise Him and serve Him for the rest of your life.

Everyone that God calls has a specific purpose for Him. No one should live life without knowing their purpose. If you do not know, ask God. Seek Him with all of your heart and soul and He will answer. The word of God is also the answer. God will bless you through His word. Seek ye first the kingdom of God and His righteousness. When you seek Him everything else that He desires for you will follow and bless you.

There are several things that God wants you to do and more. You may not finish everything but set goals in Christ Jesus. Jesus can help you make it through all of your goals. He made you and me before time. He already had us in mind before the world was formed.

Not only did He already know us, He sanctified you. He ordains the person He wanted to ordain for His purpose. It means that God has a mission for His people. He set apart specific people for pinpointed assignments. Do you know your assignment? Do you know where God wants you? Remember, before He formed you and me, He already knew about us. He knew everything about us. He knew our comprehension levels, he knew our intellect, and He knew who I would marry and who you would marry. He knew the trust level inside our heart. He knew if we would accept Him as Lord and Saviour. He knew that He would wash us in His blood for the remission of sin. He knew who would birth out a baby boy and a baby girl or even twins, triplets and even quadruplets. God knew the morning and the days of the year and times of thunder and lighting and the floods of life. He knew how much trouble you would be faced with.

PRAYERS
Father, your power leaves me speechless and in awe at times. You are so Holy, great and magnificent that words are not enough. Thank you for having all time and creation in your hands. No wonder my parents praised your name. You are magnified beyond heaven and earth by all creation.

JEREMIAH 1

GRACE BREACHED ALL ENEMY LINES

The Apostle Paul breached the lines of the enemy with the aid of the Holy Spirit as he went on multiple missionary journeys. John 16 The Apostle Paul had the audacity and the boldness to position himself where God wanted him to witness. He was led by the Holy Spirit to be a missionary in the field, touching millions of lives today. He was led by the Holy Spirit to breach all lines of the enemy's traps and devices His goal was to press for Jesus Christ by being obedient in service

It was Jesus who blessed the Apostle Paul to become the Saint he turned out to be. I believe God placed His Holy word and Spirit inside the vessel of Apostle Paul and used Him mightily.

It was the Apostle who reminds us of the word called Grace. He reminds in the word of God that all enemy lines have been breached. We are no longer in bondage by the evil one. We do not serve him. Our Savior is Jesus Christ, the son of the living God. The Apostle Paul wrote in Ephesians 2:8 "For by grace you have been saved through faith, and that not of yourselves; it is the gift of God, not of works lest any man should boast." So we have God, the Father with His loving kindness who gave us the gift of salvation through His son and the power of protection that the enemy is not authorized to breach. Grace can never be altered. Grace is untouchable, nothing can shatter it. Grace can never be breached. Noone can manipulate Grace. Grace can never be taken away or lost. Grace does not change. Grace is never won or earned. Grace will never be affected in any way. God owns it and allows us to preach His word so it will not return void. We preach grace because it is the unmerited favor of God. Grace breaches every obstacle of the enemy and every obstacle of man's bondage and fleshly desires. Galation 5. God is good and worthy of all praise. That is exactly why you and I can rest in His grace. No need to worry about anything. We have grace on our side and Jesus to back it up. The bible declares that "Jesus came with truth and grace."John 3,4 Grace covers us no matter what the circumstances. His compassion is unlimited in grace. Grace breached everything the enemy ever had.

In the military, it takes professionalism, training and discipline to pinpoint minefields, booby traps, enemy IEDs, and those around the corner aiming RPGs and missiles to take on casualties. We have grace to keep us in His perfect will. When in battle know that when you accepted Jesus as Lord of your life, you became a new creature in Jesus Christ.

We are so blessed because God showers us in grace. You see

because we stay soaked in grace by the spiritual rain of blessings from God, we can breach anything in life. If there is a challenge in marriage breach the troubles because you have grace and you have a high Priest who has already blessed you.

Grace gives you the will to survive in any and every situation. Grace carries you to the edge and back. It takes you through all enemy attacks. Grace enables me to grow. It took Jesus to breach all lines of the enemy. Adam could not do it because he had sinned with his wife. All of the old prophets and Jesus disciples could not do it. It took the blood of Jesus Christ to breach the most fortified and built up area of hell and sin.

The need to minister involves grace. The Lord will prepare all of those like Apostle Paul to run the mission outside. There is always a need for God's ministry. God put order of His ministry in place. When one falls and when one leaves for the purpose of Christ into His marvelous presence, then He alone has the authority to raise up another. You are the other. Do not allow circumstance and other people to get in your way. Seek God and ask Him for directions and purpose for your life. God is always looking for new journey men like you. He is looking for journey women also. He has a way of sending His anointing through those who seek Him and love Him with an open heart of thanksgiving.

PRAYERS

Father, thank you for grace that keeps me alive today. Your grace is the kind act that we all should reflect because of you.

EPHESIANS 2, 3

GLORIFY HIM ABOVE THE HEAVENS

PSALM 8:1 O LORD, Our LORD, how excellent is Your name in all the earth, who have set Your Glory above the heavens!

In today's society, almost everything worldly is portrayed as excellent. And when people classify something as excellent, there is a sense of glorifying it. It might be a new car, song, house, or anything of possession. We need to clearly understand that God's authority and glory is revealed throughout the world. Football and basketball players that love God get glorified by their fans in stadium and probably on their personal computers.

God's name alone has all power to shake and shape kingdoms, and loose those that are bound by the grip of the enemy. His name alone declares His glory and strength. His name is the highest name there is throughout creation. Jesus is Lord anyway we look at it. He
His name is excellent because there is no one like Him and His glory is revealed throughout the ages and eternity. His name is above the heavens because He is the creator of all things including the stars, planets, moon, earth, and even death and life. He makes the impossible possible. Imagine in your mind that God designed the man and the soul and spirit of Him. All people and everything must bow before Him in full worship. He is excellent, glorious and worthy of all praise. So now when you speak of the King of Kings, Lord of Lords, worship and praise Him with all your heart, mind, soul and strength. He is forever merciful and all loving.

Our Lord is the one who is responsible for putting a soul inside of man. He is responsible for putting a spirit inside of man. The scriptures say, that "He breathe the breath of life into man and man became a living soul." In that process, we became His alone. That is why men must bow before Him in adoration. I believe the excellence of the Lord's name was etched into the minds of men even before they accepted Him. With God's name, everything has a touch of holiness. Man must glorify Him for what He has done and is performing right now in the life of the believer and even in the natural man.

PRAYERS

Father, Thank you that your glory is above all things in heaven and earth.
PSALM 9

THE LORD'S TOUCH

John 20:27-29 Then He said to Thomas, Reach your finger here, and look at My hands; And reach your hand here, and put it into my side. Do not be unbelieving, but believing, And Thomas answered and said to Him, My Lord and My God! Jesus said Thomas because you have seen Me, you have believed. Blessed are those who have not seen and yet believed.

The bible illustrates several times that Jesus touched people in different situations. What was so important about His touch? He always made it personal. Healing was a result of His touch. It was His love that restored every possible issue in His touch. His touch in our lives is the key focus. He touched the blind, He touched the lame, He touched those with Leprosy, He touched the hands of broken men, He touched the dead, He allowed Himself to be touched. He never denies His unfailing love, grace, mercy and healing power for all people. God desires to touch each one of our lives every day.

You might have a personal experience one day that bounds you to it. But God will deliver you from it because you are one of His and He knows that you trust in Him. It was hard for Thomas for a little while but he came around to understanding it and began to understand who Jesus really was at that time. When Thomas truly understood that Jesus had risen his faith grew instantly. He believed in the resurrection.

The blind man wanted to see and finally found someone who could change the course of His life. When you ask the Lord about seeing, you might as well trust Him because you will be able to see. Your old spiritual scales will fall off. Your eyes will be open for the first time. Strange things can happen for the first in the life of the believer. Your life could be different from that blind man's experience. God might have you doing a great work to glorify Him. However, he needs you to see in the spirit.

The woman with the issue of blood just wanted to touch the hem of His garment. Her faith was noticed by Jesus. Jesus asked "who touched me?" because He knew that someone had touched him in faith. So He had to speak healing to her "Your faith has made you whole." God wants us to have that kind of faith to know that He will make you whole. Even if the physicians can not heal you, the Lord will make you whole again. You just need to ask Him to touch your situation, no matter what it is, He has the power to change it.

The men with leprosy had more than they could handle. They saw Jesus and asked for healing. They knew that they were outcast and no one wanted them around. They knew that their conditions were contagious and had to be controlled or else it would spread. But when they saw Jesus, they knew that all they had to do was ask for healing. Jesus healed them and one of them praised Him and rejoiced for His mighty act. You may have felt like an outcast because of a medical issue or because life just dealt you a blow. Call on the name of the Lord. He is our strong tower. He is our healer.

What was amazing is the fact that when Jesus rose from the dead, he did not want to be touch by Mary because as He said, I am not ascended yet into heaven and yet he ate with the disciples to prove that He was in form and that He defeated death. Jesus had gone down into the depths of hell and defeated Satan.

Next, there is doubting Thomas who was instructed to touch Jesus' side to help his belief. Some people need their belief restored, healed and delivered from the doubt and confusion. They need the Thomas experience. Jesus instructed Thomas to touch His side. It was then when Thomas believed that Jesus was and is real and that He rose from the dead. What was the blessing when Thomas touched Jesus, and made the statement that would touch the world, "My Lord and my God! Jesus said, Blessed are those who have not seen and yet have believed. My Lord and my God, Your love has touched me and made me to believe. Ask God to touch you today that you may reign in His Kingdom forever and ever. God's love will deliver you.

Sometimes in our lives we think that like the woman with the issue of blood who touched Jesus' garment and was made whole that it was just our touch of faith. But the fact of the matter is that was faith in Him and more importantly it was His touch that healed her more than her reaching out because the power of healing is in His hand. The power of love is in Him. Blessed be the name of the Lord.

PRAYERS

Father, thank you that my doubting days are over. You help me in your word so that I do not have to depend on others telling me that Jesus died and rose from the grave. Your word is truth. I trust your word Lord.

MATTHEW 16

MARRIAGE DEFINED

GENESIS 3:23-24 And Adam said: This is now bone of my bones And flesh of My flesh; She shall be called Woman, Because she was taken out of Man. Therefore a man shall leave his father and mother and be joined to his wife, and they shall become one flesh.

    The Bible speaks of marriages that are made by God. A marriage made by God is a marriage absolutely made in heaven. It is suppose to be better than the fairy tales we see on television or envision. God ordained marriages. He created it to be a union between one man and one woman. God established this blessed relationship in the Garden of Eden when he brought Eve to Adam. The other marriage is between God and His Church, the saints. These are the only marriages blessed by God Himself in accordance with Gen 3: 23-24 and Mark 10:6-9. God does not want man to drift into the mindset of what he explains in Romans 1:18-32. Remember above all the marriage has to be God centered if you want it to work. Honor must be at the center to God and to each other in respective roles of the marriage. The marriage vows are sacred in the eyes of God and witnesses.

    When people fall or step out of true matrimony, they open the gates of hell into their lives. Keep your marriage sanctified. Corinthians7:14 The enemy starts to feed off of the weakness of people then they fall for anything the enemy throws at them. The enemy makes it look good and feel good, then distorts the mind and spirit to making one believe that whatever the sin is, it is good. You need to understand that the enemy is the author of lies and confusion. He wants to destroy your blessed marriage. The one the priest and both of you vowed to live by. Keep your marriage in prayer and before God at all times. He will bless it. You do not have to allow your marriage and yourself to become a tragedy and victim of the enemy. Instead walk in the victory daily under His saving grace and power of love. You deserve to be blessed by God. Your loved ones and all of your family deserves to be blessed. Anyone who believes in God knows that there are tricks all day long and that evil exist to tear you apart. Evil wants to take over you and so we will not have a loving family. Those that marry outside of God's authority are opening themselves up for evil to take over completely. Those who love the Lord are praying that all people come on one accord and be blessed by God's true marriage principles.

Marriage defines can be complicated to so many people. But in reality it is not complicated. Too many Christian marriages fail because they stop trusting in God to lead their marriage. God has to be the center of the marriage. He must be in your marriage each and every day. The very first step to having a successful marriage is the individual relationship with God. God has to be the center of each individual person's life to make it work. So then marriage is defined by your relationship with God. Do you remember the day God entered your heart. Everyone remembers that power touched your heart and you believed Jesus entered. You were changed and knew you belonged to someone higher than anyone else. You remember your wedding day. You made a commitment before the wedding day to God. You made a commitment on the wedding day with several people in attendance as witnesses to your statement before God. Your vow was until death do us apart. I promise to love her. I promise to love him. You concentrate on being submissive to each other not the world outside your house. You concentrate on God and your marriage first and foremost. You want to know why marriages fall apart. They fail and fall apart because of those who once believed in the power of love from Jesus Christ left the sacredness of their vows. You have to recall that God ordained your marriage. You have to reclaim your marriage. You can renew vows with one another. Your marriage is your marriage, it is not anyone else's.

Marriage does require God, Honor, attraction, love and affection. You demonstrate love to your spouse because you do love Jesus. He wants you to reveal your love to one another daily.

Your marriage can be a marriage made in heaven. We all need to incorporate those five areas of life in marriage. It will make us a better person and dependent on the Holy Spirit. Remember do not allow outside forces, human nor evil to interrupt your relationship with God and your marriage. You must work out every circumstance and troubles with the Lord in prayer and go to the word of God. He is your primary and key counselor for all circumstances. Trust Him and He will bless you and maintain your marriage in your appointed times in this life. May His name be praised forever.

PRAYERS

Father, help me to be rooted in you Lord. Then help me as the man to be the best husband keeping my vows. Lord, help my wife to be the best wife as we obey your word in Ephesians 5 and Mark 10.

MARK 10

IF YOU KNEW THE GIFT OF GOD

John 4:9-10 Then the woman of Samaria said to Him, "How is it that You, being a Jew, ask a drink from me, a Samaritan woman?" For Jews have no dealing with Samaritans. Jesus answered and said to her, " If you knew the gift of God, and who it is who says to you, Give me a drink , you would have asked Him, and He would have given you living water.

God gave us the ultimate Gift. He gave us His son Jesus Christ. He sacrificed His own son for all people to destroy the work of sin. God is the only true living and loving God. He is the only one who can give such gifts. After the death, burial and resurrection of Jesus, God gave us the Holy Spirit to help us. It was after the ascension of Jesus to heaven when the Holy Spirit would come to Help us with our life issues. The Holy Spirit is our gift that God gave us from Him to be there when we need a guide and comfort through life.

God planted His Spirit in us when He breathe the breath of life into Adam's body. Before Adam became a spirit filled man, he was just a man in a dirt suit, made by God. He was fashioned by God. He was made of God with a clay body. God gave Adam the best gift. He gave Him His Spirit to walk in the image of God. So then gifts are one of God's special expressions of blessings in the life of the believer. That is exactly why I stated, if you knew the gift.

One of the things that God wants for His people is to understand that there is no difference between the Jews, Gentiles, and Samaritans. God sent Jesus to wash the sin from all people on earth. In Romans 1:16, the Apostle Paul made a statement that there is neither Jew nor Gentile. He said, "For I am not ashamed of the gospel of Christ, for it is the power of God to salvation for everyone who believes, for the Jew first and also for the Greek." The Apostle Paul, under the anointing of the Holy Spirit wanted everyone to know the message of the Good News. The good news was the news of salvation which had then and now the power to change people lives from evil to good. He was not ashamed of the gospel of Jesus Christ because it has the power to deliver a sin sick soul from that condition to claiming a place in heaven upon the return of Christ. That is the gift of God.

No one was exempt from the salvation that God gave us. No one was too special that they could be turned down. No one was better than the other person in society to receive the blessing of eternal life. If that was so, then Jesus would have had to come as a sacrifice for specific people who could earn their way in the kingdom of Heaven. The Lord wants us to know that whoever you are under the sun, He can change your life. The Samaritan woman could not in the beginning grasp who Jesus was. It took Jesus to tell her about herself. He began to tell her that she had five men in her life and now the one she is with is not her husband. With conviction and surprise, she now believes that He is a prophet or somebody that has factual insight.

Much like many other people in this world who believe that someone else is better than you, she was in total amazement. Jesus told this Samaritan women that, "if you knew the gift of God and what He can do for you. It's time to stop searching for the wrong God and the wrong religion. If you get caught up on the wrong God, life will steer you wrong under the devils influence. That is exactly why Jesus is the gift to people. They recognize Him as Savior and life becomes better.

PRAYERS

Lord, thank you for allowing us to identify you when you speak to us. Lord, you are recognized as the gift from God and the giver of living water. You bless us more than we deserve and comprehend.

JOHN 6, 8

SEEK FIRST THE KINGDOM OF GOD

MATTHEW 6:33 But seek first the kingdom of God and His righteousness, and all these things shall be added to you.

One of the most important things in life is to seek God with all your heart and soul. Do not allow blessings and opportunities for the abundant life pass you by. Time moves fast and you can lose out on opportunities and particular moves of God that can bless you in abundance. Also, God has priorities for your life. His priority is that all of us seek Him first in all things. When we seek Him, we must trust Him. Matthew 6:33 tell us to put God first. He gives us the ticket to success and if I may say so, the lottery that you have always been trying to win. When you go after Jesus with everything you have, all of your might, you strike it rich automatically.

Make Him your priority in life. Seek Him with interest like you do other things. So many people seek everything else in life such as new homes, cars, companionship or spouses, fantasy vacations, retirement and so many other things in this world. But the truth of the matter is that God comes first. The Lord knows who is putting Him first in their lives. He will bless you with an overflow. He will touch your life and make you prosper. Stop listening to those that tell you opposite of God's blessing. Just in case you want to drop a word to them, ask them who are they seeking in life for self satisfaction and blessings and inheritance. The inheritance you get from God is eternal and never exhausted. People can bless you but they bless you different from God. Continue to concentrate and seek Jesus first and seek Jesus always.

Jesus is the first and the last, the Alpha and Omega. That means you have everything you need to survive in life. When you get Jesus, you have the beginning of life and the end. He is eternal so He can not end but we in the flesh and carnal state will perish. We need Him for everlasting life.

At one point in my life, basic training was the most important event for me to achieve. I had made up my mind that I was going to be a soldier and serve the Armed Forces for several years. My focus became clear in my life. I needed to get through those eight agonizing weeks of hell with those crazy Drill Sergeants. If I could make it through all of the demanding physical training and the draining mental effects, then I knew that I could now be called a United States Armed Force "Soldier" When you know that you are a real soldier, then you know that everything that you sought after was pleasing and rewarding in your life. It will benefit you in combat. I needed to be prepared period for any and everything that the enemy would throw at me. I can rest now knowing that those years and the training was not done in vain. I know that I was a Soldier ready to fight in any battle.

I liken the military career to seeking first the Lord's Kingdom and His righteousness. I need the help of the Holy Spirit in God's Army. Nothing can be sought after and achieved if you do not have the Holy Spirit working in you and for you. As a Christian today, sometimes I believe that I need to revisit God's basic training camp. I need to retrain or get a special tune up inside my heart. I need the Lord to take hold of me and make me over. When He makes me over then I will be able to see the reality of seeking Him first. How is that so? He put His spirit in me and made me over. I will be more than what we think. What is clear to me now is that whatever comes to mind as a desire, a want and even a need, I must put God first no matter what.
I thought about the fact that military forces use heat seeking missiles to destroy enemy targets. The missile has a special seeking devices to locate the enemy. What makes it so valuable is that it does not get off target and course. God want Christians to be like heat seeking missiles, always abounding in the work of the Lord.

There are various kinds of people in the world. Some enjoy the outdoor game of hunting. When you hunt, you are searching for the kill of the game. God wants that kind of attitude in His children. Hunters have a seeking mentality for the game that they chase. Some hunters score big points for big game. In this kind of game, you keep and eat it. For some they transformed it into trophies. The same happens when you play football and basketball. The best players are highlighted and given huge contracts. They seek after being the best player. God wants us to be the best players for His kingdom.

PRAYERS

Father, thank you for your goodness and tender mercies. You are first place in my life. I need your Holy Spirit to be with me as I seek you for counsel in the ministry, as husband, and a Father. ISAIAH 53:8

SHAKE OFF ALL WEIGHTS

HEBREW 12:1 Therefore, since we are surrounded by such a great cloud of witnesses, let us throw off everything that hinders and the sin that so easily entangles, and let us run with perseverance the race marked out for us.

    No one can run a race and make progress, let alone win the race if you are weighed down. You can be weighed down and have all kinds of excessive weight on you that is harmful and stressful. If you want to live the good life, lose that weight that causes sin. In order to live the good life, you need to be healthy in body and in spirit. God will fill you with His strength to help against life's challenges. God, our Father did not make us to be unhealthy. He made us to be healthy naturally and spiritually. Set a new goal in your life today to exercise and eat the proper food groups. You will be happier and feel better. You will also live longer. A proper diet is essential for your health. Take a look at the proper breads, fish, dairy products, and fruit and vegetables. Take the necessary portion each day to maintain a healthy diet. You already know you and you know how to discipline yourself. If you do not know how maintain a healthy diet, then seek God and a nutritionist to develop a plan. Then stick with that plan. When you start your diet, just think of it as going on a diet for the Lord. You can also look at in a view of fasting, though they are two separate actions. The two key things about both of them are that they result in a breakthrough and a balanced life. You will see as time goes by. You will live a better life. You can do it. Do not let yourself down! Love yourself, Jesus loves you.

    Your health means a lot to the Lord. He gave you this earthen vessel to take care of it, not worship it but to live a good life. I was thinking of the proper diet spoken of earlier. When you go on a diet, imagine how you study the word of God. Well use that method of training your body. At the same time, when you are fasting and praying, you will also get a breakthrough if you are vigorously doing it. Fasting gets your spiritual breakthrough.

    There was a hard downpour today and it seemed as if the rain just would not cease for a long period of time. You know sometimes it can immediately stop pouring down. When it does that it seems like a tease. It makes you want to say Lord, stop teasing me. Well, I had all kinds of thoughts when I saw the rain just pouring down at a seemingly nonstop flow. The only thing I knew I could still do at the moment was to rejoice in the Lord even in a down pour with a day so cloudy and dark.

Usually we think of getting soaked and wet to the max and end up changing out of wet clothing because of that feeling of soaked and being unbalanced. We are so used to being dry. It rained so hard that it seemed as though the sky had burst open and released tons upon tons of water to revive this planet. God knows how to send blessings down. God waters this planet with more than we can imagine. He pours down from heaven and blesses us. God rains on the just as well as the unjust. He has no respect of persons when He rains down. He is the God of judgment and blessings. He can pour out any kind of blessing He wants to reward us with. Nothing is impossible for Him. In Malachi, He says, in referring to tithing, He will pour out blessings that you will not have room to receive.

Believers know that God has the power to control everything from heaven and any place that He wants to control. He owns an operation center everywhere, in every country, in every nation, in every city, in every state, in every house and in every temple, every Church, and on every mission. No one can stop Him from controlling all things. That right, He controls the waters, the skies, the valleys, the rivers, the oceans, man, woman, children, spiritual things, life on earth, death, and everlasting life and anything the imagination can think of.

PRAYERS

Father, Remove all the heavy weights in my life so that I can serve you and exalt your name.

PSALM 37, PHIL 4

JESUS' HAND

John 20:19-21 Then, the same day at evening, being the first *day* of the week, when the doors were shut where the disciples were assembled, for fear of the Jews, Jesus came and stood in the midst, and said to them, "Peace *be* with you." When He had said this, He showed them *His* hands and His side. Then the disciples were glad when they saw the Lord. So Jesus said to them again, "Peace to you! As the Father has sent Me, I also send you."

You know Jesus, the Son of the Living God. He is always revealing miracles and demonstrating His love again and again. Thank God that He is always taking care of us. As I was playing with my granddaughter, I placed her hands in my hand and really just looked to see how tiny they really are. I was amazed as always thinking of how God can do such a miracle in creation and in birth. I was playing the little game itsy bitsy spider with her and what got me is when she just stared at my hand. I kept showing her my fingers and placing her hand in my hand. Something about that moment just blessed me and struck me in complete awe and amazement of God's gentleness and loving kindness.

I thought about the hand of God. Our Father's hand covers us every time we are in need and every day that we breath and walk. Every time we need Him to lift us up from falling into the pits of hell, He reaches out His hand of unfailing love and mercy. Every time we stumble into the enemy's camp, He reaches out His hand to place us on the right path of life. Every time we drift back into the mindset of sinful living, He reaches out His hand of to find and rescue that of the ninety-nine to show His love. The writer say, do not remove your hand from me. Every time we call on Him in marriage situations, He knows exactly where to place His hand.

When Thomas had doubt about the resurrection, it was Jesus who told him to put his hand in the side of Jesus and in the nail prints in His hand. The purpose was so that Thomas would believe in Jesus' resurrection. Then Jesus said that those who have not seen shall surely be blessed. Thomas needed to touch Him to see if He is real.

Today is your day. If you want to find out if Jesus can touch you with His loving hands, ask Him to come into your life. Receive salvation for it is eternal and you will reign in His Kingdom Forever. His hand will keep you in perfect peace on earth. His hand will bless you in ways man cannot imagine.

PRAYERS

Father, help me to be rooted and grounded in your love. I pray to be filled in your love. thank you for transforming me into your kingdom of righteousness.

PHIL 2, 3

RECOVERING UNDER HIS GRACE

2 Corinthians 12:9 And He said to me, "My grace is sufficient for you, for My strength is made perfect in weakness." Therefore most gladly I will rather boast in my infirmities, that the power of Christ may rest upon me.

I was riding in my tactical vehicle being as tactical and technically proficient in my skills as anyone else. Suddenly, a blast, a loud explosion hit the Hummv and flipped it over. There were casualties and too many of them. It was suppose to be an easy day of patrolling the streets of Bagdad. I had my game face on and I was observing every obstacle, scoping out every potential hidden improvised Explosive Device (IED). Everybody knows now that an easy day can turn into your worst nightmare when least expected. The only thing I wondered about the most was if God truly loved me and where would I go. I wondered if grace was sufficient enough to get me through this war zone. Some days even in your calmest state of mind, you are saying get me out of this hell hole of mess and confusion. It is already enough to be wondering about if I am going to heaven or hell. It is the grace of God that kept me through and through all the times. It is important that all soldiers recover under grace.

When it rains, it pours and it seems like it will never end. Today is your day to look the enemy in the eye and denounce all demonic powers and speak blessings over your life. God is the one who helps me to recover. He helps me to recover from injures. He helps me to recover mentally when the enemy tried to still my mind in combat and after combat, Jesus was there to help me by the Holy Spirit. God is the one who ensures that I recover from all the attacks that left marks and scars and hurt and pain. Jesus Christ is my healer and I will confess it daily for my healing all over my body. I will look to the hills in which my help comes from. My help comes from the Lord.

When I was in Iraq, I saw many vehicles get turned over due to damage by enemy attack. The next thing that had to happen was the security and recovery operations. Some vehicles and equipment may have had such severe damage that it was almost impossible to recover it and tow it to the nearest mechanical shop for assessment and repair. In many cases, it would take a long period of time to do so. God is the one who helps wounded warriors and all soldiers recover from their combat experience.

Today, God has made Himself available to touch all that desire healing and comfort. God is available to help anyone who desires to recover from sickness and depression, PTSD, anxiety, body dysfunctions, brain injuries, physicals, IED attacks, injuries. As believers, we know that God has the power to control everything from heaven and any place that He wants to control. He owns an operation center in heaven. He is calling the shots. He wants to recover you. If you look at the twelve disciples, He had prayed to the Father in Heaven that the Father would keep these men and protect these men that He had spent time with on Earth training for the gospel's sake(John 17). Some of you are in God's Army and are located in Iraq and in Afghanistan and need a helping hand in Spirit. Call on Jesus who will lift you up. He will quicken your Spirit. He has not forgotten about you. Whatever you do in life, make sure you call on the name of Jesus and accept Him as Lord and Savior. You will never go wrong. He is real in our lives.

PRAYERS

Father, help me to be rooted and grounded in your love. I pray to be filled in your love. Thank you for transforming me into your kingdom of righteousness.

EPHESIANS 2, 3

STRIPPED FOR GOD'S PURPOSE

GEN 37:23 So when Joseph came to his brothers, they stripped him of his robe, the richly oriented robe he was wearing. And they took him and threw him into the cistern. Now the cistern was empty; there was no water in it. So when the Midianite merchants came by, his brothers pulled Joseph up out of the cistern and sold him for twenty shekels of silver to the Ishmaelite, who took him to Egypt.

When I was growing up, I learned a valuable lesson by watching people strip cars of their car parts and use them for the purpose of putting a new car together. Piece by piece would disappear from the car across the street that was left unattended. Sometimes a person would come in the morning, some at night and some all day long until that car had nothing left but the blocks it sat on. Then the owner would come and take that frame away. Somehow the owner either used that frame because the foundation was still strong or he sold it to someone who would use it and make it better. Nevertheless, there was still a purpose for that car frame. It was used to be a rebuilt car for someone who never had one. The car was better and faster.

You can strip many people and objects but know that there will be results. You can strip a floor to make it appear clean to the point you can eat off the surface. The point of that is to polish it and make it look brand new again. That is what happens in the military. When it comes to striping a person, you have to be careful not to rob their dignity and break them down. In the military, civilians line up before that thirsty Drill Sergeant for a strip down. This strip down makes sure you do not have anything illegal on your possession. He is also breaking you from the old man. The Drill Sergeant makes it plain that the trainee will become a Soldier ready to win in combat and any battle. There is also a flip side when dealing with families. Families have to be careful not to strip a loved one. So we see that there can be good stripping and bad stripping.

Joseph was stripped by his brothers to be used by God. Joseph's brothers and His entire family did not understand the anointing on his life. They did not have the vision or the dreams he had. Joseph's brothers thought that they had broken his spirit. Instead they just pushed him into the favor of God. They stripped him down for the purpose of getting rid of their father's favorite son. They did not know that by stripping him of the coat of many colors, they set him up for God's favor and blessings. There is no way to stop the blessings that God has in store for you and me. Certainly, Joseph's blessings were not going to be stopped. When the Lord set something in motion, it will not be stopped by anyone or anything. Please understand that the move of God is too powerful for anyone.

Joseph's coat was representation of royalty. His father gave it to him because he favored him. Joseph coat had colors as of rainbow. Some viewed his coat as a representation of a priestly robe. His father saw it as a gift and a blessing for his favorite Son. We need to know that God has made all of us royal priest in the army of the Lord. We need to know that when we have family situations, God does not turn His back on us. There are blessings on the way. The robe was a blessing and that is exactly why the enemy wanted to twist things in the family, causing jealousy. It is clear that when Jesus rose from the dead He wore a priestly robe. He wears a priest robe in heaven.

Jealousy can cause all kinds of trouble. But when trouble comes our way, He always makes everything alright. He walks with us and protects us. The Pharisees were jealous of Jesus because He went about healing, making miracles happen, and teaching disciples. Jesus was punished because of jealousy by the Pharisees and His own people. Joseph was punished by his own brothers. No matter how much you feel like somebody has broken you like a slave, keep your head up and look to the hills where you help comes from. Jesus always looked up to the Father when things got so rough. He prayed in the Garden of Gethsemane. Joseph just kept the faith in knowing who his God was during that time in the pit, prison and palace. He knew God.

You have an advocate to take you back from the enemy. You have an advocate to set you up for blessings innumerable to count. You have an advocate that will help you when someone sells you out. God is always on your side. You can be just like Joseph and be positioned second in command or you can be first in command according to God's favor and will for your life. Do not give up even if you feel like you have be placed in a pit and sold out. God is on your side and He has multiple blessings for you. You need to know that God strips all of us clean of the sin Life. We were stripped by the precious blood of the Lamb.

PRAYERS

Father, help me to be rooted and grounded in your love. I pray to be filled in your love. Thank you for transforming me into your kingdom of righteousness.

Psalm 34

HEARTS ON FIRE, HEART OF FIRE

REV 3:15-16 I know your works, that you are neither cold nor hot, I could wish you were cold or hot. So then, because you are lukewarm, and neither cold nor hot, I will vomit you out of my mouth.

God sees everything and hears everything from the Throne Room of Heaven. He knows who demonstrates truth and commitment with their ability in the church. He knows the ability of those who proclaim His name. He knows who has backslidden and fallen from the faith. He knows what caused it and who caused it and the situation behind it. God is no respecter of persons. No one can hide. No one can get away with anything. He is omnipresent. There is nowhere to hide. He is everywhere and all knowing. He is looking for a church without spot or wrinkle. God knows the heart of man. God knows the heart of the Church.

The Lord wants men to have a heart that is on fire for Him. He said either cold nor hot. The point is to go all the way for Him. He wants men to have a servant's hearts that will continue in obedience. He wants men to follow in His will for their lives and the ministry of the Gospel. Do you remember the first time you felt the change and the conversion? You were on fire for the Lord. God is saying do not leave your first love. He was there when you first fell in love with Him. Do not let somebody or something steal your joy and your anointing. The enemy is sly enough to make you think otherwise. He comes to steal, kill and to destroy your dreams in the Lord, your service for the Lord. You do not have to stand by and let the enemy snatch you away. Listen to the voice of the Lord.

Noah did, he was on fire for the Lord. He built an Ark and saved the world from total devastation. Abraham was on fire. He moved when God told Him to move. He move in faith and became the Father of many nations. God has something in store for you. You are a child of the Most High, so start walking in the anointing placed in your life.

You might lose some friends. But God is on your side.

PRAYERS

Father, thank you for transforming me into your kingdom of righteousness. You made my life better. Thank you for making me over into a child of God and a Priest to serve you. Lead me to witness on this earth that I might be pleasing to you.

REV 1, 2

VICTORY IS IN JESUS CHRIST!

1 JOHN 5:4-5 For whatever is born of God overcomes the world. And this is the victory that has overcome the world-our faith. Who is he who overcomes the world, but he who believes that Jesus is the son of God.

    To be born of God already reflects that you have the victory in the Lord for your life. No one can walk victorious without Him. You must be born again to walk in victory. You must have faith to be an overcomer of the world. The world is tricky because it is attractive to so many people. It has so much that looks so good that entices you to live a life without Christ. It is vitally important that you make Jesus the head of your life today. Do not wait any longer. It is like suicide without Him. He will bless you more than you know. Never let someone tell you that they predict your relationship and victory. You get yourself up and you make it happen with the Lord. You tell Jesus that you want to make a date, time and place for you and Him to meet. You talk to the Lord for yourself. When you get Christ Jesus in your life, you can tell any and everybody that no one can snatch victory away from you because of who you are now. Make a change.

    Don't misunderstand the blessings that God gave us in this world. Just do not get caught up with all the misleading things in life that are not of God. As a soldier in the Army, I remember telling about 64,000 soldiers or more about what the bible says is victory in the Lord. I was absolutely shocked when I was able to tell some of the highest ranking Officers and Enlisted about nothing is better than having victory in the Lord. You see victory comes directly from Him. Our strength, our knowledge, our technical skills, our strategy and planning, our decision making, our creativity, the sound mind, the best of judgment, all of our tactical skills and abilities, all of the future planning and the past reviews of war, all of the war gaming tools and techniques had to come from the one who holds and gives intellect to man.

    It must be faith in God that drives senior leadership and subordinate leaders and the soldiers who attack on ground and by other means necessary to secure victory in war and battle. Faith must be the corner stone, it must be the absolute ingredient in the heart of man that enables him to survive and secure victory for the sake of peace and tranquility in the land of the free. All believers and all that battle against enemy must overcome every obstacle so that all nations live in a peaceful environment and relationship in foreign policy and trade will be in the best interest for everyone.

Victory is not substitutable when it comes to saints of the Lord. We have it in Christ and will not be changed because He promised it. Victory relies on faith. You must have faith. it can be the faith of a mustard seed. It can be the faith of a person newly converted as long as that faith is true Godly faith. The faith you have whether you are in Iraq, Afghanistan, Africa, Asia, Korea, Kuwait or even the United States is the faith needed to believe in Jesus and accept Him in your heart as Lord and Savior. Then, you will walk in a continuous life of victory in the Lord.

You can start over from where you are now. You are never too low. Read Psalms 139. God said if you made your bed in hell, He is there. He will not leave you. Certainly, if you have fallen from the faith, God is there to pick you up again. Let the Lord carry you. You just ask the Holy Spirit to ignite your heart that it will be on fire again for the service of the Lord. The bible says to pick up your cross and carry it. When you are on fire, God will use you in ways to glorify Him.

It is time to pick up your sword again. Pick up your bible and read again. The enemy has worked hard trying to destroy you. Some of your companions worked hard to keep you down.
If they are encouraging you then fine, but if not you might have to break away. Do not let anyone tamper with your soul salvation. Be strong in the Lord and in the power of His might. Stay focused and God will see you through.

Preach the word and be instant in season and out of season. Tell of God's plan of salvation. Be a witness on fire and tell that God loves you more than anybody and everybody could even imagine. Tell them that God listens to a repentant heart. Tell them that God has a plan for them and for you. Remember to keep the faith and let the love of God shed abroad your heart by the power of the Holy Spirit. Praise His righteous name forever.

PRAYERS

Father, thank you for transforming me into your kingdom of righteousness. You made my life better. Thank you for making me over into a child of God and a Priest to serve you. Lead me to witness on this earth that I might be pleasing to you.

1 JOHN 3, 4

FASTING AND PRAYER

Matthew 4:1-12 Then Jesus was led up by the Spirit into the wilderness to be tempted by the devil. And when He had fasted forty days and forty nights, afterward He was hungry. Now when the tempter came to Him, he said, "If You are the Son of God, command that these stones become bread."But He answered and said, "It is written, 'Man shall not live by bread alone, but by every word that proceeds from the mouth of God.'"Then the devil took Him up into the holy city, set Him on the pinnacle of the temple, and said to Him, "If You are the Son of God, throw Yourself down. For it is written:

> **He shall give His angels charge over you, and,**
> **In their hands they shall bear you up,**
> **Lest you dash your foot against a stone.**

Jesus said to him, "It is written again, 'You shall not tempt the LORD your God.'"
Again, the devil took Him up on an exceedingly high mountain, and showed Him all the kingdoms of the world and their glory. And he said to Him, "All these things I will give You if You will fall down and worship me." Then Jesus said to him, "Away with you, Satan! For it is written, 'You shall worship the LORD your God, and Him only you shall serve.'"Then the devil left Him, and behold, angels came and ministered to Him. Now when Jesus heard that John had been put in prison, He departed to Galilee.

Jesus began His Galilean ministry after He fasted for forty days. When you fast and pray, you may have a wilderness experience that will change the course of your life. Jesus had experience that was set by the Father in heaven.

It appears that one of the most effective ways to begin your ministry is by fasting and praying. This allows you to seek the Lord and get closer to Him. Fasting opens up channels of communication between you and God. You get the connection properly when you leave flesh out of the matter at hand. God loves it as it appears when we put our plates aside for a while. He wants us to fast properly and not publicly announce it. It is personal between you and God alone.

God wants us to have breakthroughs. Jesus illustrated exactly what we need to do. We fast and use the word of God for the enemy who chases us daily. We fast to get the mission done if need be. We fast out of devotion to Christ Jesus to let go of things that entangle us and bound us. We fast and pray because we are committed to live a life in Christ Jesus.

Today, ask yourself what is it that I need to fast from that has a necessary hold on me? If you need it each day and can't do without it outside of water, then it may have a hold on you. Remember, when you fast, get ready for some attacks as well because you operate in the spirit even more. Also remember that God is on your side whenever you are going through. It is important that you seek God before fasting. Ask the Lord to help you make the right choice. When you fast, you do not have to boast about it and tell everyone. It is between you and God. However, you can let your wife know and if the community church is fasting together, it is necessary to keep each other in prayer. Seek your breakthrough in Christ Jesus.

PRAYERS

Father, thank you for transforming me into your kingdom of righteousness. You made my life better. Thank you for making me over into a child of God and a Priest to serve you. Lead me to witness on this earth that I might be pleasing to you.

MATTHEW 1, 3

HEALING

Matthew 9:1-8 So He got into a boat, crossed over, and came to His own city. Then behold, they brought to Him a paralytic lying on a bed. When Jesus saw their faith, He said to the paralytic, "Son, be of good cheer; your sins are forgiven you."And at once some of the scribes said within themselves, "This Man blasphemes!" But Jesus, knowing their thoughts, said, "Why do you think evil in your hearts? For which is easier, to say, *'Your* sins are forgiven you,' or to say, 'Arise and walk'? But that you may know that the Son of Man has power on earth to forgive sins"—then He said to the paralytic, "Arise, take up your bed, and go to your house." And he arose and departed to his house. Now when the multitudes saw *it,* they marveled[1] and glorified God, who had given such power to men.

    This day is your day to get out of the paralyzed conditions of life. It may seem impossible but it is not. It may seem as though no one cares or will help you but that is not the truth. God is able to do the impossible and He alone can do it for you. Today is your day to arise and walk. You have the power if you believe in Jesus Christ who rose from the dead.

    You probably have just like myself found yourself walking into convenient stores near some corners and even just at a stop at a red light in some towns have encountered a person in a wheel chair or crippled for some reason. There are some things we do not have the power to do in our own strength. But the God of a second chance, the God of healing power and miracles can change things in an instant.

    There are many people who do not have the external hurt, or the injury that is visible before our eyes. But inside, they have a crippling mentality that is even worst. That mentality of religious battles and principalities keep them from accepting Jesus as Lord of their life.

    I watched a man on television preaching the gospel with a scarred face and legs that were not visible because he had a car accident that severed them. So now his life is without legs. But he does not go around sad and acting like he has no hope. Instead, he gives all that he has to service for Christ. He inspired me to a new level of thinking.

    Believers all over the world should see this man who has the tenacity to walk in faith and be healed in mind and soul and spirit. He believes that Jesus is his Lord and there is no other like Him. This is your time for healing. Keep the faith and walk in it. Believe that God can remove any crippling situation in your life. Stop allowing the old past of sin to speak barriers and brokenness in your life. Instead listen to what Jesus said, arise and walk. Your sins have been forgiven.

PRAYERS

Father, thank you for transforming me into your kingdom of righteousness. You made my life better. Thank you for making me over into a child of God and a Priest to serve you. Lead me to witness on this earth that I might be pleasing to you.

MARK 4

PATIENCE WINS

GALATIONS 5:21-26 But the fruit of the Spirit is love, joy, peace, longsuffering, kindness, goodness, faithfulness, gentleness, self-control. Against such there is no law. And those who are Christ's have crucified the flesh with its passions and desires. If we live in the Spirit, let us also walk in the Spirit. Let us not become conceited, provoking one another, envying one another.

You have to have patience in just about all the things you do especially for raising a family and taking care the home. You have to be patient with friends and family members, co-workers, church members and basically all the public business, especially restaurants where you and I expect the best in the meal that we are waiting to receive upon arrival. We also want the best seat in the house. Sometimes we settle for just a seat. Sometimes we are just content with what we have in life. Patience helps us to be content with what we need to be content in. Patience is needed to be successful. Patience is the key to many issues in the natural as well as in the spirit. We need to let the Holy Spirit work for us.

More importantly, you have to have patience to walk faithfully in Christ Jesus. The Apostle Paul illustrated in the book of Acts a great deal of patience as he went on several missionary journeys. It was patience that helped him make it through those journeys that God sent him on. Patience helps you to be confident in God in all things because you will have discovered that the things you do so well in impacting and changing lives is not of your own strength. It is of the Holy Spirit. Patience helps you understand that you do not have to give in to anything in this world. What will take you over in this life and the life to come is the possession of the Fruit of the Spirit.

The scripture say, "**But the fruit of the Spirit is love, joy, peace, longsuffering, kindness, goodness, faithfulness, gentleness, self-control" Galatians 5.** We need these God given character traits and blessings to live like God wants us to live. These powerful fruit of the spirit helps us walk in the spirit pleasing to God. When you express a fruit filled lifestyle to those around you, the God in you comes forth to shine and witness to others. He wants us to demonstrate to other people His power working on the inside of the believer. He wants His Saints touching multiple lives with His word. These God given fruit are necessary for changing our lives and those we approach. Many people are looking at us. So we must constantly be ready to give an answer and demonstrate the love of Christ. The fruit of the Spirit is a lifetime anointing for success in the ministry and life itself.

Patience wins no matter what the obstacle or barrier may be. If you are sketching something on a canvas for a painting project, you must be patient with all the tender touches and designs for your painting. You are an artist with expert creative thoughts and you want to apply it. Did you know that you have the ability to sketch in the next super million dollar convention at the art center?

PRAYERS

Father, thank you for transforming me into your kingdom of righteousness. You made my life better. Thank you for making me over into a child of God and a Priest to serve you. Lead me to witness on this earth that I might be pleasing to you.

MARK 4

PASSOVER FOR YOUR CHILDREN

EXODUS 12:13-17 Now the blood shall be a sign for you on the houses where you *are.* And when I see the blood, I will pass over you; and the plague shall not be on you to destroy *you* when I strike the land of Egypt. 'So this day shall be to you a memorial; and you shall keep it as a feast to the LORD throughout your generations. You shall keep it as a feast by an everlasting ordinance. Seven days you shall eat unleavened bread. On the first day you shall remove leaven from your houses. For whoever eats leavened bread from the first day until the seventh day, that person shall be cut off from Israel. On the first day *there shall be* a holy convocation, and on the seventh day there shall be a holy convocation for you. No manner of work shall be done on them; but *that* which everyone must eat—that only may be prepared by you. So you shall observe *the Feast of* Unleavened Bread, for on this same day I will have brought your armies out of the land of Egypt. Therefore you shall observe this day throughout your generations as an everlasting ordinance.

EXODUS 12:25-27 It will come to pass when you come to the land which the LORD will give you, just as He promised, that you shall keep this service. And it shall be, when your children say to you, 'What do you mean by this service?' that you shall say, 'It *is* the Passover sacrifice of the LORD, who passed over the houses of the children of Israel in Egypt when He struck the Egyptians and delivered our households.'" So the people bowed their heads and worshiped.

    The Exodus is one of the most important events in Jewish history when comes to Gods people. The Exodus is when God freed His people from the slavery and bondage of Egyptian task masters. Before God has set the Israelites free from Egypt, He had commanded them to eat the Passover meal.
    This time was like no other. God sent neither rain or a storm to take care of sin in this land. During this particular time, God had had enough of this wickedness with Pharaoh. God is not someone who plays with others. God is serious and loving and just and merciful. This night would be like rain but instead it would be a death angel pouring out death door to door. People are used to God pouring out blessings. In this particular time, they weren't blessings.

Our children need a down pour today to keep them from falling prey to other people and other sinful lifestyles. Too many teenagers are living to impress other peers in their lives. Peer pressure is one of the leading causes to stumble and not achieve the level that is inside of you. You have the ability to do anything. Our children have to remove their minds from the old traditional setting of standing in place and being idle and complacent. It is time for them to live out their dreams. No one can stop you from living your dream. One of the reasons that this is being written is because the enemy wants to carry out his version of this scripture and wipe you out. The only sure way of not being wiped out is to except Jesus as Lord and Savior.

It is time for fathers in the house to act as priest and mothers as the true help meet. Start marking your homes. It is time to start identifying and equipping young people who have talent to work hard and be successful.

PRAYERS

Father, thank you for transforming me into your kingdom of righteousness. You made my life better. Thank you for making me over into a child of God and a Priest to serve you. Lead me to witness on this earth that I might be pleasing to you.

Exodus 11

LIKE LIGHTNING STRIKE

LUKE 10:18-22 And He said to them, "I saw Satan fall like lightning from heaven. Behold, I give you the authority to trample on serpents and scorpions, and over all the power of the enemy, and nothing shall by any means hurt you. Nevertheless do not rejoice in this, that the spirits are subject to you, but rather[1] rejoice because your names are written in heaven." In that hour Jesus rejoiced in the Spirit and said, "I thank You, Father, Lord of heaven and earth, that You have hidden these things from the wise and prudent and revealed them to babes. Even so, Father, for so it seemed good in your sight. All things have been delivered to me by my Father, and no one knows who the Son is except the Father, and who the Father is except the Son, and the one to whom the Son wills to reveal to Him."

God used His power and authority to send Satan from Heaven to Hell. He still has all authority to send Satan to the Lake of Fire in the end and He will according to His word. God is so
 powerful that everything must bow before Him and everything must worship Him in the beauty of His Holiness. No one is exempt from bowing down. God is so powerful that He gave us the power and authority to walk over serpents and scorpions. The Holy Spirit has given us powers to live in authority.

In Philippians men who were righteous in His eyes received the blessing directly from God. Noah found grace for several reasons and I believe it's important for you and I to know so we can be obedient like Noah was. Noah found grace because he loved the Lord. Noah found grace because of His obedience to do what God said no matter what people around him were saying. Noah found grace because He listened and heard what God had to say. Noah found grace because it was in God's plan.

 Lightning comes down fast. It will hit whatever is in the path. When lightning hits an object it makes an impact or destroys whatever object it hits. It is the power in the lightning the counts the most. The second thing in the lightning is the affects of it. God sends more power and grace in His word. What is so unique about this scripture is that God said in Luke 10:19," I give you authority to trample on serpents and scorpions and over all the power of the enemy." The authority

God is referring to is His authority and power. God also gives the power to call down the rain in our lives when we have a dry spell. God is able to make His servants rejoice even in the times of evil trying to break us and separate families, friends and churches. God is on the battlefield for us. He runs the enemy out of town and sets the captives free.

PRAYERS

Father, thank you for transforming me into your kingdom of righteousness. You made my life better. Thank you for making me over into a child of God and a Priest to serve you. Lead me to witness on this earth that I might be pleasing to you.

Luke 9

MY FATHER, THE PRIEST

Luke 15: 20-21 So he got up and went to his father. "But while he was still a long way off, his father saw him and was filled with compassion for him; he ran to his son, threw his arms around him and kissed him. "The son said to him, 'Father, I have sinned against heaven and against you. I am no longer worthy to be called your son.'

Your Father is the priest in your house. God is the head Priest in your life and house. Everyone falls under His complete authority. Everyone in the house must know that God ordained your father to bless the house. God made the order and it is not changing. You just have to live by His order and know it and love it. He orders our footsteps. He orders the marriage because He alone ordained marriage. He orders everyone in the house. He ordained the seed to be birthed. He knew which child in the house would be the way they are at this very moment. God knew then and knows now exactly what each person is in need of for their lives. God our Lord knows if you Honor your father and mother (Ephesians 6). It is a good thing to know that the power of God is in your house. So God has His own strategy for your house.

He placed the man as the head of the house because that is simply His order. He desires to keep order in your house. The moment the order is broken, those that assist in breaking the order have to deal with God. It is God's will for your house to walk in blessings. If you step out of order the enemy wants to come right in and disrupt more. In the bible Job had a visitation. His entire family was wiped out except his wife. All the children were killed by the enemy's attack. But because Job continued to trust and walk in the faith of God, he was blessed with more abundance. Tell children to obey their Father so that it will be pleasing in the sight of God.

In Luke 15, the prodigal did not recognize the extent of the blessing on his father's life and in the house. The prodigal son left home thinking with arrogance that he could make it on his own and He did not need the blessing and inheritance of his father. But to his surprise, life became complicated and challenging to the utmost, beyond his ability to maintain himself. When you find yourself in a condition that forces you to go to the pig pin and slop around with the swine, who are known as the filthiest animals on earth, you need to get a new attitude and return to God. Jesus is calling every son to return home now. You do not have to wait until times get so difficult, He deserves the praise now. What you see in the story of the prodigal son is that the father never lost the ability to shower his son with the blessing of love. The father threw a celebration in his house regardless of what happened. He threw a party for his son's arrival back home.

There are people today that need to come back home to the father. He is the priest of the house. He answers to the Most High God. He sets the condition for you to prosper as long as you remain under obedience and the truth of God. I tell you that the Father in heaven will never let you down. He will not turn you away. He will never leave you.

He specializes in love grace, mercy, salvation, deliverance, blessings and getting all the glory. With your lost son or daughter, do not give in, do not allow the enemy to take authority, you take it. Do not give up; God is working on them right at this moment. God is speaking to them at this very moment. Give them a call and ask them what is God saying to them. Tell them what God is saying to you as well. Make it a family revival. Open the word and tell them what scripture the Lord has shared with you as well at the right time. Then pray together. That will make the enemy flee and get mad about his defeat he just experienced. Your victory is in the Lord Jesus Christ. Jesus, our high Priest is the Lord of Lord and King of Kings. Come back home to the Priest at your house and worship the Father in Heaven with all your heart.

PRAYERS

Father, thank you for transforming me into your kingdom of righteousness. You made my life better. Thank you for making me over into a child of God and a Priest to serve you. Lead me to witness on this earth that I might be pleasing to you.

LUKE 3

UNCOVERED IMAGINATION

Mark 2: 4 And when they could not come near Him because of the crowd, they uncovered the roof Where He was, So when they had broken through, they let down the bed on which the Paralytic was lying.

Some places allow you the front entry. But sometimes the crowd can force you to make a different entrance. That is what happened with this paralytic man's condition. When you need healing, you need to come up with a positive imagination and a prayer life in Christ. Let the Lord know your desire. He wants you to use your mind and allow the blessing to be poured out. You have much potential in your imagination, just uncover it for God's purpose. You have an imagination that can cause you to make millions. Think about it that is all people need is their positive God given imagination.

In this story, the paralyzed man needed a healing. What was so powerful about these men is that they were not about to let anything get in their way. They had already made up in their minds that there is a way to get healing. They used their imagination to get to the roof of the building Jesus was inside of to let the man down to Jesus. These men must be considered God sent!

We live in a society that have many people who have need of healing. Many lives have been paralyzed by the enemy. They also remain paralyzed because men and their families have not accepted Jesus as Lord and Savior. Today is your day to uncover you imagination and uncover the roof, and uncover your heart to let Jesus inside. He will keep you eternally in His hand. If you are around crowds, leave the crowd and go and get saved by Jesus Christ, the son of the Living God. You will never have to be paralyzed again because your spirit and you belong to God and no one else.

When I played football, I ran hard and strong over the defenders and had the potential like so many others to play professional football. But one day something happened to me in football practice on a rainy and muddy day. I was tackled by at least five defenders, which piled on me. They did not realize that my legs had twisted. I left that day with a hip pointer. I had to sit out of the games for a while until I healed properly. In my mind, I lost a little confidence and a little spark because I felt paralyzed. There was no need for me to feel that way. I just told myself that. I come to tell you that you never have feel that way.

Today, if you feel like the enemy has paralyzed you from head to toe and even broken your hip to keep you from running for the Lord, call on the name of Jesus for healing. Call on Him to help you to run for His purpose and call His Holy and Righteous name. He will be there to remove the scales that keep you paralyzed.

PRAYERS

Father, thank you for transforming me into your kingdom of righteousness. You made my life better. Thank you for making me over into a child of God and a Priest to serve you. Lead me to witness on this earth that I might be pleasing to you.

MARK 4

GOD GIVES THE INCREASE

1 CORINTHIANS 3:5-7 Who then is Paul, and who is Apollos, but ministers through whom you believe as the Lord gave to each one? I planted, Apollos watered, but God gave the increase. So then neither he who plants is anything, nor he who waters, But God who gives the increase.

The focus must be kept on God granting blessings and the increase the way He gives. When we take our eyes off the prize then we begin to sink and drown in our own spiritual abilities. Neither Paul nor Apollos gain the credit for service for the Lord. Everything we do and what they did must be to the glory of only God. In their preaching, it had to be the Lord who blesses others with the power to deliver His word of conversion, conviction, transformation, and salvation. It has to be the power of the Holy Spirit who reveals carnality and those who are in need of being spirit filled. It is He who gives the increase that blesses us with the infilling of His Spirit.

The Apostle Paul was tasked with giving the word even to those who were babes in Christ and carnal in mind. The scripture says, I fed you with milk and not with solid food, for until now you were not able to receive it, and even now you are still not able. But in Christ, men of God don't give up. Men might be able to identify weaknesses and what the enemy tried to destroy. Remember that God always steps in to rescue us. You see your salvation does not depend on these two men. But it is dependent solely upon God whose Spirit changes, who also gives the increase.

Churches are not successful because they have great preachers. Churches are successful because the Holy Spirit shows up and does the work that God requires for His glory. Worship is not happening unless the Holy Spirit leads the congregation. Praise from the heart is not going forth unless the Holy Spirit ushers it through the sanctuary and the heart of people. Surely God has work for His saints, however, we must remember our position is to plant and water as God requires of us because God gives the increase in all ways. He is the God with all power in His hand.

God gives the increase because only He can sanctify. God gives the increase because only He can justify. God gives the increase because He owns cattle on a thousand hills. God gives the increase in any way

He sees fit. If He wants 100 or 1000 new members in one Church on one set day, He can do it. If He wants 10,000 or 20,000 new members two settings, He can do it. God oversees the church with power. God grows the church and sustain its blessings. The scripture is clear in Psalms 127:1, "Except the Lord builds a house, the work of the builders is wasted. Unless the Lord protects a city, guarding it with sentries will do no good." He has His hand on the pulse of all service and servants. He know what will prosper to give Him glory.

When I was a young boy, I use to think that the man in the pulpit was God's man and He made it happen. It helped me to learn of His word and become a minister in His grace and will.

Today, allow the Holy Spirit to minister to you. Know that He will enter the heart of man and reveal His love to you right now. He will help you to grow in the faith regardless of what happened in the past. Jesus Christ loves you and always shines His tender mercies and grace on your life. He gives the increase for the glory of the Father. Speak increase in Jesus Name. Blessings to His Holy Name.

PRAYERS

Father, thank you for transforming me into your kingdom of righteousness. You made my life better. Thank you for making me over into a child of God and a Priest to serve you. Lead me to witness on this earth that I might be pleasing to you.

1 CORINTHIANS 3

KNOW HIM FOR YOURSELF

Philippians 3:10 that I may know Him and the power of His resurrection, and the fellowship of His sufferings, being conformed to His death.

When you get into His word, when you get intimate with His word, He will commune with you and your fellowship will become habitual. Your relationship will be stronger than ever before. You will begin to delight yourself in the Lord. You will know Him and experience a glimpse of His resurrection. You will experience even more than you can imagine. An experience with the Lord is more than enough. It is a life of fulfillment. You will never want anything outside of His perfect will for your life. Know Him for yourself. Scripture says, "To know Him and the power of His resurrection." Imagine knowing Him! Your heart changes when you know Him. More blessings come when you know Him, Love flows better when you know Him, life changes for the better when you know Him, and your life changes with abundant blessings ready to enter your life. Now that is a thought! When you commune with God in prayer you might as well get ready to break through because Now you are in the right place and position.

I would not want to know anyone better than knowing God. You need to make Him your number one priority to know. You can know someone with the highest education but they cannot get you into the Kingdom of Heaven, they cannot get you into salvation, they cannot bless you like Jesus does every day. Knowing someone means you had to get a closer perspective of them. Knowing someone means you know a lot about them. You know about their family, you know more personal information. When you go to the doctor, the doctor really does not know your heart but he knows your organs and how to diagnose you. He knows how to treat you with the best medicine. The doctor gets intimate with your case because it could mean life or death in the balance. That is exactly what Jesus wants. He wants us to get to know Him intimately. Our lives in the balance for a place in heaven. People need to get to know better than knowing their spouse. Jesus will always be there in the midst of a storm, He is there. When you go through marriage storms, He is there to rescue you.

I always go back to the day that God illuminated His word for me. He made the scriptures come alive and burn in my heart. It was John 1:1-12. He made Himself come down from Heaven to live among His people and bless them. God just loves when we want to know Him. It is when we take the time to fellowship with Him is when we know Him better. The more you study His word, the more you get in touch with God. He is the word according to John 1:1 In the beginning was the word and His word was with God and the word was God. How can this be? He is God. No one can fully express all of God because God is above all things. He is the ruler of the universe and all of creations. He calls the shots. No human in society calls the shots. They may have a role but they do not call the shots. Otherwise, they would be false Gods. No one wants that to happen because it is an abomination to God.

When you get to know Him and the power of His resurrection and the fellowship of His suffering, you will be blessed. One thing He does is destroy demons entering into your life. In 1997, the enemy came into my house and we had a show down. I was just born again, the second time so many years later. He came in to rise up against me and my family. He wanted everyone destroyed in my house. The enemy wanted my wife destroyed and he wanted my career destroyed. The enemy wanted the family to hate instead of have peace. Peace that surpasses all understanding will guard your hearts and minds in Christ Jesus.

Get yourself a new place where you can meet God and talk to Him. Get to know your redeemer and worship Him in the beauty of Holiness.

PRAYERS

Father, thank you for transforming me into your kingdom of righteousness. You made my life better. Thank you for making me over into a child of God and a Priest to serve you. Lead me to witness on this earth that I might be pleasing to you.

MARK 4

WHO MEASURES YOU? THINK FOR YOURSELF

2 Corinthian 10:12-13 But they, measuring themselves by themselves, and comparing themselves among themselves, are not wise.

God is the one who does the true measuring of a man. One of God's key missions of the believer is to help one another in love. Love a brother like a brother because a brother will tell you the truth. A brother will help you overcome shortcomings. But first things first, you must ask God to remove the scales from your own eyes. It is just like Matthew 6 says, remove the beam or plank from your eye so you can see as well. You do not have to settle for what anybody says, you should get the advice from the Holy Spirit. Your trust should always be in the Lord. He will guide your decisions for you. Trust the wisdom of God.

I particularly take interest in this because of the way our society has shaped itself under the enemy's umbrella. There is too much false pretense and false advertising and strange commercialism by people who want to get ahead but misuse what they have for gain. I always tell my children one key statement. Do not sell yourself to the Devil because of someone else's perception and opinion of you. They do not hold the key to heaven nor access to hell. I am sure they really do not want to hold Hell's key. I believe it is valuable to train your children to know that they have a mind and no one controls their mind except they give it to Jesus, the author and finisher.

Look to God for all your answers. Never look to see who is measuring you because they have no power to put you before the throne of God. Our Father in Heaven measures you and knows all things about you. He can review you entire life in a flash of a second and allow you to see it. We serve a mighty God, who is omnipresent, sovereign and omnipotent. He is everywhere. He is the God who can tell you all about yourself. Be careful not to judge. Matthew 7:7

PRAYERS

Father, thank you for transforming me into your kingdom of righteousness. You made my life better. Thank you for making me over into a child of God and a Priest to serve you. Lead me to witness on this earth that I might be pleasing to you.

2 CORINTHIANS 9

ROLLING IN THE SAND

GALATIONS 5: 16-21 I say then: Walk in the Spirit, and you shall not fulfill the lust of the flesh. For the flesh lusts against the Spirit, and the Spirit against the flesh; and these are contrary to one another, so that you do not do the things that you wish. But if you are led by the Spirit, you are not under the law. Now the works of the flesh are evident, which are: adultery, fornication, uncleanness, lewdness, idolatry, sorcery, hatred, contentions, jealousies, outbursts of wrath, selfish ambitions, dissensions, heresies, envy, murders, drunkenness, revelries, and the like; of which I tell you beforehand, just as I also told *you* in time past, that those who practice such things will not inherit the kingdom of God.

There are some people who do not mind rolling in the sand for recreation. I found it interesting that someone use it for a lie in relations. They love the dirt and sand because it seems good and for one it was an excuse. What does sin and sand have in common? They both come in multiples and both require washing and cleansing. They both must come off of us. The issue is that one is on the inside without outward results. The other, dirt comes off from the outside and it is usually not associated with something evil. Sin does not have to be your friend. The bottom line is that sin is not your friend. Cast it off and cut it away from your life.

A friend of mine told me a story that her friend had to go through. She said its hard having a companion that can be true and faithful in heart with real love. She said, they both stated their vows publically and sounded so committed to each other and their guest and before God. She said that she was so startled at what happened later that she almost lost her hope in a love lasting forever. She made it absolutely clear to me that she did not want any part of rolling in the sand over and over.

One of her sayings to me was that it is hard having someone you can love and they love you back 100%. She said, I can't believe that my boyfriend lies to me every night. He says one thing and does another. He says that the troops are meeting at the unit tonight and I believed him. But for some strange reason, he announces every week at least three times a week. Well what gave him away is that the dirt he had on his body. She said my husband would leave for hours and come home covered in dirt. She wondered what would make you get so dirty. Well, one night she followed and discovered that her husband was cheating and to cover it up he wallowed in dirt in his uniform.

This was not funny but it was because of the piece. I thought for moment this must have truly hurt her. It was a good thing that she left the relationship because it seems that it would not work, cheating is not an option, deception is not an option. The primary means to relationships are love and trust, commitment and honesty, loyalty and honor. You must have Christ at the center focus of your relationship and nothing outside of him.

No matter how you see it. God is watching every move of married men and married women and all single people. You do not have to roll in the sands of sin, nor the sea of sin. My God is able to deliver you from all that binds you. He is able to touch the heart of anyone who is committing adultery. He loves it when you call on Him for help. Today ask God to deliver you from all that deceive and try to take hold of you with evil.

I am reminded of how often people allow sin to force them to roll in the depth of sin. The good news is that you will never be able to cover it up and God is a forgiving God who can set you free from all manner of deception. If you are rolling in the sin of jealousy or fornication, let God be your God today. If the enemy wants you to roll away from God's work of witnessing to others, do not allow yourself to get caught up in it. The enemy will do his best to make you imitate the manner of sin that he enjoys watching you perform and commit to. God wants you to walk in the Spirit to be fruitful. God will lead you to live a victorious life.

PRAYERS

Father, thank you for transforming me into your kingdom of righteousness. You made my life better. Thank you for making me over into a child of God and a Priest to serve you. Lead me to witness on this earth that I might be pleasing to you.

GALATIANS 4

GOD'S ALTAR IN THE HEART

GEN 8:20-21 Then Noah built an altar to the Lord, and took of every clean animal and of every clean bird, and offered burnt offerings on the altar. And the Lord smelled a soothing aroma. Then the Lord said in His heart, I will never again curse the ground for man's sake, although the imagination of man's heart is evil from his youth; nor will I again destroy every living thing as I have done.

Your challenge today is to build God an ark and an altar. It only makes sense that Noah would build an altar unto the Lord. When you walk with God and know Him for yourself, you will do nothing less than reverence Him in the way your heart is lead by the Holy Spirit. Please understand first that Noah received the word from God to build an ark for the saving of God's people. If you ever want to walk with God intimately, in the sense of true holiness, build an altar in your heart for the Lord. Let the Lord know that your heart is open for Him to come and dwell to make you over with praise and worship. God is looking for those open vessels, those that are seeking Him, those that are in need of Him, those that desire to meditate day and night in worship with Him, those that desire to sup with Him and those who desire to be transformed and translated like Enoch who walked perfectly with God. Listen to what happened. Noah built an ark to save his family and start the seed process over in being fruitful and multiplying. He did it because God recognized Noah's obedience. Noah built an altar for the Lord after the flood and this time God promised not to destroy man. God blessed future generations through Noah's obedience in the ark and the altar. Noah was God's sacrifice because his heart was clean before God. He was faithful before God and righteous before the Lord and it pleased God. So then that is why God chose Noah for these tasks. Noah presented clean animals to sacrifice and offered burnt offerings to God that pleased Him. By Noah's action people live through the power of God recognizing your blessing. However, never forget the only true sacrifice that took away the sin of the world is Jesus Christ. In Hebrews 10:5-12, Jesus is our sacrifice for eternal life. He took away the sin of the world by the power of His love.

PRAYERS

Father, all glory to your name. Guide me by your Holy Spirit to build an altar in my heart daily. My sole purpose is to glorify your Lord. I pray for an everlasting altar in my heart to glorify Jesus Christ, the son of God and my Lord.

MATTHEW 25

KEEP THE HOPE OF THE LORD

1 PETER 3: 13-16 Who is going to harm you if you are eager to do good? But even if you should suffer for what is right, you are blessed. "Do not fear what they fear; do not be frightened."But in your hearts set apart Christ as Lord. Always be prepared to give an answer to everyone who asks you to give the reason for the hope that you have. But do this with gentleness and respect, keeping a clear conscience, so that those who speak maliciously against your good behavior in Christ may be ashamed of their slander.

There will always be those that Mock God because they do not know Him and recognize His power in their lives. But when you discover the power of His grace, love and sheer magnitude of his creative power, the lights will come on and the heart will be transformed because the fear of the Lord will be ignited in you. You will learn about love and reverencing the one who sits on the throne. You will learn to bow down before Him. Don't feel alone for one moment. Many atheist and idol worshippers, big bang theorist, intellectual scientific believers, Pharisee minded people, and religious people in general have crossed over. You will accept Him after this! There is no other God to accept and bless you the way He does. There is simply no one like Him! You can search anywhere you want. My goal is to keep you from wasting time and putting your life in the devils hand and fake kingdom and fake ideologies, fake belief systems and the list of fake things go on. That is not where God wants our mind. You were made to be in God's Kingdom with the abundance of life. The scripture tells us as believers to be ready to give an answer. The Holy Spirit will speak to the believer and tell us what we must do to help that brother or sister out. You might be standing at the Shopping Mall and over hear people discussing the Lord in a negative way. How do you approach it? You approach with meekness and wisdom. The Holy Spirit will give you a way to approach and open your mouth gently. We do not run people off; the devil is busy enough doing that. This is really called a form of persecution not only to the saints but to those that are lost.

The Apostle Paul wants us through the word to take a stand in the Lord. We are already more than conquerors in Him. We are committed to His perfect will because we know that He is our maker. I have had several challenges with people using the Lord's name in vain. For the most part, they do not understand that they are in a sense using profanity and unintentionally mocking God. No one can curse God nor can anyone move Him from His throne. Regardless of those that speak negative words without knowledge of Him, God is still God eternal and can never be changed for anyone or anything in existence. One of my best witnesses when it comes to giving an answer is found in Romans 1:18-21. I believe it's important that people just look around and see what was made by the voice of God. See what His hands can do. See what His voice can do. See what His power can do. You cannot be you unless God allows you to be you. The big bang cannot take care of you each day. It takes someone who has all power in His hand. Why? I am glad you asked! You cannot sustain you. You want an answer! How can you activate all of your senses without God? How can you activate your energy level without God? Who gave you sight to see? Who made your heart beat each moment of life? How can you breath? Where did your oxygen come from in your body and out of your body? Who formed you? Have you ever heard of the foundation center? He is the only CEO of the foundation center. He founded planet earth by speaking it. He founded the universe and its evolving cycles by speaking it. God is beyond human imagination, thought pattern and all makeup.

 God asked a question to Job. Job was a righteous man whom God allowed the enemy to attack but not kill (Job 39). Where were you when I laid the foundations of the earth and stretched out the sky? This was enough to close not only Jobs mouth, but drop his jaw in awe. But is it enough for man today? The same question applies, where were you when God laid the foundations and stretched out the sky? The answer is simple, we were not yet formed. But God's intent was that we understand that we can not do anything without Him. We did not create anything. We did not create the universe. We did not lay any foundation. We do not have the power to make anything let alone stretch anything. God wants our imagination in Him. Meditate on the one who made you whole. The one who gave you life and breath in you that you could be human and walk and talk. Ask God to renew your mind today. Roman 12 will always get you. Romans 10:9 will help you get delivered in Christ Jesus, the Son of the living God. Today believe in Him. Let go of the doubting Thomas attitude and be renewed like Thomas when He saw the nail prints in His hand and the piercing in His side. Understand and know that He died for a wretch like you and I. Jesus is your hope in all the blessings you can get. Jesus is the hope that will deliver you now and eternally. Count on Him only for His everlasting love, peace, joy, faith, and hope. May the name of Jesus be praised forever.

PRAYERS

Father, we thank you for the blessed hope. We celebrate your life, death, and resurrection. Lord, we await your coming to bring your Saints home. You are Lord of my life. Praise and glory to your righteous name.

1 Corinthians 11

BREAKING STRONGHOLDS

2 CORINTHIANS 10:4-5 The weapons we fight with are not the weapons of the world. On the contrary, they have divine power to demolish strongholds. We demolish arguments and every pretension that sets itself up against the knowledge of God, and we take captive every thought to make it obedient to Christ.

    Most people remain in their strong hold because they think like the rest of the world. Many people have been lowered into the device of the enemy. They often forget about the more than a conqueror attitude that God gave us. You don't have to be a part of the world's thinking tank. That, my friend, is a large amount of worldly thinking. You don't have to impress anyone. You were born to think in the spirit to be close to God who lives in heaven. Get your mind in the right gear. Start shifting it to make a difference in this world. Somebody needs you to encourage them because of a bondage situation they were kept in for years. Someone is in need of encouragement to stop allowing the enemy to place sickness on you and believing your are dying. Someone needs to know that the wildness experience is over. It is your time to walk in freedom and in the abundance of God's blessings. Always remember when God has something good ahead for you, the enemy is laying in the trench ready to ambush to set you back and to take away the goods that the Lord has given you. Hold on to your faith in Jesus. He will keep you under His perfect protection and care. He will anoint you to get His mission completed because His mission involve lifting up others that have been bound to different pits and shackles. Be strong in the power of His might. Break every stronghold that the enemy throws at you. You are a born again, sanctified believer and child of the most High God.

    The other half of society needs to know that Satan does not give you true benefits. Satan falsely gives you things that make you think that life is full of wonders. Don't you let him grip your spirit and soul like that over some material stuff that will not benefit the Kingdom. The enemy can't wait for you to give him God's glory. Why don't you start today reminding God that it will never happen because you are making a new commitment to God. Why don't you tell God that you are ready to take a big step in obedience. Tell the Lord that you desire to serve Him, ready to step up to the plate an no longer be bound to those strongholds. Make it clear and make your confessions know to the Lord that you are stronger and better now that you walk under the power of the Holy Spirit. Tell your past bye.

PRAYERS

Father, thank you for breaking strongholds from my life. You have the power to remove any stronghold that seeks to destroy my life. Lord I pray for your infilling Spirit to take hold of my life and give me the knowledge of your Holy word. Lord, keep my in the palm of your hand. In Jesus name, amen

Isaiah 53

ILLUMINATE THE WORD IN MY EYES
OVERCOME BLINDNESS

2 CORINTHIANS 4:1-4 And even if our gospel is veiled, it is veiled to those who are perishing. The god of this age has blinded the minds of unbelievers, so that they cannot see the light of the gospel of the glory of Christ, who is the image of God.

We once crossed a bridge that was set in place overseas for multiple night missions. At one point it got so dark and one of the components broke in the middle of crossing huge tonnage equipment, no one could function in the dark to repair that component. It was so difficult to the point that we couldn't even disconnect the old piece to put on the new piece. Darkness had crippled us for a moment. It wasn't until the commander gave the go ahead to turn the lights on. Then we could connect and repair the components for the bridge. Afterwards the mission was a success and promotions were in order to so many of the soldiers. They were successful because of the illumination given from the light.

You might be wondering why so many people refuse to accept God. They do it because the enemy Satan has blinded them in the worst way. Satan has kept them in darkness. But it was also a choice that people made for themselves and their families. Today you have a chance to get the light in your eyes and overcome blindness. You can help your family. Jesus is the light of the world. More importantly, Jesus is the light of the word of God. He illuminates Himself in your eyes and your mind and spirit to become one of His children. When you look in your Bible, you see Jesus explained in scripture. Furthermore, as you look at the word, it will leap out into your eyes and you will see Jesus all through the Bible. You will be blessed to see the things that God shows you. Do not miss out on your blessing. They come directly from God.

You might even be wondering what does it take to get a person to see the Lord at work in their lives. Remember one of the most powerful statements Jesus made on the cross, Father forgive them for they know not what they do." The mind, your mind and everybody else mind is already equipped upon conversion. I believe that Jesus see us in the same ways so often. We reject the light that He shines in our lives even for the good of our lives. One the worst reasons why He is rejected is because often people allow the enemy of darkness to blind the minds and hearts of God's people and those that have full potential in crossing over into the Kingdom of God. Thank God that it is not over until He says it is over. The enemy really does not have enough to keep you blinded. You have the authority and the access to God and His angels to shake off any hindrance in your life.

PRAYERS

Father, thank you for removing the veil from my mind so that I can receive Jesus as Lord of my life. I pray to remain steadfast in your word so that your light will empower me to serve you and receive the blessing. I pray for your word to illuminate my heart daily. In Jesus name, amen.

JOHN 1

TURN ON THE LIGHT SWITCH!

2 CORINTHIANS 4:5-12 For we do not preach ourselves, but Jesus Christ as Lord, and ourselves as your servants for Jesus' sake. For God, who said, "Let light shine out of darkness," made His light shine in our hearts to give us the light of the knowledge of the glory of God in the face of Christ. But we have this treasure in jars of clay to show that this all-surpassing power is from God and not from us. We are hard pressed on every side, but not crushed; perplexed, but not in despair; persecuted, but not abandoned; struck down, but not destroyed. always carry around in our body the death of Jesus, so that the life of Jesus may also be revealed in our body. For we who are alive are always being given over to death for Jesus' sake, so that his life may be revealed in our mortal body. So then, death is at work in us, but life is at work in you.

Any person sitting in a board meeting with executives briefing a marketing plan to capture more consumers and increase profit sits in total anticipation to gain something out of that meeting. One of the primary efforts is to advance the business to a greater advantage against competitors. Soldiers are sitting in the battle plan room getting briefed by superior officers and leaders listening intently to understand the strategy that has to be executed on the battlefield. In order to execute you must take something away with you from each briefing. You had to take away something in order to be effective for the mission at hand. When you get out there on the battlefield the action and sense of awareness will cause a switch to be turn on in your mind. A light switch in your mind causes you to see clearly what is going on and how to respond on the battlefield to survive.

Much like the battlefield experience that soldiers encounter, Christians need to respond accordingly as they are led by the Holy Spirit. All the information and facts of life are fine and great, but without the light switch coming on, there is not victory or success. Everyone is in need of the Holy Spirit helping us to turn on our minds and hearts and to be receptive of the Lord and becoming an effective witness on the battlefield.

Every believer needs the light of God to shine forth most in our walk and at home. My walk with God starts inside me and at home. Don't you let anyone tell you differently! Ask our Lord Jesus to come into your heart now. The toughest ministry starts at home. Win your wife and children into the ministry. Let them see the light of the Lord shining in your life. Let them know that the light switch is on by your sound decision making and the way you love them and treat them. It is at home where you try your best to get everyone in the house to listen, learn and apply it under the obedience of the Lord as the head of the household.

The light switch came on when I was called to ministry. When I first read the qualification of a Deacon and a Bishop in 1 Timothy 3, I thought about the strictness and the holy life that an apostle and man of God has to live for service in Jesus Christ. I saw the importance of God setting the qualifications for man to observe in obedience to Jesus Christ. It made me think about Moses and the Ten commandments that God gave him for people to live by. Can a man truly live by this standard in his appointed position? The answer is yes. He may not be able to live the law out. But that is why God gave us grace. But he definitely can live those qualifications in position that God placed him in as long as he entrusts the Holy Spirit for strength and obedience. It is only the Holy Spirit's guidance that will see us through all of God's standards. We can't do it on our own. Remember, all things are possible by God. At the same time, He put them there because He knows our potential strengths, and weaknesses.

I took away the blessings that will come if you operate in obedience to His will for your life. He has so much for His Servants that they can't help but to win. Believers are not to walk in defeat. We are winners in Jesus Christ. We do not cave in and quit the mission that God has purposed for us. We have crossed over and there is no turning back. You can lose some things out of your life. But when it comes to ministering to God's people, He will enable you to stand for the perfection of the five fold ministry. If He has to take another route, just remember, God is not a respecter of persons.

PRAYERS

Father, thank you for turning on the light switch in my mind to receive Jesus Christ as Lord and Redeemer. Because of your love and kindness, I will preach Jesus Christ and believe in deliverance from darkness and from those things that press us on every side.

2 Corinthians 2,3

UNSEEN BLESSINGS

2 CORINTHIANS 4:18 So we fix our eyes not on what is seen, but on what is unseen. For what is seen is temporary, but what is unseen is eternal.

If you visited the Grand Canyon and saw the sights of mountains, you would be amazed at the awesome beauty, size and structure of those mountains and all the surroundings that God made. Somehow because of the beauty, your eyes get fixed on it and wonder of God's splendor and power. Nevertheless, what you can't see are the hands of God that shaped all of those mountains and the surroundings. If you saw God's hands you would be amazed. However, you do not see His hands although they are there shaping and upholding the sheer beauty and massiveness. It really settles in your mind that God's hands are ready and available to hold you up when the mountains in your life are too heavy and threaten to squeeze the life out of you, the hand of God is there, invisible but almighty blessing your life.

We do not see God but we see what He has done in our lives. We do not see the Holy Spirit but we see the work that He does by guiding our lives and helping us to glorify Jesus who lives forever. God did not make us to get tied up with this world and its stresses and lose focus. He did not make us to walk in the darkness of this world. He did not make us to get all distracted and frustrated. Everything on this earth is temporary. It can change at any time. These things on Earth are not permanent. So do not get your mind fixed or dependent on them. Nothing on this Earth is going to Heaven except those that He alone selects. He selects based off of His word. If you accepted Him, then He will accept you. Romans 10 puts it into context: if you confess that Jesus is Lord and believe He died for you, and accept Him, then you are one of His born again children. You are heaven bound.

God's word is your lead by the power of the Holy Spirit. Since you are unable to see the Lord, your help is the word and the Holy Spirit. You and I could have never made it this far if it had not been for the Lord on our side. We serve a God who is eternal and has all power to bless in every way. Too often people look at their current situation and believe that they must remain in that zone. That is false. God did not make you so you feel cursed and broken. He made you so you receive the promise and walk in them. He is the God that will supply all your needs according to His riches and glory. No one else can do what He does for us.

God sees all attacks of the enemy when we do not see. He sees every diseases that the enemy try to plaque this society and household with. God sees all things and He gets rid of it because of your prayers. You may not see your prayers but God sees all things especially in the unseen world. He can see things better than we can with the naked eye and even a microscope. Start focusing your attention on God and not the things that you can see. Focus on the grace, mercy, and truth of the King of Glory. Focus on knowing that He sees all things and opens your eyes as well. He will never let you down. He is Lord and King over all creation and unseen worlds.

PRAYERS

Father, thank you for fixing my eyes on the eternal and not the natural things surrounding my life. This spirit filled life from you O' Lord blesses me more each and every day.

COLOSSIANS 2

DO NOT GIVE THE DEVIL A FOOTHOLD

EPHESIANS 4:25-27 Therefore each of you must put off falsehood and speak truthfully to your neighbor, for we are all members of one body. "In your anger do not sin": Do not let the sun go down while you are still angry, and do not give the devil a foothold.

When you wake up in the morning, give your wife a kiss that she will remember and set love date, private between you and her. The intent is let love move to a higher level. Keep your marriage strong. If you allow the devil to come into your house and shake up everything, then you will see for yourself what he is capable of destroying. If you really don't want it to get that far, you can stop his manipulations and lies in its tracks with a leap of faith in Jesus Christ. Jesus will stop it for you. Do not give that Devil an inch. Start by glorifying Jesus in everything you do today. That is how you get house back in order. Start praying daily a simple prayer. Lord, I love you and need your helping hand in every situation of my life. Lord I worship and praise your name forever, in Jesus name. Then you can watch all of those demons flee at the name of Jesus.

Use that little member in your mouth that you use everyday anyway. You need to use it because the enemy has strategies and all types angles that he is trying to use to destroy you and your family and friends. Stand against it using the word. Let the word of God be spoken from your mouth. Use your tongue to confess the word and the power in it. Use Psalm 23, The Lord is my Shepherd, I shall not want. Use Psalm 27, The Lord is my light and my salvation who shall I fear. The Lord is the strength of my life, who shall I be afraid. Ask Jesus to strengthen in His holy word. Ask Jesus to keep you under His shelter. Ask God to allow you to dwell in His secret place.

You need to start making decisions today. Make four key decisions. One Lord, I will accept you as Lord and Savior. Second, Lord I will deny myself and pick up my cross and follow you. Matthew 16 Third, Lord I will be obedient to you under your Holy Spirit. Forth, Lord I will walk in faith while staying in your word.

PRAYERS

Father, deliver me from all footholds that entangle my life and

distort truth. Help me to be honest and speak the truth in love and peace. Lord deliver me from anger to a mind of peace and joy in your kingdom.

1 JOHN 1:9

JESUS OPEN DOORS

REV 3:7-11 "To the angel of the church in Philadelphia write: These are the words of him who is holy and true, who holds the key of David. What he opens no one can shut, and what he shuts no one can open. I know your deeds. See, I have placed before you an open door that no one can shut. I know that you have little strength, yet you have kept my word and have not denied my name. I will make those who are of the synagogue of Satan, who claim to be Jews though they are not, but are liars. I will make them come and fall down at your feet and acknowledge that I have loved you. Since you have kept my command to endure patiently, I will also keep you from the hour of trial that is going to come upon the whole world to test those who live on the earth. I am coming soon. Hold on to what you have, so that no one will take your crown.

The door is vital for every home and every building. The door is in most cases the first thing that people notice upon entering a building or a home. Whether it is beautiful or it lacks the best taste, doors attract people. There is always something behind closed doors. Business deals are made behind closed doors. We end up behind closed doors each day of our lives. You go behind closed doors because of privacy, security and you need your special space. At home, there are doors all over the house. Which one is yours? How much time do you spend behind closed doors? The Lord talks much about doors. No man can open doors for you that God opened. No man can closed doors that God opened for you. Blessings are associated with the behind doors scenes. The good thing about all the doors is that when God opens doors no one can shut them. No one can make deals for God behind any doors. There are those closed doors that are designed to stunt your spiritual growth. But God has an open door for those that call on His name and believe in Him. There is nothing too hard for God. He opens doors that no one can shut. When God puts things in order for you to prosper because He has a plan for you, no doors can shut you out. When God wants you to succeed in a business plan that He gave you to layout the vision and goals, no doors can be shut. Instead all doors have to open because of the Lord. God will be glorified no matter what it looks like. When the ministry seems like its dying because the enemy has trampled on your life, do not worry God will open doors for you that no devil in hell or man alive can shut. You need to be reminded that we are more than conquerors through Christ Jesus. Romans 8:37 I am reminded of Alex Haley who authored the book "Roots" and became a model to millions because he helped to set people free from a slave mentality to understanding that God opened doors for everyone.

PRAYERS

Father, thank you for opening doors that no man can shut. Thank you for blessings that only you can give. Thank you for favor. Thank you for kingdom authority. You made my life better. Thank you for making me over into a child of God and a Priest to serve you in your Kingdom. Lead me to witness on this earth that I might be pleasing to you. Lord, I exalt you with all my heart, soul, strength and spirit. In Jesus name, amen.

ACTS 1, 2

GET A GOOD SHAKEDOWN

ACTS 28:5 But Paul shook the snake off into the fire and suffered no ill effects.

The military does it well in basic training day one. When the drill instructor really wants your attention on day one, he or she conducts a shakedown, which also a pre-inspection of what you are bringing in to the unit and what illegal items you are bringing that must be taken away. In many cases it takes a while and in some it only takes a few minutes. The shakedown is necessary because a newly arrived soldier could have possessions that are harmful to the other Soldiers and people in that environment. Normally the basic training takes about 8 weeks and the newly arrived civilian becomes a soldier because not only did he receive the shakedown in the beginning, things of old nature were shaken off during all the training for eight weeks and a new mind set has taken hold of the new soldier. Now he is reminded that he must conform to the Army Regulation and the training he has learned.

God has helped us in so many situations time and time again, shaking off things that bounded us and kept us in a deep sense of captivity. There are things that can shut you down in your tracks and only the enemy employs those things. So whatever is keeping you at a standstill or stagnant or lost, bound, in mental prison, or scared, it is time to have a shakedown. You can do a self inventory and find out what is holding you down and causing upset in your life and start by asking the Lord to shake them off of your life. The most commonly know issues are in the fifth chapter of Galatians.

The Apostle Paul shook off what was stated as a snake bite. Anyone who has been bitten by a snake will tell you that you just don't shake them off. God was with Him to shake those venomous bites off. You have received similar bites; we all have, by the enemy who wants to control our lives. One bite by the enemy could destroy you if you allow it. The answer is calling on Jesus to rescue you. Ask Him today to be your Lord and savior. Surrender completely to Him.

Today, you need to make a choice because the enemy is not playing with you. He is not joking with you. He is in it for the kill. He wants to steal and destroy you and your family. Be the priest of your house and stand against it by surrendering yourself first and ask God to cover your family. Ask God to help your entire family to surrender to Jesus

Christ, the son of the living God. Pray to Him and walk in His word. It is the power in His word that will change things in our lives. When you accept Him just watch your life change and watch the power of the Lord and His blessings move in your life. Remember once God shakes you down, the only thing that will remain is His goodness inside of you. He will fill you with the fruit of the Spirit, with love leading the way. Today, ask a neighbor politely if they need God to do something in their life. Ask them if they want a blessing. Then tell your story of God shaking off the things in your life and filling you with good fruit, salvation and everlasting joy

PRAYERS

Father, I pray for courage to shake off the things that try to poison my spirit and take my life. I pray for strength to shake off the adversary at all times. Lord, I humbly ask for you help to deal with the enemy. It is only by your strength that I am saved from sin and attacks. Praise your Holy name, Jesus Christ.

ACTS 2

LISTEN TO GOD'S VOICE

EXODUS 15:26-27 He said, "If you listen carefully to the voice of the LORD your God and do what is right in his eyes, if you pay attention to his commands and keep all his decrees, I will not bring on you any of the diseases I brought on the Egyptians, for I am the LORD, who heals you."

One of the things that touch the hearts of most people when they are experiencing health issues is a get well card or flowers. It works almost every time. It lifts the spirit of people to know that you care. We call it in the word to get well. You can find it from Genesis to Revelation, get well scriptures. You just might have a friend that will bring you a get well message from God. Yes, you are right. It is your time to witness His everlasting love and tender mercies and deliverance.

Did you hear what God just said, He said "for I am the Lord that heals you" No one else can take that claim. If you hear it by anyone else, it is not God. It is the devil lying to you, the deceiver, manipulator, false lies, a hell catching net for you to get tangled up in. God is the only loving one that can save a sick soul, heal, deliver, bless beyond all measures, and still rock you in the midnight hour. God is the one who will comfort you when you feel like there is no hope in the sickness that the enemy pronounced on your life. You need to and have to take a stand in the Lord Jesus and rebuke all those false accusations of sickness and bad health. Today, stand up and turn your lips toward heaven and speak to the Lord with reverence and praise for His righteousness and goodness.

Tell Him thank you for His healing power for this very moment of life and believe Him and trust Him. He will never let you down. You have to keep your faith activated in Him no matter what it looks like. You need to keep reading the get well card. The get well card is more than a card. It is the Holy Bible which contains words that restore and gives healing power to all people. Christians refer to it as the word of God. Ask the Holy Spirit to help you with scripture that will heal you. There is nothing too hard for God.

His word has all the perfect ingredients of healing. Whatever healing you need, it's in the get well card, the word of God. All the proper prescriptions are in the get well card. The Bible as the perfect get well card always manages to restore what is needed to be restored.

I found out that too many people are afraid to speak to God for some off the wall reason that was conveyed by the enemy. Speak to God today. Do not allow other people to stop you. The enemy specializes in using people against you. Stand your ground in the Lord, Jesus Christ. Remember that you are highly blessed, highly favored among all people. Your blessings do not stop based on anyone's belief and thoughts. God reminds that His thoughts are not like ours. His thoughts are beyond our comprehension. I can live over 100 years old or even 200 if He wanted me to and still not comprehend the great mystery in His healing and blessed power. Instead what we need to grab hold of is our individual faith in God.

You had a medical issue that required seeing a doctor, go see the doctor. God gave the doctor faith also to help you. Use your faith as you are traveling to see him or her. Use your faith through the procedure. God made doctors to treat people. Everything will work out for God to get the glory. His will is in operation so let it flow. It just so happened that God gave us the power of faith to be dependent on Him in every situation of life. Real faith will help in any case if you really surrender and allow the Lord to have His way with your life. God always reminds us that when you really want a breakthrough, try faith and fasting in Jesus' power. He can break all strongholds of disease and sickness. You just have to believe in Him and activate faith and fasting. God never runs out of His blessed power.

Today, you need to make a choice because the enemy is not playing with you. He is not joking with you. He is in it to kill, steal and destroy you and your family. Be the priest of your house and stand against it by surrendering your family to Christ. Pray to Him and walk in His word. Watch your life change and watch the power of Lord blessings upon you.

PRAYERS

Father, I pray to hear your voice daily and to walk in obedience. I pray for the Holy Spirit to keep me in your word and on the right path. Lead me to witness on this earth that I might be pleasing to you.

Exodus 16

RECEIVE YOUR SIGHT BY FAITH

LUKE 18:35-37 As Jesus approached Jericho, a blind man was sitting by the roadside begging. When he heard the crowd going by, he asked what was happening. They told him, "Jesus of Nazareth is passing by."

Have you ever called on Jesus to have mercy on you? Have you ever found yourself sitting on a roadside lost? Blind Bartimaeus was a character who sat on the roadside waiting for the move and miracle working power of Jesus Christ. When you call on the Lord to have mercy on you, He hears you no matter what the distance or circumstance may be in your life. Can you imagine what Blind Bartimaeus was thinking when He knew he needed Jesus' help. It appears that up to that point perhaps in his mind, his days were cloudy and dark days in Bartimaeus' life because he could not see. He was blind from birth. Brighter days are approaching Blind Bartimaeus in this story because a blessings is about to be demonstrated by our Lord, Jesus Christ. We must be reminded that life has lessons also that help us so many ways. Jesus was about to show us a level of faith and what we should exercise in our life's lessons and expectations. Jesus has ways of doing things that defy odds, nature, fear and all things because of His attitude to bless and restore. Jesus is the one who loves us so much that He desires to heal all that call on His name. He heals according to His purpose and His timing. It may not come when you want it, but Jesus is right on time. Your blessing is between you and the Lord.

Blind Bartiamaeus cried out to Jesus for healing upon hearing that Jesus was walking by. In Luke 18:38, Jesus, Son of David have mercy upon me. Jesus will heal when you request healing from Him. Have you ever heard of someone who sat by the wayside and just waited for some help? There are plenty Bartimaeus out there in this culture and other countries as well. Try calling on Jesus with the same kind of attitude Bartimaues had and wait for your miracle.

Whatever your wayside is or wherever it is, it is not big enough and it can't hide from God. You need to release the blind areas of life. Call on Jesus, He is waiting to set you free. Maybe you are tired of the same old conditions of life and need someone to open your eyes to see the light of the world, Jesus is the answer to open those eyes and the levels that are blinded. When you can't see yourself through, Jesus is the answer to walk you through all of life's circumstances.

If you go to the gym to workout, be looking for Jesus to touch you during your workout. As you reach the peak of your workout, expect Jesus to do a new thing in you whether your sight or your heart and mind, He will do it for all areas of your body.

If you find yourself on the highway this morning and have a little meditation time on your mind, call on the Master to visit you while you are rolling down the highway. If you allow Jesus to role with you, there is something in it for you. I would not want lose my blessings.

When you find yourself watching football, basketball, baseball, or hockey games of your favorite teams and players, since almost everybody has one, give Jesus a chance to touch you so you can see better the games of life. Allow Him to show you something through one of the player moves on the court, field, or ice. Allow Him to show you something even at the Olympics, the biggest event all year long. Watch for the Lord to give you a sign of a better sight and awareness of who you really are in Christ. His unfailing grace and mercy is always revealed to everyone. Grab hold of your blessings in His grace.

Today is your day to see like blind Bartimaeus did after Jesus healed him. You are encouraged to seek Him while He may be found. It is the day of salvation for you. If you never ever do anything in life worth something, do this and you will be blessed forever. Salvation is freedom from everything and it guarantees eternal life. You have everything to gain. Repeat this prayer. Lord Jesus, I repent of my sin. Please forgive me. Come into my heart as my Lord. I believe that you died for me on the cross and rose from the grave to set me free from sin.

LUKE 18:42 Jesus said to him, "Receive your sight; your faith has healed you." Salvation is like receiving new vision and new sight.

PRAYERS

Father, thank you for restoring my sight when I could not see the things that you were revealing to me. You made my life better. Thank you for making me over into a child of God with new sight and new vision. I pray to use these blessings to exalt and serve you. Lead me to witness on this earth that I might be pleasing to you.

LUKE 18

PUT YOUR EYES ON GOD

2 CHRONICLES 20:11-12 See how they are repaying us by coming to drive us out of the possession you gave us as an inheritance. O our God, will you not judge them? For we have no power to face this vast army that is attacking us. We do not know what to do, but our eyes are upon you."

You will never go wrong when you put your eyes on Jesus. Make Him the center of your life. Make Him the focus each and every day. King Jehoshaphat's Army was being surrounded and perhaps overrun in so many ways. King Jehoshaphat had the best idea of the day. Call upon the Lord in prayer for everything especially the moment of war. Can you imagine what would happen if general officers and enlisted men and women of the Armed Forces of every branch, Army, Air force, Marines, Coast Guard, Reserves, National Guard, and any other forces called upon the name of the Lord during war and even during peace time. God would respond to all request because He is God and He holds to His word. God hears your prayer every time you pray. He hears the distress call in your prayer and everything else in it. He hears the battle cry in your prayer. King Jehoshaphat spoke these word, "we do not know what to do, but our eyes are upon you" This sounds like a plea and at the same time a total submission to God to deal with the circumstances of war and all troubles involved and around it.

God has ways of blessing His people. Have you ever had a bully that was just ready to take you out and you knew that the bully was going to win. That is exactly how Satan works. He bullies folks in war and in trials and in suffering and in all cases that bind them. Listen, God has an Army so big that nothing can stop Him. In one blink, He can summon every angel and some to come at your request and take out all the demons in hell and those around you. In response to King Jehoshaphat's prayer, He made it clear to "be not discouraged, for the battle is not yours, but God's." The Army at this point had only one responsibility. The Army's responsibility is to stand still and watch the mighty hand of God work in this battle. He will resolve things according to His power and authority. He will also show His tender mercies toward King Jehoshaphat and his Army. The King only needed to obey God.

One of things God loves for us to do is to praise Him at all times. Praise can do marvelous things in the sight of God during any battle, even those battles at home. God wants us to praise Him even in war. King Jehoshaphat appointed men to walk ahead of the Army while praising God. They praised Him for His love that endures forever. They praised Him for His everlasting goodness. They praised Him because He can be trusted in all things. They praised Him because He is the God of deliverance. The victory was won because God said it would be won.

The Lord is good and He deserves the praise by all of His wonderful creations. We must praise Him continually. For His mercy endures for ever. He has graced us with His loving kindness.

Do you have enemies coming against you today? What seems hopeless to you? What seems to be impossible to you in your life? If you feel hopeless and powerless, call on the name of the Lord and begin to praise Him for what He has already done. Believe it and walk in it. He steps in to hold back all those issues that try to flood you out of His Kingdom. He opens His arms to those that are lost with unlimited love. God loves your praise. So praise Him in the morning. Praise Him in the evening. Praise Him for His marvelous acts.

PRAYERS

Father, thank you that I can put my eyes on you in heaven for all situations. When the enemy surrounds me, you come to my rescue every time. I praise you for your faithfulness and love.

Psalm 27

REIGNING KING OF KINGS

REV 11:15 The seventh angel sounded his trumpet, and there were loud voices in heaven, which said:"The kingdom of the world has become the kingdom of our Lord and of his Christ, and he will reign forever and ever."

A king's crown gives him a distinguished look above everyone else. He is set apart as the king of that land. We are kings as well ever since we crossed over into salvation, accepting Jesus as Lord. Jesus is the reigning King in my life and the entire world. He is identified by everyone who sees the crown on his head as King of Kings, Lord of Lords.

Some crowns may be locked up in museums for show purposes of history. The crowns of kings of old are with precious stones, gems, diamonds and gold and eloquently shaped perfectly to fit the head of a designated or appointed king of a particular kingdom. When David was ruler of Israel and all the land, General Joab would bring kings crowns to King David so that he could know that victory had been taken from those heathens.

During the appointment or installation, thousands show up to watch the crown and the appointment to a throne for a new king. This ceremony has to be one hundred percent flawless and spotless. When the crown is placed on the head all bow down and the applause is perhaps more than a football game at the largest dome.

There is nothing on earth that can compare to the crown placed on Jesus' head when He carried the cross on cavalry. The crown of thorns was pushed into His head as blood came streaming out. He was being beaten and ridiculed and spat upon and whipped as though He was lower than a slave. Blood was everywhere on Him and the cross was stained in blood. Nevertheless, He carried the cross and barred all suffering as the living sacrifice atoned for you and I.

This same Jesus was the one sent from God who loved me with an everlasting love. He paid the cost without hesitation. The love He demonstrated was beyond my mind's comprehension. Why didn't He just give up on us? His love endures forever. He is Love.

PRAYERS

Father, thank you for coming into my heart and placing me into your kingdom over the power of darkness. In your kingdom, I find peace and joy and love. In your Kingdom, I reign with you Lord. In Jesus name, amen

PSALM 34

LET IT GO TODAY!

MARK 16:9 When Jesus rose early on the first day of the week, he appeared first to Mary Magdalene, out of whom he had driven seven demons. She went and told those who had been with him and who were mourning and weeping. [11]When they heard that Jesus was alive and that she had seen him, they did not believe it.

Possessions can hold your back at times in your heart. Let some things go! Do not try to explain everything, you already have enough attacks coming your way. As I was going through clothing that my wife said was too little or too big or even you never wear it. It was still kind of hard for me to get rid of my things. You get so connected to material items that it can easily draw you in and make you kind of selfish without thinking about it. When I thought about the plenty that the Lord had already provided for me, it was easy for me to adopt the right attitude. I simply said to myself just let it go today! In my mind, I was saying I do not want possession to have control over me nor to hold me back from what God is saying to me. Give something to somebody in one way or another and I will bless you. Those are the words that He could have been speaking to me. I am not sure if they were, but one thing for sure is that He had spoken to my heart.

God is always reminding us of His infinite blessings, love and kindness. He is always somehow, even just in the atmosphere He reminds us of what He has provided and the love on cross. He gave His life for me. How can I be selfish to others? When I think about God giving up His only begotten son, my heart rejoices and I praise His Holy name. Jesus gave up His life on Earth as a sacrifice for all mankind. Jesus gave up His life for sinners in every place throughout the world. There is no place exempt from His compassion and love. There is no need to hold to any bondage or anything that puts a hold on us. Let it go today! I need to tell myself let it go every time some old womb opens in my mind. I need to let the past go every time it attacks me. Let the hurt and pain go today! Let the violence go today! Let the abuse go today! Let the adultery go today! Let the addictions go today! Let the drugs, go today! Let the prostitution go today! Let the needles go from shooting up! Let the cocaine go! Let the alcohol go today! Let all the illegal substances go! Let evil obsessions go today! Let things that mean you no good go today! Let all those sinful things go in life that snare you and pull you down. Never let Jesus go!

Hold on to the Lord with all your might. Call on the Holy Spirit to help you. He will help you and make intercession for you as well.

When reality set in my mind of what Jesus did for me, I simply had tears bursting out of my eyes and a heart ready for another entrance of His loving kindness. I simply adapted the attitude let it go today to a different degree. I pray that my life is a prisoner of His love and kindness and His unlimited grace.

Jesus let everything go except divinity! He did not access His divine power though He could have called on every angel to destroy planet earth at one word or thought. then have them to return to the throne of grace to bow down and worship the Father. Obviously He did not summon them because of His mission to save the world from wrath. He did it because of love. Jesus let go of life that very day. Jesus let go of all power that very day. Jesus allowed Himself to be stripped of everything so He could carry the cross on Calvary and save a sin sick soul and spirit like mine. Jesus let everything go to become the perfect sacrifice for you and I. He made Himself the ransom that had to be paid on the spot for our freedom from sin. Jesus let go of the wrath that was prepared to be poured out on humanity. No wonder in the book of Revelations, those that sit around the throne bow and cast their crowns before Him. It was God who gave His son Jesus for me.

The Father let everything go that day to redeem me. He let His Son go! The grave could not hold Him. He washed us in the blood and rose from the dead to defeat death at every angle to ensure that we are secure in Jesus Christ. Let everything go today that you might know Him and live and reign with Him forever. **When the Sabbath was over, Mary Magdalene, Mary the mother of James, and Salome bought spices so that they might go to anoint Jesus' body. ^{2}Very early on the first day of the week, just after sunrise, they were on their way to the tomb ^{3}and they asked each other, "Who will roll the stone away from the entrance of the tomb?"MARK 16:1.** The stone was rolled away from Jesus' grave. When you let things go, stones can be rolled away. Nothing will block you again. No one of any authority will block you ever again.

PRAYER

Father, thank you for giving me strength to let go of the things that had me in bondage. You strength is what I need to sustain me daily. The power of the cross and resurrection saved me. Because of you Lord, "I can do all thing through Jesus Christ who strengthens me." Praise to your glorious name, Jesus.

MARK 16

MY CLIPPED WING ANGEL

ROMANS 3:23 for all have sinned and fall short of the glory of God,

As I was cleaning my office at home, I ran across a small glass angel. When I looked at this glass angel, I automatically thought of it being a delicate piece of art material that had such beauty and was well crafted with excellent designs. It looked so light in weight that it could fall over if I just passed by it with the slightest wind. Well, I did walk by it and made a false move trying pick it up which led to me breaking it. If you are anything like me, I really dislike breaking anything, not to mention if it is associated with God. I believe in the utmost of reverencing Him and I don't mind going beyond the limits praising Him. I kept that angel beside my bed for several years until I decided to move it to my new office. On that particular day I decided to rearrange some things, that is when the accident happened.

As I moved something I accidently pushed the angel over and one of the wings fell off. I felt so bad! I told my wife about it looking for sympathy. I never told anyone that this one angel was a special piece of art to me. Because I know God makes angels in heaven and place them where He wants them throughout the world and heaven, I felt some connection to that glass angel I believe for that reason. When I looked at it, it always made me think about us having a guardian angel that watches over each person. Please understand, this piece of art was just a special gift from someone. It was never an idol nor did I worship it. I need to say that because so many people do worship things and it causes so many people to fall into sin.

I was just fascinated with the creative skills God gives to people to make such pieces of art. No one likes to see things broken especially when you see the beauty God allowed in it. I thought about a lot of things. Romans 3:23 came to mind. I thought about for sure " we all fall short of the glory of God." We all make mistakes. Even being His best design on earth, man still falls short. Thank God for His unmerited favor known as grace. He knows that man will always break things. He knows that sin will cause man to break more things. We need to learn to discern attacks and sinful things that tempt us and snare us because they are the reason people fall along with the choices they make. Our emergency rescuer is Jesus. When we fall short, grace picks us up. That grace can only be found in Jesus Christ. So, don't worry too much. The Holy Spirit will help all of us. Just call on Jesus and believe in Him.

I still have that same angel sitting in my office with the broken wing laying next to the angel. I placed it there as a reminder of the delicate design of the Lord's creation of angels and all things. It is also there to remind me that Jesus loves me so much regardless of my sin and all of mess ups and brokenness. I placed it there so that I am reminded of the love Jesus placed in us and His love in creating angels to guard His people. He made it from love that knew no sin. He made it from love that it might conquer sinful natured people. He made the perfect angel that in time of rescue, He would see you through. I placed it there to remind me always that He even takes care of His angels. I believe if a real live angel had a broken wing, God would immediately repair that wing and send that angel out with full force on mission with blessings.

I believe sometimes the enemy seek to challenge believers to walk away from the anointing of God on our life. The enemy wants us to be derailed at all cost and turn our backs on our risen Lord. The enemy can never out do the power of God's love for us. We just need to be reminded as we go before the altar with thanksgiving, laying aside bondages because God never breaks promises and He answers prayers and delivers timely. He is the God who surrounds us with His blessings.

Today is our day to clip away the sin that so easily beset us and walk in the righteousness of our Lord, Jesus Christ. Clip away all the misdeeds and the temptation. We need to clip away those sinful things in Galatians 5 and put on the fruit of the Spirit. God is calling for leaders in every church to clip off the old nature and start a new thing in your church that He has already ordained. Yes, the Lord has already blessed that new thing. You have been told things by God and He is waiting for your response. Clip off the attitude of pride and self rebellion and go after the Lord Jesus with all your might to please Him. We can help restore that old clipped wing person in whom the enemy is trying to destroy. We help by prayer and praising God at home and in worship service. We call on the Lord at all times of the day. If you have a problem pull over and start praying and worshiping our Lord in the Spirit. Let your request be made known to Him. This time allow our service to be a service of exalting our Lord Jesus Christ. Give Him praise with Alleluia. Clip the enemy in every way possible by calling on the name of Jesus for help. Lord we exalt you forever and ever.

PRAYERS

Father, thank you for redeeming me from the sin that held me down for so many years. It was you who set me free my sinful habits. I recognized that I fall short of your standards of holiness and living. Thank you for allowing me to call on you anytime for deliverance. Keep me near your heart Lord so that my life will be transformed to glorify you in spirit and truth.

ROMANS 5

THE MAGNITUDE OF "IT IS FINISHED"

JOHN 19:29-30 Now a vessel full of sour wine was sitting there; and they filled a sponge with sour wine, put it on hyssop, and put it to His mouth. So when Jesus had received the sour wine, He said, "It is finished!" And bowing His head, He gave up His spirit.

    When you look at a court case on television, often we just see a vivid discussion of the charges that are against an offender who violates the law. We hear of the accusations and so forth but we don't always see the actual offense unless there is a video or photographs of the crime. It is discussed on almost every news broadcast to the point that it is extremely magnified to a level that the entire world knows about it. In some cases it even becomes entertainment for people all around the globe to view and hear about, some to ridicule and cast judgment. Crime scenes and all kinds of analysis are presented on national television. There is the battle back and forth of the prosecutor and the defense attorneys. "Who will win the case?" is always out there. Contrary to offenders, those that do good acts are often observed and examined just as much as one who commits crime. Nevertheless, all of these things are visibly seen on a larger scale through the media on television. I would imagine, millions of people view all the media broadcasting shows and other televised broadcasting channels to see such cases along with other spectacular and heroic acts. The impact usually occurs when these cases and heroic acts are finished. The work and mission is finished. Jesus said, "It is finished."

    The heroic acts is what turns people on the most in this world because they set out to do good and the result is normally saving someone in a specific area of their lives. Those kind, gentle and loving acts of heroes in this humanity matter most to all people and need to be displayed and magnified much more frequent than negative news broadcast. We need the good news to be magnified just like the world now knows that Jesus died on the cross to destroy sin. He destroyed sin because of His love for all people. He made a way for every man and woman and their households to accept Him as Lord. Jesus, said it is finished to bring us into relationship with our Father in heaven.

    My mother gave us the good news every day as children up to becoming teenager. When I was growing up, my mother had a picture of Jesus in a double golden medal frame with beautiful flowers in the center of it. On one side she had Jesus hanging on a cross and on the other side, there was a photo of Jesus. As a young child and teenager, I really did not understand the fullness of what it meant to my mother and to the family. No wonder God puts mothers in place to bless us in His love. What I learned about it is that she was magnifying Jesus in our home to anyone that entered the house. She was a witness that Jesus was her Lord because of what He did on the cross. When I think about it, Jesus gave up everything for us. Jesus gave His life. The scripture says, " He gave up His spirit"

    I pray today that fathers, mothers, saints, the media, every news station, every business, every home, every church, and everyone that is able to call on the name of Jesus will glorify Him as we magnify His name and all of His goodness. He deserves all the praise, worship and glory. The next time we look at the news being broadcasted, maybe one anchor man or anchor women in charge will send out to the entire world that Jesus said "it is finished." Let the word of God be sent to the world that Jesus said, "it is finished." They will feel the magnitude of Jesus carrying the cross and dying on it, completely washing away and destroying the power of sin. The magnitude is that Jesus died to give us life and to save us from the wrath of God, His Father in heaven. Wherever you go today, let His name role off your tongue and lips magnifying Him with all your strength in the spirit. If you have never accepted Jesus as Lord, do not wait. Accept Jesus Christ as Lord of your life. Ask Him simply to come into your heart today. Acknowledge to Him alone that you repent of your sin. Just say Lord, I believe that you are the son of God and you died for me and rose from the dead Romans 10:9. After that very moment you are a new creature in Christ. Now you see the magnitude of "It is finished." Praise, Honor and Glory to His Holy and Righteous name.

PRAYERS

Father, thank you for a life changing relationship. Thank you for finishing the work that our Father in heaven entrusted you with. We have been redeemed because of your precious blood. Your name is magnified because of who you are. Today, I am finished with my old nature so that I can magnify you in service because of your love for me.

ROMANS 8

GUARD YOUR HEART

PROVERBS 4:23 Keep thy heart with all diligence; for out of it are the issues of life.

    Guard your heart above all other things. Your heart is what the roaring lion seeks to destroy. Your heart is where you form relationships. Your first relationship should be with our Lord Jesus Christ. Your heart is where you attitude is formed.
    The attitude is extremely important when it comes to relationships and success. When you walk in the best attitude people notice you each time, everyday. In fact, your good attitude serves as a witness to people in a dark place. Your act of good instead of evil impresses Jesus. Romans 12:21 You just might help someone come out and enter into the light of Jesus Christ with your smile and attitude. Keep a good heart. Matthew 5 refers to the beatitudes. which translates into attitude. It describes the characteristics of a believer. The beatitudes start with blessed which means happy and ends with a condition like vs8 Blessed are the pure in heart , for they shall see God etc.. God wants us to walk in it because it is His way and blessings are constantly upon us when we trust and obey God. He blesses us anyway but imagine if we obey. The best thing for any person is to talk to God and ask Him to give you a new walk, a new attitude and change of heart. Ask God to make your heart new in the Sprit so He will be pleased. It's all about pleasing God.
    It really does not matter about other distractions and complicated puzzles and all sort of unimportant things that hinder you. It is about asking Jesus to change your heart and guard it no matter what you do. Guard your heart so you can walk with Him in faith and keep your relationship strong with the Lord through all troubles. John 14:1-6 It is only then you and others can see the effects you have on other people's lives and God sees you as pleasing Him. When you ask God to guard your heart not only will He do it, He will comfort it and fill it with a joy unspeakable.

PRAYERS

Father, my trust is in you for all things. Lord, continue to guard my heart against things that are unpleasing to you. Open my heart to receive blessings from you. May your name be magnified in my heart and the heart of your people. In Jesus name, Amen

PROVERBS 3

NEVER LET GO OF HOPE

Psalm 39:1-7

I said, "I will watch my ways
   and keep my tongue from sin;
   I will put a muzzle on my mouth
   as long as the wicked are in my presence."

But when I was silent and still,
   not even saying anything good,
   my anguish increased.

My heart grew hot within me,
   and as I meditated, the fire burned;
   then I spoke with my tongue:

"Show me, O LORD, my life's end
   and the number of my days;
   let me know how fleeting is my life.

You have made my days a mere handbreadth;
   the span of my years is as nothing before you.
   Each man's life is but a breath.
   Selah

Man is a mere phantom as he goes to and fro:
   He bustles about, but only in vain;
   he heaps up wealth, not knowing who will get it.

"But now, Lord, what do I look for?
   My hope is in you.

   Hope is a powerful word that we all should apply in our lives. Hope helps us to dream again when dreams sometimes seem distant. Hope helps when dreams seems like they are snatched out of the mind and heart. Hope helps you keep the zeal in your life. Hope helps you to thirst for that goal in life until you achieve it. Hope does not concentrate on forgetting dreams; it is to help you remember to don't ever give up on dreams. Increase your efforts in your plan. Stay focused. I knew in when I played football, I had to stay focused on the in zone instead of the hardest hitter tackling me to cause pain or break a bone. When we stay focused we weaken obstacles. In fact obstacles and barriers just fade always because hope builds confidence. We need that confidence in Jesus. In 1 John 5:14 it says, "Now this is the confidence that we have in Him, that if we ask anything according to His will He hears us."

    We can always count on the Lord to help us in our dreams. The Lord never leaves us nor forsakes us. He has given us a call, a gift, a talent and the edge over the enemy to serve Him. God gives unique abilities that qualify us in areas to be a blessing and used by Him. We have to remember that these gifts are for His glory. He has already endorsed what you desire in your heart for His purpose. Did you know that God has already endorsed your dream because you believe in Him and He knows it is for His kingdom? He has sealed it because of the love in your heart for Jesus. Listen everyone has a level of hope inside them. All have hope on a daily basis, for example, I hope my better half pays the rent next week. That is an average hope. This hope that Jesus refers to is through salvation. We as Christians must seek God for those blessings that he has laid up in earthen treasure. At the play I visited, I heard a woman speak of the dreams she had for so long to write plays. It was ironic because I had been thinking the same thing at one time off and on, just like a faucet with running water overflowing. The only problem is that I did not stay focused, she did stay focused. She kept on hoping that life would allow her to be successful in the area of theater. You can do it also. You can send that message of love through the theater. Just like one of the actors said on stage at the end of the play. She quoted Philippians 4:13. I can do all things through Christ who strengthens me. Imagine that! We have hope and at the same time the love of God and His strength to carry us for His purpose.

    Never let go of your dreams. Never let go of God's unchanging hand. Let go of all the other things that cause bondage and troubles. Just get freed up and walk away from it with the help of the Holy Spirit. Today, make it your priority to concentrate on Jesus. You see it was the shedding of His blood that gave us life, keeping us from the wrath of God. So you have a right to live and have the hope in Christ to guide your life.

PRAYERS

Father, I put my hope and trust in you because you never let me down. I will call on your name for the rest of my life. Praise to your Holy name.

PSALM 40

PROVEN RESURRECTION

Mark 16:6-7 "Don't be alarmed," he said. "You are looking for Jesus the Nazarene, who was crucified. He has risen! He is not here. See the place where they laid him. But go, tell his disciples and Peter, 'He is going ahead of you into Galilee. There you will see him, just as he told you.'"

Make no mistake about the resurrection of Jesus Christ, it happened and no one can change it. A discovery was made of the Shroud of Turin in the late 16th century in Turkey during a holy crusade. Around 1988, the Vatican allowed the shroud to be dated by several sources such the University of Arizona, Oxford University and Swiss Federal Institution of Technology. Clearly it was examined by several scientist with the most precise instruments. They determined that the image in the shroud was indeed Jesus Christ. The image was fuzed by God's power into the cloth. For those who believe in the Father, the Son and the Holy Spirit, you cannot help but to believe that God the Father sent His only Son to die on a cross for the sin of the world and then raise Him up from the dead on the third day. Read the scripture and believe in the resurrection. God can not lie. It fully supports what Jesus has spoken through Mark, his disciples. These scriptures were divinely inspired by God. To say that this did not happen, would be to say that God is not real and that there is no truth, we know that is impossible. God is the only true and wise God. God cannot lie. God is truth. God is Holy and divine. He does not have to argue with men about anything with Jesus. There is no case with Jesus because it is already done. Jesus rose from the dead with all power. No one could explain it better than the word of God. The Apostle Paul was consumed with the blessings and power of Jesus. He knew that there was and is a God because He met Him. For anyone who does not believes or having difficult, go back to the tomb and see if He is there. You will not find him. He is risen from the dead. He did it for you and me. No story compares to Jesus Christ death, burial and resurrection period. Jesus is our Master and Lord. Nothing is history nor present, and ever could compare to what He did for us. A few months ago, I watched a movie entitled " I am Legend". Please understand it does not compare to Jesus. Several thing stood out in the film. One thing was the desire to get a cure for the virus that had wiped out thousands of people in the town. The researcher in the in the movie was sincere in his quest for a cure for that virus. At one point, he held captive a women who was infected with the virus and her entire countenance and body was transformed into a different creature. The doctor conducted test and at the conclusion, her mate hunted them down . At the end, the doctor had discovered a cure and sent two survivors to deliver it. Then the doctor and the male creature collided in mid-air and exploded destroying all other creatures. The point is that a cure was discovered through all manner of evil. Thanks be to God, who had a cure for all the people in the world. John 3:16 Jesus is our cure for life and eternity. His blood washes us whiter than snow. John 19 He destroy the enemy so we could live in the blessings forever with him. You should give God all the glory and praise right now for your life. We were dead but now we are risen with Jesus Christ. Romans 6 He is Lord, He is the physician who cured us and made us whole. It took the second Adam to bless us and save our souls. Glory to the name of Jesus Christ. Revelations 4

PRAYERS

Father, thank you for proving the resurrection of your Son Jesus Christ. You proved it in your word. Your word alone stands as proof over all things. Your word is the authority on resurrection and things you have made known to mankind. Thank you for resurrecting Jesus so that I can live a free life. I pray that you resurrect my life in all areas that I might serve Jesus.

MARK 15, 16

CLEAR JUDGEMENT

Matthew 7: 1-2 "Do not judge, or you too will be judged. For in the same way you judge others, you will be judged, and with the measure you use, it will be measured to you.

This scripture is about clear judgment You need clear vision with your clear judgment. True Judgment really starts with God. Judgment is a part of the human race and in the heart of man. Judgment is an everyday factor of life. It simply involves decision making. However, in this case it starts in the heart, mind and eyes. It appears to focus on the eyes. What you interpret with your eyes can usually expand to a new level of thinking and also concentrating on the unthinkable. You have to be careful with what is planted in your thoughts. What thoughts registered from your heart and mind in the first place?

Many things can take over your heart and mind and cause you to judge negatively. God wants positive and true judgment. He wants that kind of judgment that will help others get into God's Kingdom. Once on national television, Oprah Winfrey conducted a scenario with her audience. It was a test with groups that had blue eyes and groups with brown eyes. The brown eyes were treated better. The blue eyes people were very upset and angry. The point behind it was to gain a clear vision of how people specifically, African American had been treated because of skin color. We all need a clear vision of how to love people regardless of race or gender or anything. Jesus set the example.

Jesus is allowing us to see how it works in his eyes of judgment. He gives us the basic strategy to stop judging others, which we know it can easily start conflict and destroy families and friends. The wrong judgment can make Christians fall away and non-believers stay away. He tells us in verse 3 basically how we can look at someone else in judgment and see the beam in your own eye. In other words, that person might be falling short and is blinded by the dust in his or her eyes. Nevertheless don't cast a negative judgment on that person. They just need your prayers and love. You do not have to accept the sin of a person. You do not have to cast evil thoughts on them. Jesus makes it clear that we need a clear vision and mentality that points to love. That clear vision and mentality is to look at people like Jesus looks at them. He looks with grace and mercy. He looks with loving kindness. The Bible is clear about us drawing people with love and kindness. We are reminded by the Lord that we are not perfect in this fleshly body. I was thinking of how we see different scenes in movie that portray Holograms. A Hologram is a three dimensional photographic image of an object. It may be used to portray a image of a person or thing. It is not real. The enemy does it very often to entice millions of people. We need to see through false illusions and put our eyes on God, who blesses us. We need that spiritual sight from the Lord to recognize truth and discern the enemy's motives. Remember Jesus is telling us that God will judge us at the appointed time. So be careful how you judge others. Be careful how you view others. Be careful how you treat others and do not look down on them. . Be careful how you treat people because Jesus will judge the world and every Christian will be judged as well those who have not accepted Jesus.

The other day a young man told me a story of how he use to go to church and upon his arrival before worship started, he received some good looks from a few people but when he went up closer, he received the most dirty looks that he had ever received in church. He said to me that all of these people were in the ministry. He felt hurt and left the church. But one day after a few years of leaving the church because he felt judged because of his clothing attire, he came back because someone told him about this scripture. He also came back because he remembered the love of Christ who touched his heart in those early years of his life. He found out that in this scripture it is not the speck in a man's eye nor the beam in the judgmental person's eye that saves a soul. It is the power of Jesus Christ who comes into the heart and renews a person into a totally different identity and creature. If you want to truly be connected Jesus Christ and live the life in Christ, get the beam out of your eyes. More importantly get the negative judging out of your heart and ask Jesus to come into your heart today. Get a clear vision on what to do for your life. It must be in Jesus' hands. Watch with your own eyes the Lord's hand on your life, changing thing for His purpose. You will glorify Him. Get ready because you will live with him forever. Believe in his power working on your life. Reign with Jesus because He is Lord. Philippians 2:1-10

PRAYERS

Father, thank you for removing the beam out of my eye so I can see clearly and not judge others. Give me a heart to walk in faith and not by sight. Keep me near you by the power of your Holy Spirit.

MATTHEW 8

ABOUT THE AUTHOR

Joseph Harris is a Pastor for Jesus Christ, His Lord and Savior. He is married to LaDonna and they have two children, Lamar and LaMonique. He and his family currently live in Texas.

He is the founder and Pastor of the Christian Worship Outreach Center Ministries in Harker Heights, Texas.

www.ingramcontent.com/pod-product-compliance
Lightning Source LLC
Chambersburg PA
CBHW071704160426
43195CB00012B/1576